Aristotelian Philosophy

Aristotelian Philosophy

Ethics and Politics from Aristotle to MacIntyre

KELVIN KNIGHT

polity

First published in 2007 by Polity Press

Polity Press
65 Bridge Street
Cambridge CB2 1UR, UK

Polity Press
350 Main Street
Malden, MA 02148, USA

ISBN-10: 0-7456-1976-2
ISBN-13: 978-07456-1976-7
ISBN-10: 0-7456-1977-0 (pb)
ISBN-13: 978-07456-1977-4 (pb)

A catalogue record for this book is available from the British Library.

Typeset in 11.25 / 13 pt Dante
by Servis Filmsetting Ltd, Manchester
Printed and bound in Great Britain by MPG Books Ltd, Bodmin, Cornwall.

The publisher has used its best endeavours to ensure that the URLs for external websites referred to in this book are correct and active at the time of going to press. However, the publisher has no responsibility for the websites and can make no guarantee that a site will remain live or that the content is or will remain appropriate.

For further information on Polity, visit our website www.polity.co.uk

Contents

Acknowledgements

My greatest thanks are to David Held and Emma Hutchinson at Polity for their practical wisdom and their patient insistence, without which I might never have forced myself to free up sufficient time from more pressing academic duties to write this book. I am greatly indebted for comments upon drafts of the text to Andrius Bielskis, Paul Blackledge, Sarah Dancy, Alasdair MacIntyre, Jeffery Nicholas, Mary Ruskin, Benedict Smith, Alberta Stevens and Polity's two readers, whom I now know to be John Horton and Mark Murphy. I also thank Kamalita for her encouragement and for reminding me of the reality of managerial oppression, Aidan Rose for demonstrating that a good practitioner can be a good manager, Lee Salter for technological assistance, Ron Beadle, Keith Breen, Tony Burns, David Charles, Philip Gorski, John Haldane, Duncan Kelly, Arthur Madigan S.J., Keith Tribe, Stephen Turner and especially Alasdair MacIntyre and Cary Nederman for copies of papers, and everyone who has responded to the papers in which I have, over many years, presented aspects of this book's argument. I apologize to those scholars (Terence Irwin and Jim Lennox spring most immediately to mind) from whose work I have tried to learn but who receive no acknowledgement below, and to those to whom I would have wished to allow time to respond to certain lines of argument before publication. They, like others, should know that the book would have been composed differently had I known that it would be dignified with its present title. Now that the text is committed to print, I look forward to learning how to tighten up, straighten out, clarify and elaborate – even if never to complete – its developing argument.

As MacIntyre's *Selected Essays* appeared between my submission of the manuscript and receipt of the proofs, I have been able to update numerous references to this more accessible source. All references to texts by MacIntyre in chapter 4 omit his name. All quotations are reproduced without any addition or omission of italicization throughout the book, and no mention of this is made within references. Where quotations are repeated, they are unreferenced. References to the works of Aristotle, Kant and the like include observation of the relevant conventions in ways that will, I hope, prove sufficient to enable a reader to locate a passage in any standard edition. Such works are only included in the References when published translations are cited.

Introduction

Aristotle's practical philosophy – his philosophy of ethics, politics and economics – has had two great attractions. One is the image it presents of
human excellence. The other is the notion that this image is projected by a
theoretical philosophy – of nature, of logic and of being – that is awesome
in its magnitude and influence.

Even if the ethical image is still bright, its theoretical projector is now tar-
nished. Aristotle's account of nature has been contradicted by such heroes
of modern science as Galileo, Newton and Darwin. His logic has been
replaced. His metaphysics has been deconstructed. In sum, his theoretical
philosophy is discredited. Nonetheless, the image remains. It is an image of
personal excellence, of moral and intellectual virtue, of *arete*. Politically, it
is an image of a community of such excellent individuals, sharing in discourse and in active pursuit of their common good. Unfortunately, when
we look at the image more closely, we also see exclusion and oppression. In
Aristotle's Athens, the oppressed included women, slaves and workers. We
might now try to project the image onto the screen of Britain or America,
hoping to exclude the exclusions and see a modern picture of political
freedom and moral harmony. But can we?

Karl Marx gives us one reason why we cannot, and Martin Heidegger
another. Marx agreed with Aristotle that a good life is one of freedom from
material necessity and freedom to rationally determine one's own actions.
He also observed that only a few have ever been able to enjoy such leisure
and opportunity, and that they have only done so by commanding the
labour of those producing the material goods they consume. We should
surely agree that there is something profoundly wrong with such a situation, and with any ideology – such as Aristotle's – that is used to justify it.
We might therefore welcome Heidegger's deconstruction of the traditional
projector that is Aristotle's theoretical philosophy, and we might approve
the claim that what its deconstruction reveals is a contingent collection of
components and, behind these, human being in all its immediacy, particularity and difference. What is claimed is that, even if it cannot free us from

oppression, this deconstruction of philosophical tradition at least frees us from illusion.

But perhaps we wish to retain the picture of moral, intellectual and political excellence. Can it be saved? Even if the theoretical tradition is no more, might a tradition of Aristotelian practical philosophy somehow stand alone? To answer affirmatively is to deny that Aristotle's practical philosophy need be understood as projected by, or based in, his theoretical philosophy. Recently, this has indeed been forcefully denied. The most famous of these denials is entitled *After Virtue*. We might therefore regret that its author, Alasdair MacIntyre, has since changed his mind. He still calls himself an Aristotelian, and he still calls Aristotelianism a tradition, but he no longer argues that an Aristotelian ethics and politics can be sustained apart from any Aristotelian metaphysics or biology. Without a philosophical understanding of the potentiality and good of human beings as such, any solely practical philosophy of human excellence is likely to become a self-serving and self-deceiving justification for arbitrary elitism, exclusion and exploitation.

If we look into the history of Aristotelianism, we might question our distinction of practical from theoretical philosophy. For Aristotle, theology was central to philosophy. With Christianity, the two were separated. Right and wrong were understood to be ordained by God. After a long period of revival, philosophy was itself divided between theory and practice by Wolff and Kant. Theoretical philosophy dealt with what is universal and, for Kant, how we can know of it. Practical philosophy dealt with what applies universally to human action or, for Kant, what ought to so apply. Hegel protested their division. Others abandoned theoretical philosophy for what had evolved, out of the subdiscipline of natural philosophy, into science. It was Heidegger who then urged us to abandon ideas of universality in our concern with practice. And it was Heidegger who invoked Aristotle as his principal source for the claim that an original concern with practical existence had been hidden by a philosophical tradition that pretended to universal knowledge.

Heidegger's reinterpretation of Aristotle has pitted a supposedly authentic Aristotle against the Aristotle of tradition. Central to this revelation of a new Aristotle, and to the creation of a 'neo-Aristotelianism', is the conceptual distinction of action, or *praxis*, from not only theory but also production. A concern with action is simply with being and doing, and not with its temporal effects or products. A concern with effects, and with the techniques by which to produce those effects, covers over that original concern with being and doing. Such a distinction can indeed be found in Aristotle,

who differentiates those engaged in acting from those employed in producing and denies to producers the possibility of human excellence.
Producers work for the sake of actors, and actors alone are admitted to the
political and ethical community.

In returning to the Aristotle of tradition, MacIntyre diminishes these
conceptual distinctions and disputes their ethical and political implications.
Instead, he distinguishes between what he calls practices and institutions,
goods of excellence and goods of effectiveness. He agrees with Aristotle,
and with Marx, that excellence cannot be attributed to workers as a class,
but he denies still more emphatically that it can be attributed to their managers. His Aristotelianism is a particular tradition of theoretical reflection
upon practical rationality, unafraid of conflict with more powerful rivals.

Such an Aristotelianism would have appeared strange when it could still
be maintained that 'Aristotle's special glory [is] that every thinker is his
pupil', and that ' "Aristotelianism" ' has never 'in the history of philosophy'
been used to indicate any distinct 'speculative tendency' (Stocks 1925: 155,
154). When Heidegger attempted Aristotelianism's deconstruction, it was
identified not as *a* tradition but as *the* tradition. Aristotle would himself
have been less surprised that his philosophy should be understood as contending with others, but he would nonetheless have contested MacIntyre's
identification of excellence with those who resist rather than exercise institutionalized power. Aristotle advised how to conserve political order, not to
overturn it. This thought does not perturb MacIntyre because he argues
that a progressive philosophical tradition comprises an ongoing argument
and enquiry, and that this enquiry is not merely into the tradition's norms
and their application but also into its first principles. The question con-
fronting contemporary Aristotelians is that of the extent to which their first
principles require revision in order to sustain pursuit of human excellence
as the final end of human action, and in order to sustain the claim that
Aristotelianism constitutes the best theory so far of ethical practice and its
political implications.

1

Aristotle's Theoretical and Practical Philosophy

To begin the history of an Aristotelian tradition with Aristotle is not to diminish the importance of such predecessors as Socrates or Plato, nor even of Heraclitus, Parmenides, Empedocles, Anaxagoras or Democritus. Aristotle's love of wisdom was inspired by theirs, and it was in critical engagement with them and others that he based many of his arguments. Therefore his influence upon Stoics and neo-Platonists, and upon us, is also often theirs. Nonetheless, in historical hindsight it is clear that Greek and classical philosophy reached its culmination in his work.

Aristotle is now widely regarded as the first philosopher who dealt with both theoretical and practical philosophy whilst differentiating incisively between them. On this view, *theoria* concerns that which is universal and cannot be otherwise, whereas *praxis* concerns particularities that are subject to human choice and change. Theoretical wisdom is about truth whilst practical wisdom is about action, and therefore, whereas his teacher, Plato, would have had theorists rule, Aristotle tells us that theory is one thing and practice quite another. There is much that is valid in this view. However, in this chapter I shall sketch some aspects of Aristotle's philosophy in another way, suggesting that the distinction between his theoretical and practical philosophies can be overdrawn. There is continuing merit in the more traditional interpretation, according to which what Aristotle writes of practice should be understood in the light of what he writes of theology, of ontology and of nature. That said, my representation of Aristotle's philosophy will be less sanguine than its portrayal by tradition.

Aristotle as Innovator

Aristotle inherited Plato's robust philosophical realism (Gerson 2005). Like Parmenides and Socrates, Plato thought that what is most truly real, what most really is, is that which is unchanging. He developed this idea of absolute being into his famous doctrine of atemporal, universal and immaterial forms. Aristotle tells us that Plato believed these forms to be entirely separate from our world of sensuous particulars. Aristotle agrees that God (*theos*) and such celestial entities as the Sun enjoy a kind of eternal and self-sufficient (*autarkes*) being and activity (*energeia*) which we cannot share but only contemplate. Crucially, he also agrees in regarding the best life for human beings as that of *theoria*, the activity of such contemplation.

Aristotle explicitly *disagrees* with Plato when he brings the forms down to Earth and recasts them as natural kinds, such as plant and animal species. Nonetheless, even here he remains significantly Platonic. Individual animals may come and go, but, he insists, the species of which they are particular instances are themselves universal and eternal forms. Although revising Plato, in retaining a robust account of forms Aristotle may be understood as siding with him against Heraclitus' perspectivism, Empedocles' evolutionism and Democritus' atomistic materialism. For Aristotle, atemporal and universal forms inform – genetically determinate the nature (*physis*) and temporal development of – individual animals. A species is real and conceptually separate from the particular individuals in which it is instantiated, but, he emphasizes, it has no substantial existence apart from those material individuals. Therefore, he reverses Plato's order of priority in describing the form of a species as only a 'secondary being' and the reality of a substantial individual (a 'this'), combining form with matter, as 'primary being' (*Categories* 2a11–14). Such primary, individual subjects are the basic entities of which such insubstantial things as qualities and changes (*metabolai*) may be predicated. That the world of such sensuous particulars is one of change does not entail that it is one of Heraclitean flux or of mere chance. As forms imbue nature with an elemental order, much of changing reality can be analysed, explained and specified in terms of determinate processes of coming-into-being (*genesis*), of contingent movements (*kineseis*) of substantive beings, and of different species' characteristic activities (*energeiai*).

Energeia is a word of Aristotle's own coinage. Literally, it means being in (*en-*) work (*ergon*) or at work or, more simply, working. When not translated as 'activity' it is usually rendered 'functioning'. It is something predicated of an individual being, or of a specific kind of being. We could understand it as denoting the condition of being energetic, so long as we understand this energy as expended in the performance of a specific activity; that is, in the activity, work or function characteristic of the way of life (*bios*) of some species, or characteristic of the craft of some kind of worker, or even characteristic of some kind of tool. For Aristotle, all beings are to be understood in terms of the activity characteristic of their kind, but kinds of being differ in the degree of self-sufficiency of their specific activities. Whereas the constant activity of the Sun requires nothing external for its sustenance, plants and animals require light and nutrition if they are to live and reproduce, artisans additionally require external direction of their activities, and tools require artisans for their very movement.

Developing an idea from Plato and Anaxagoras, Aristotle argues that the most self-sufficient activity is that of the divine, or God, because this comprises self-activating intelligence (*nous*) thinking of itself. God's activity is performed for its own sake and is therefore complete (*teleios*) and good (*agathon*) in itself. As such, Aristotle hypothesizes, it is an object of attraction to every other intelligent being in the cosmos, including human beings. God is, in this sense, the cosmos's prime mover.

We may note here that *energeia* should not be understood as 'functioning', at least if description of something as functioning is taken to imply that it is essentially a means to some further end. Aristotle's God has no further end. Nor is it (*it* is not the personal God of Judaic or Christian theism) the world's creator or originating cause. Aristotle's theological postulate is that God causes movement as an object of attraction, through its perfect activity, to other beings. Conversely, the postulate of an utterly complete being does not imply that it is a final end in relation to which the *energeia* of every other being should be understood as a means. God's simple activity of pure thinking (*noesis*) is utterly self-sufficient, and this self-sufficiency is what comprises its perfection. It is self-causing and has no need or use for anything external to it. Aristotle therefore proposes no great theocentric chain of beings or of ends and means. Nor does he propose any such anthropocentric chain (Johnson 2005). Aristotle theorizes neither the cosmos nor sublunary nature as a providential or interdependently functioning system.

What Aristotle does propose is that each kind of being has its own characteristic kind of activity, engagement in which constitutes the good for that kind of being. If other beings imitate God in their own *energeiai*, then what those other beings and their activities imitate is something self-sufficient and complete. In order to get this central point across, he resorts to a second terminological and conceptual innovation. This second coinage is *entelecheia*. Rather as he neologizes *energeia* from *ergon*, so he invents *entelecheia* from *telos*. *Telos* is commonly translated as 'end', but 'completion' would often be more accurate. A being's *entelecheia* is its state of completion, its 'actuality' in the standard translation. Just as God is perfectly constant *energeia*, so too is God perfect *entelecheia*. In contrast, the actuality of a temporal being is the fulfilment of its natural potential. Its *entelecheia* is its complete or final good. These two terms – *energeia* and *entelecheia*, or activity and actuality – are often interchangeable, as *energeia* denotes the activity characteristic of a form of being and *entelecheia* denotes the fully developed or completed being of some form of actor. For Aristotle, what is most essential to being – including human being – is not its material constitution but its working, not what a particular being is made of but what it does.

Aristotle follows philosophical tradition in affirming that the best activity of which human beings are capable is contemplation of that which constantly is. In engaging in such activity, individuals are fulfilling their highest potential, so that *theoria* is good in itself and a means to no further end. This is because it is in contemplating the divine that humans come the closest of which they are capable to participating in divinity. Not only do they contemplate what is immutable, but their contemplative activity is in a sense itself atemporal. It is at once being done and done, completed, and it is not a means to any further, future end.

Contemplating is not the only human *energeia* that allows of *entelecheia*. An activity comparable to *noesis* is *aisthesis* or perception or, especially, seeing. The activity of seeing, like that of contemplating, cannot be divided into temporal parts and cannot be done more quickly or slowly. However, Aristotle has an altogether less elevated understanding of seeing than of contemplating, and this for at least four reasons: seeing gives us knowledge of external beings only as changing individuals and not as unchanging forms; it is not an *energeia* of the human psyche (*psyche*) or of the human being as a whole but of a bodily part, the eye; seeing is an activity that is not unique to humankind but is shared with other animals; and it is an activity that is not only an end in itself but also a means to other ends, as when an animal sees food to eat or another individual with which to mate and reproduce. Reproduction of its form is the closest that a plant or a non-human animal can get to immortality and divinity. Reproduction is a second way in which humans can approximate to divinity but an inferior way to contemplation, both because it is shared with lower beings and because it is for the sake of the child and not just of the actor. Aristotle identifies human completion with the activity of *theoria* most of all because it is the activity that is most unproductive or 'useless' (Nightingale 2004). If it were a means to some further end it could not be our *telos*.

Change

A particular being has the potential to engage in the *energeia* characteristic of its kind and, in so doing, to actualize its good. Another potential, common to all terrestrial beings, is that to undergo or undertake temporal and contingent changes. All animals have a potential for locomotion, or change of location, but, although seeing is an activity, walking is not. Walking is a *kinesis* rather than an *energeia* because it involves what we might call an ordered succession of temporal stages (rather than, as is often said, events) with a beginning and a terminus, and more particularly because it is done in order to reach some destination or some other, further goal, such as health. Deliberating is another temporal process, undertaken in order to reach some conclusion.

The processes of a being's *genesis* and of its later decline and death are not *kineseis*, Aristotle occasionally stipulates (especially at *Physics* V: 1), because a *kinesis* is predicated of a continuing being. Nonetheless, *geneseis* are changes as distinct from activities. They are processes of coming-into-being, not workings or completions characteristic of some kind of being. Aristotle denies that beings can come to be from nothing, either materially or formally. The form of individual animals exists before they do, because species are eternal, and each animal inherits its form from its parents (to be more exact, Aristotle proposes that it inherits its matter from its mother and its form through its father).

Aristotle argues that an analogous process of coming-into-being occurs in manufacture, and says that all art (*techne*) involves *genesis* (e.g. *Nicomachean Ethics* (*NE*) 1140a11, *Generation of Animals* 734b21–735a4). The building of a house resembles the conception, gestation and birth of a horse in that it is a temporal process with a beginning and an end. The coming-to-be of each, when happening, has not yet happened, and when it has happened is no longer still happening. Only when the house is built or the foal born is the process (not the being) *teleios*, complete or at an end. Its completion is the initial formation of the foal or the house.

It may be tempting to assume that Aristotle's term *telos* here confuses two different ideas of an end: first, that of a temporal terminus, as in the ending of a process of walking, building or gestation; secondly, that of the intentional aim or goal of the actors who bring a house or foal into being. But there is no such confusion. Aristotle does not here intend *telos* to denote either the termination of a process or the intention of an actor. If a house remains half built or a mare miscarries, then the process has terminated but nothing is completed. Nor does Aristotle display the confusion often attributed to his refrain that 'art imitates nature' of fallaciously imputing purposiveness or intentional agency to nature. Although it is the case that intentionality can be attributed to human builders in a way that it cannot to equine parents, Aristotle regards conscious purposiveness as inessential even to manufacture. If the house is built or the foal born, then what is completed is not any intention of the producer but a process of coming-into-being. Conversely, if any process occurs by chance rather than intention, then it may be completed just the same. *Genesis* is not an *energeia* that occurs in an actor, but a *metabole* that occurs in a product.

For Aristotle, what we call purposiveness introduces contingencies into artificial processes, which diminish the necessity that is fully present in their natural analogues, and this is a major reason that he proposes it to be art that imitates nature and not vice versa. However, this is not the most important disanalogy between art and nature. With regard to generation, there is an absolute difference between the two in that the products of art have a different form from the producer, whereas in nature they are the same; a foal and its parents are beings of the same kind, but a house and its human builder are not. Artefacts, unlike animals, have no internal source of growth, completion or reproduction (or, rather, had no such source in any of the artefacts of Aristotle's time). An artificial form exists only as a paradigm (*paradeigma*) in extant and substantial artefacts and as an account (*logos*) in both the shared craft knowledge and the individual psyches of artisans, who then apply it to inform raw material. What changes in building is not the being of the builder but that of, for example, the wood which is hewn from a tree to make beams. To repeat, production (*poiesis*) occurs not in the producers or their actions but in that which those actions bring about. It is with this theoretical reason that Aristotle justifies his insistence that *poiesis* is a process that occurs for the sake not of the producer but of the product.

The explanatory capacity of Aristotle's concept of *telos* is most famously articulated in his juxtaposition of four types of 'cause' (*aition*) of beings, found most fully in the *Physics* (II: 3) and *Metaphysics* (Delta: 2). The first type of cause that he mentions is that from which something is made, and his examples – the bronze of a statue, the silver of a bowl – are often taken to indicate how important is reflection upon material production to his focal idea of causation. The second type of cause is the form or paradigm of something, although he does not here (where he is distinguishing between that matter and form which together compose substantial beings) refer to any such simple instance as a statue, bowl or house. The third type is, in translation, variously called the generative, productive, efficient, moving, motive, prior, agent or, even, acting cause, and Aristotle himself describes it as the source (*arche*) of change (and conversely of rest), having just said that 'all causes are sources' (*Metaphysics* 1013a16). It may return our attention to processes of production and of what I have already called the *re*production of form; he here cites a father as the cause of a child. Crucially, this cause, as that *from* which change occurs, is some being external to and separate from that which is produced or otherwise changed, and in this natural generation is again analogous to artificial. This is therefore an entirely different type of cause than the fourth type, a thing's *telos*, which is that *for the sake of which* something undergoes change.

A thing's *telos* is its *hou heneka*, its that-for-the-sake-of-which, and the common translation of *telos* as 'final cause' is understandable in the context of Aristotle's general account of causation. He argues that what comes first in nature or reason is the form for the sake of which something happens, even though he acknowledges that it is not what comes first temporally. As we have seen, what comes first temporally he describes not (as in most modern accounts of causation, such as that of Donald Davidson) in terms of some discrete event, such as an act of conception, but in terms of a process of *genesis* of which *this* particular individual is the product. His example in his fullest account of causation (as often elsewhere in his texts) is health, which was, in the developing Hippocratic tradition, the subject of an ethical craft (Miles 2004) about which he, as a doctor's son, knew much. He notes that a person may walk for the sake of her health, or that drugs or medical instruments may be used for the sake of a patient's health. When lacking, health is a good to be produced by some process. It is that for the sake of which some process may be begun, whether the taking of drugs or the taking of a walk or a doctor's administration of a treatment or performance of an operation. In such cases, the *telos* could be described as an end in relation to which such processes as those of walking, taking medicine or operating may be regarded as means. Accordingly, in first deliberating about and then prescribing or executing some such means, a doctor may herself be regarded as a means to the health of the patient; or, more accurately, on Aristotle's account, the generating means is the craft that is operationalized by the doctor acting specifically as a doctor (*Metaphysics* Zeta: 7). In any case, the doctor is not engaging in a veritably human *energeia*. Her setting in motion of a process within the patient is for the sake of the patient's health and not of herself, either as a doctor or as a human being. What is normative and causal is health, and both the doctor and the medical process are mere means to health's restoration and actualization in some particular patient.

Aims and Beneficiaries

Aristotle tries to draw an absolute distinction between activity and production. *Energeia* is internal to a being; it is necessarily present in the same being as is its source. In contrast, the source of artificial change is entirely separate from that in which the change occurs. Even in the case of a doctor curing herself, Aristotle insists that if we are to explain what is going on we must differentiate between the individual as possessor of productive craft knowledge and as patient receptacle of change. As a doctor, she is the external producer of health; as a patient, she is the beneficiary of the process that occurs within herself.

We might think that this contrast between activity and artificial change is a contrast of teleological with efficient causation, but this is not how it is presented by Aristotle. He both refuses description of doctoring in terms of activity and describes the process of health coming to be in terms of the completion of a process for the sake of which the efficiently causal doctoring occurs. A particular case of doctoring occurs for the sake of the individual patient and, also, for the sake of the universal form of human health, which is the aim of the medical craft.

Aristotle also expresses his distinction between activity and production in terms of a cross-cutting distinction between 'two senses of "for the sake of which"'. This latter distinction has been perspicaciously enunciated by Monte Ransome Johnson, after careful reading of classical commentators. In one sense the phrase signifies 'the aim of something'; in the other it signifies 'the beneficiary of the achievement of that aim' (Johnson 2005: 66; cf. *On the Soul* 415b2, *Metaphysics* 1072b2 and *Physics* 194a35–6, where Aristotle refers to a more extended discussion in his lost dialogue *On Philosophy*; Ross 1936: 509). In the sense of 'aim', that-for-the-sake-of-which is not any particular intention but some such universal form as that of a healthy human being. In the sense of 'beneficiary', that-for-the-sake-of-which is a particular being such as *this* individual patient. Once again, we may note that in neither sense is doctoring for the sake of a doctor qua doctor, who is, for Aristotle, *merely* the source and agent of change. In the same way, or so Aristotle argues, when a builder builds it is for the sake of bringing the form of the house or the temple (i.e. *the* building, in the nounal sense of a completed object) into substantial being and, also, for the sake of those who will live or worship in the building. In the sense neither of aim nor of benefit is the *process* of building for the sake of the builder. We might at least wish to add that a builder builds or a doctor cures for the sake also of pay (or perhaps as a favour, or under compulsion), but, for Aristotle, this social relation is entirely incidental and inessential to the process and its explanation. His ontology of causation is, at this basic level, not at all sociological. Theoretical philosophy precedes practical philosophy.

Johnson follows Aristotle in saying that an 'animal reproduces both for the aim of participating in the divine and eternal form, and for its own benefit', because such participation is the closest that it can get, as an individual, to immortality. He identifies this understanding of benefit with another: 'furthermore, the process of reproduction directly benefits the animal insofar as it is just this process that has brought it into being and life' (Johnson 2005: 74; cf. 175–8). But it is *not* one and the same temporal process of *genesis* that the individual animal causes as parent and was caused by as offspring, and therefore what we have is not just one 'primary being' as candidate for the status of beneficiary but two. A birth benefits both that which is born, in bringing it into being, and its parents. But we might well ask why, if this type of *genesis* can benefit the producer, the process of artificial production cannot do so also. Of course, manufacture cannot benefit the manufacturer in the same way that procreation benefits the father (as both moving and formal cause) in reproducing his own form. Nonetheless, we should at least acknowledge that such a productive process as doctoring or building is not rendered incapable of producing some benefit internal to the producer simply because it is undertaken for the sake of some external aim and of some external beneficiary.

Aristotle differentiates little between the good of individuals of the same species in his natural philosophy, and in his several biological treatises he normally applies the same principles to humans as to other animals. However, craft and manufacture, like language, are more or less unique to human beings. In his works of both theoretical and practical philosophy, he says that the beneficiaries of manufacture are the consumers of those products which are the aims of productive processes and of crafts. He intends (as we shall see below) both a hierarchy of consumers and a separation of producers from non-producers. Even though the crafts were once invented (*Metaphysics* 981b13–23), production is not, on his account, a matter of innovation or imaginative creativity, still less of rational invention. In imitating nature (rather than divinity), craft aspires merely to the reproduction of pre-existing but inferior forms.

The Good of Activity

The concepts of *energeia* and *entelecheia* not only denote what is most importantly distinctive in Aristotle's concept of nature; they also denote what is elemental to his concept of virtue or excellence (*arete*). What is excellent is what is most good. Goodness is not (as argued by Plato) a form in itself but something predicated of other beings, and what is good for a substantive being is the actualization of its specific potential and form. Therefore, an excellent being must be one that has actualized or completed its form. Teleological explanation of change is explanation couched in terms of some final end, some that-for-the-sake-of-which or completion. A veritable *telos* is nothing less than the achievement of some such condition, the enjoyment of some such *entelecheia*. It is therefore incumbent upon Aristotle to identify and describe such constant actualizations of form in terrestrial and temporal beings.

Much of what Aristotle intends by the 'form' of a living being is detailed in his book *Peri Psyches*, better known by its Latin title, *De Anima*, or by its standard English translation, *On the Soul*. The soul or psyche is not, for Aristotle, anything immortal. On the contrary, it is inseparable from an individual living body. Even plants have specific psyches, and therefore the term denotes a kind of life and not simply of either psychology or animation. Here and in his biological treatises, Aristotle writes of nutrition, reproduction, locomotion, perception and thinking as *energeiai*.

Aristotle extends the concept of *energeia* in writing of the activity, the being-at-work, of the parts of animals. Terrestrial beings are composites not only of form and matter but also of different organs, each of which has its own *energeia*. As we have noted, an eye is defined not in terms of its material composition but of its essential activity of seeing, and an eye that sees clearly is a good eye. Seeing is an activity that is in a sense both self-sufficient and atemporal, and therefore an end in itself. However, seeing is also for the sake of the horse or the human that sees and is an integral part of what it is to be and to act as a complete horse or human. This is the central point of both *On the Soul* and *On the Parts of Animals*. As so often, Aristotle argues from common sense when he equates the actualization of an animal's natural potentials with its *telos*, and its *telos* with its good. To say that an animal's eyes see and lungs breathe for the sake of the entire animal is to imply that it is good for that animal to see and breathe. Each being's good is its actualization of the characteristic *ergon*, work or self-moved activity of a being of its kind. We can, for example, talk of the good of Bucephalus and of the good of horses, and we can postulate that what would constitute the good life for Bucephalus is what would also constitute the good life for other horses, universally: seeing, breathing, grazing, galloping, interacting with other horses, mating, having foals, seeing those foals grow, and so on. Each form of animal is characterized by certain activities, and perhaps it is the actualization of its natural potential to engage in all of those essential activities that constitutes an individual animal's *telos*. But presumably the animal's *entelecheia* is something more than a simple aggregate of the activities of its different parts, with their respective activities and goods. So, alternatively, perhaps its highest and final good is that for the sake of which it not only comes into being and grows but also breathes and sees, and this is the actualization of the most distinctive or refined capacities of a being of its kind. In this case, the *entelecheia* of a composite being – unlike that of such a simple being as God, with its single, intellectual *energeia* – comprises an ordered hierarchy in which lesser activities are for the sake of higher ones and the excellence of an individual is the fullest development of those highest activities. This is an idea elaborated less in either Aristotle's metaphysics or his natural philosophy than, as we will see, in his practical philosophy of what is humanly changeable through action (*praxis*).

The Best Human Life

That there is a human *telos*, a good life of specifically human work or activity, is the premise of Aristotle's practical philosophy – his ethics, politics and economics. But his introduction of this premise in the *Nicomachean Ethics* – and also in his other ethical texts, the *Eudemian Ethics* (*EE*) and (if it is indeed by him) the *Magna Moralia* – contrasts with his usual accounts of the *tele* of other species. He indicates the peculiar singularity of the human good by adopting as its name the popular term *eudaimonia*. Literally, this means being possessed of a 'well demon'. Our standard, subjectivist translation is 'happiness', but translations that more happily relate the concept to Aristotle's biology or metaphysics are 'flourishing' (Anscombe 1958: 18–19, Cooper 1975: 89–90) or 'well-being'. (Another, increasingly prevalent translation is 'success', leaving open whether *eudaimonia* is success for an individual in actualizing the human *telos* or, say, in simply out competing rivals.) Keen to identify this good as one of characteristically human activity, Aristotle proposes that *eudaimonia* is generally agreed to denote 'living well and doing [acting, faring] well [*eu prattein*]' (e.g. *NE* 1095a19). No Socrates, he considers the plausibility of this move to depend upon identifying the best life with those activities that his audience finds pleasurable or esteems, and then expends his persuasive efforts in establishing that what is most eudaimonistic is what is most lastingly admirable rather than most sensually and subjectively pleasurable. We might therefore understand him as accepting some of the received opinions of his wealthy Athenian listeners in order to argue against others. He does not deny them the benefit of pleasure, which we share with other animals and which supervenes upon various activities (*NE* X: 1–5), but he wants to persuade them that some aims are more rationally deliberated (*NE* III: 1–5) and defensible, and therefore better, than others.

What might seem to be more important here is not the content of the aims but the very process of deliberation, as this actualizes those rational capacities that are distinctively human and therefore allow of specifically human excellence. Accordingly, we might suppose that even though the deliberation of a doctor benefits her patient, it also benefits her as it actualizes her own potential as a human being. But this is denied by Aristotle on the basis of his absolute distinction between activities and processes, not only because healing is clearly a process, but also because even deliberation is a temporal process. The highest human good is the leisured activity of contemplation of what is unchanging, and this activity issues in the production of neither an artefact nor a decision. As we have seen, it is, on Aristotle's account, our potential for such activity that most surely distinguishes us from other terrestrial beings, and its actualization is what in human nature comes closest to divinity. Knowledge and understanding are permanent achievements of a human being. Although other animals also have their own pleasures, their own reproductive activities, and even their own kinds of practical wisdom (*phronesis*) in pursuit of their specific goods (*NE* 1141a22–9), neither 'horse nor bird nor fish can be *eudaimon*' because none of them has any such share in the divine (*EE* 1217a24–8) as that which humans enjoy through its contemplation. Pleasures, like movements, are transient; knowledge is permanent.

The *Nicomachean Ethics* announces that we should aim at what is 'the good and the best [*tagathon kai to ariston*]' (1094a22), and Anglophone commentators have debated for the past 40 years (Hardie 1965; Lear 2004) or more (Greenwood 1909) as to whether this single aim should be understood to be 'inclusive' of a plurality of different activities and 'ends' or, alternatively, to be constituted by a single 'dominant' activity for the sake of which individuals' other activities should be ordered. What has been agreed by the participants in this debate is that if *eudaimonia* is to be identified with a single, dominant activity, then this must be the purely intellectual activity of contemplating unchanging forms. If the 'inclusivist' interpretation of Aristotle were correct, his practical philosophy would be freed from 'intellectualist' domination by this single activity of *theoria*, and *eudaimonia* would instead comprise a plurality of *energeiai* and *praxeis*, of activities and actions. And yet, even though freeing *praxis* from *theoria*, the inclusivist interpretation would render Aristotle's practical philosophy similar to his theoretical and natural philosophy in that it would make the human *telos* an aggregation of various activities in the same way that he describes the *tele* of other animals. But, even if what is at issue between inclusivist and intellectualist interpretations of Aristotle is not settled in the first book of the

Nicomachean Ethics, then it surely is in the last. This clearly states that the best or most excellent human life is one of *theoria*, because contemplation is the most self-sufficient and complete activity available to us (*NE* X: 6–8).

What this leaves out of account is politics. Being naturally incapable of self-sufficiency as individuals, humans are naturally political animals. This human activity of politics involves the domination of other activities and, for Aristotle, their hierarchical ordering. For this reason, Aristotle considers politics the highest non-theoretical activity or type of *praxis*.

The most decisive contribution to the debate between intellectualist and inclusivist interpretations of the *Nicomachean Ethics* has been made by Richard Kraut. He argues that Aristotle considers the most perfect and therefore best life to be one of contemplation for the sake of which all other activities are undertaken, including politics, the task of which is to order all other, lesser activities. He qualifies this intellectualist interpretation only in adding that a life of specifically political action comprises a 'second-best' kind of *eudaimonia*, itself subserved by all activities other than *theoria*.

Kraut follows his interpretive argument about Aristotle with an argument *against* Aristotle. He acknowledges that philosophical and political lives can be good lives, but denies that they are necessarily the best. This denial is based in a rejection of Aristotle's teleological 'for-the-sake-of relation', according to which 'only lives organized around' reasoning and 'ends that are not pursued for the sake of further goals' 'deserve to be models of human flourishing' (Kraut 1989: 356–7). Kraut's objection to Aristotle's argument is that it makes the best and second-best lives enemies of a more morally compelling account of the good life as something actualizable through any one of a plurality of human activities. His argument may be described as inclusivist, but not in the sense that a good life must include a uniform set of different activities. Rather, his argument against Aristotle is socially inclusivist. Kraut's moral claim is that lives organized around any of a number of different activities may be considered good.

Theory, Action and Production

The plausibility of Aristotle's denigration of lives spent in occupations other than those of philosophy or politics depends upon establishing the similarity of *praxis* to the activity of *theoria* and their shared dissimilarity from the process of *poiesis*. One necessary condition of this is the drawing of some consistent distinction between actions and productions. A difficulty facing any such comparison and contrast is that – unlike *theoria*, which produces nothing beyond itself and leaves everything as it is – *praxeis* are, like *poieseis*, often useful and effective. Indeed, Aristotle differentiates *theoria* from *praxis* on the very grounds that the one is concerned with what is immutable whereas the other concerns what is humanly changeable. Whilst what is paradigmatic of theoretical reasoning is the activity of thought timelessly thinking of itself, what is paradigmatic of non-theoretical reasoning is thought thinking of the form of something that is to be brought into being (see *Metaphysics* Lambda: 9, especially 1074b38–1075a5).

Another necessary condition of establishing the superiority of philosophers over politicians and, then, of both over producers is the drawing of a conceptual distinction between *sophia*, the intellectual excellence of those engaging in *theoria* (and also in natural science, insofar as this also involves knowledge of unchanging forms; as he does not foresee natural science becoming the handmaiden of technology, Aristotle proposes that the study of nature is also a complete activity because a means to no further end), and *phronesis*, the intellectual excellence of those engaging in political and other ethical *praxeis*, and, most especially, a distinction between both *sophia* and *phronesis* on the one side and, on the other, *techne*, the craft excellence or expertise apparent in production. This Aristotle attempts in Book Six of the *Nicomachean Ethics* (repeated as *EE* V). He notes that technical expertise has often been dignified as '*sophia*' and that it is in some ways analogous to the knowledge of philosophers, but he is far keener than those philosophers he follows to pin down what is disanalogous. His distinction between *sophia* and *techne* is underpinned by his distinction between *energeia* and *genesis*, in that contemplation is a human activity, a being-at-work, whereas craft causes a type of coming-into-being. As coming-into-being occurs in the product and not in the producer, Aristotle discounts it as a human *energeia* (despite etymology, and even though he elsewhere describes the weaving of webs and the building of nests as *energeiai* of spiders and birds). As technical excellence is manifest in the product, he describes it as a quality of the product and not of the producer. This corresponds to his description of the efficient cause of manufacture as the craft rather than the craftsperson. On his account, the artisan substitutes for the necessity operative in that natural generation which art merely imitates or completes; she merely facilitates the productive process. Aristotle takes care to conceptualize both the form of the product and the technical knowledge required for necessity to guide its production (as opposed to when, occasionally, this occurs through luck) in isolation from any account of the attributes of the producer as a human being. On his account, both the form and the craft are (respectively, formal and efficient) causes of the product in a way that the individual producer is not. He therefore reveals that, just as production is not a human activity in the same way as are contemplation and action, nor is craft skill an *intellectual* excellence inhering in humans in the same way as do theoretical and practical wisdom.

Aristotle also argues that craft skill is a capacity rather than either an activity or a virtue. It can be used or not, and can be used for either good or bad purposes. In this, craftiness or artifice differs from theoretical and practical wisdom alike. Theoretical wisdom is good in itself and so too, he stipulates, is practical wisdom, because it only pursues aims commended by the moral virtues. In this sense, practical wisdom does not deliberate. This lack of deliberation about practical wisdom's ends might again appear to draw it close to craft skill in that 'a doctor does not deliberate about whether to cure' any more than does 'a politician whether to produce good order', but only about the means by which to do so (*NE* 1112b12–16).

Although Aristotle implies that a doctor is at least as likely to act Hippocratically as is a politician to act virtuously, he insists that to act Hippocratically is not the same as to act out of a virtuous character. To act as a doctor or shipbuilder is to refrain from deliberation about ends in a way that is similar to that in which deliberation is absent from natural processes (*Physics* 199b26–31). Art's aim is given by necessity, as is nature's. What Aristotle asserts is that, in this, both differ from virtuous action. The aims of such action are given not by necessity but by the actor's excellent character. We have seen that a doctor deliberates about *how* best to bring about health before acting to do so, but, for Aristotle, medicine's need of such technical deliberation merely evinces art's inferiority to the spontaneity operative in nature. Once deliberation has apprehended what is necessary to secure art's necessary aim, movement follows with a similar necessity to that of natural processes.

This argument is undermined elsewhere. Both the *Eudemian Ethics* (VIII) and Book Six of the *Nicomachean Ethics* conclude with the analogy between politics and medicine. Aristotle here again distinguishes practice from theory in proposing that, just as doctoring does not direct health but is for the sake of bringing health into being, so politics does not direct the gods but only those things that subserve our contemplation of the divine (*EE* 1249b12–15; *NE* 1145a6–11). Similarly, at the end of the *Nicomachean Ethics* he compares education into the works (*erga*) of law-making with that into the products of medicine. As he repeats in Book One of the *Eudemian Ethics*, politics is itself a 'productive science', its product being good order in just the same way as health is the aim of medicine (1216b16–19). What all this indicates is that, even if a consistent distinction between *poiesis* and *praxis* were maintained, Aristotle's more elemental conceptual distinction would remain that separating *theoria* from *praxis* and *poiesis* alike. But it is not, in any case, clear that a consistent distinction can be drawn between the production of artefacts or performance of services (so that, for example, the production of music is a *poiesis*, as distinct from its 'aesthetic' contemplation) and, conversely, the performance of actions that effect such states of affairs as military victories and well-ordered *poleis*. We might ask whether a speech by Pericles is any less a production than is a poem (*poiema*) by Solon or a play by Sophocles or a statue by Polycleitus or an operation by Nicomachus senior, and whether all are not as much expressions and examples of human agency as are Solon's laws, Pericles's securing of political order, Alexander's victories, or Alexander's impatient cutting through of perplexities.

Action, Production and Interpretation

The instability of Aristotle's distinction of *praxis* from *poiesis* may be found in his account of the very logic of practical reasoning. The deductive structure of theoretical reasoning about forms is exemplified in the *Prior Analytics'* account of the syllogism. Elsewhere Aristotle suggests that practical reasoning is exemplified in the logic of what commentators have called a 'practical syllogism', in which what is deduced from the premises is the proposition – or, as Elizabeth Anscombe argues (Anscombe 1963: 59–60), the performance – of an action. However, when we turn to the two clearest examples of such a practical syllogism, we find that neither is concerned with action as distinct from production. The clearest example outside the *Ethics* concerns the 'production' of a cloak, which Aristotle calls an 'action' (*On the Motion of Animals* 701a17–22). The clearest example within the *Ethics* is concerned with nutrition and the production of health (*NE* VII (*EE* VI): 3), and he here describes what he contrasts with theoretical reasoning as reasoning about 'productive activity [*poietikais prattein*]' (*NE* 1147a28).

That Aristotle fails to maintain throughout his corpus any consistent semantic distinction between *poiesis* and *praxis*, production and action, was not considered a problem when Anglophone scholarship on Aristotle really took off. This was less because of any historical thesis about Aristotle's development than because of the spirit of the time and place in which that take-off occurred. In the early decades of the last century Oxford University still felt the influence of T. H. Green's reception of German idealism and, also, of his appeal to Aristotle's authority in theorizing a political community within which labour could be newly included. Ernest Barker, in dealing directly with the *Politics*, agonized over the difficulties of such an appeal, accusing Aristotle of mistaking 'an *external* and unreal teleology' for 'a true' and *'internal'* teleology in describing workers as 'means to an end external to themselves' (Barker 1906: 226–7). However, we might well suspect that it is Barker who is contravening this Kantian and Hegelian distinction (see below, pp. 75–6, 77–8) in postulating what may be called a communal functionalism (see below, pp. 51–2) in which 'there is no relation of means and end between the lower and higher workers' but all are 'parts of one whole . . . each giving, each receiving, and all contributing to the common life by that which they supply' (ibid.: 372). The issue could be dealt with more obliquely with reference to the *Ethics* (notwithstanding Barker in Aristotle 1948: 10). Even if W. D. Ross, editor of the Oxford Translation of Aristotle, was himself less ready to translate *poietikais* as 'practical' than is sometimes suggested (compare *NE* 1147a28 in Aristotle 1925 and Wiggins 1996: 258–9; it can still be claimed that *poiein* is usually translated as 'action', as in Wildberg 2004: 222), commentators who were more influenced by Green had ethical, political and even 'sociological' (see below, p. 39) reason to minimize any difference between *praxis* and *poiesis*. Harold Joachim eulogized 'the man who embodies' productive science, 'the skilled craftsman or the artist, whose "making" is alive with his own intelligent purpose' and whose *techne* is 'confirmed [in] thoughtful mastery of his materials' and 'incarnated in the "making" which it illumines and controls'. This man Joachim compared with one who embodies practical science, 'the statesman or wise agent whose conduct is alive with his own intelligent insight' (Joachim 1926: xv). In the lectures he delivered on the *Nicomachean Ethics* from 1902 to 1917, he emphasized the priority of Aristotle's distinction of 'speculative science as contrasted with practical and productive' science, although noting that a distinction should be drawn between *'praxis'* as *energeia* and *'praxis'* as production (Joachim 1951: 2–3, 206–7). Later, G. R. G. Mure objected that 'when Aristotle abstracts and considers the basis of moral conduct in the individual, he tends perhaps to overemphasize its difference from art', and that he does not offer 'a plausible account of art'. Habituation into virtue is 'formally of the same nature as' habituation into skill, and 'the more a man's talents and interests are absorbed by the steady direction of his energies in an important profession, the less chance there is of his being a bad man' (Mure 1932: 137, 139).

The Oxford tradition of commentary has become decreasingly tentative in its treatment of Aristotle. J. L. Ackrill critically analysed Aristotle's distinction of *energeia* from *poiesis*, *kinesis* and *genesis* in the *Nicomachean Ethics* (X: 4) and elsewhere (Ackrill 1997c), going on to raise 'the real difficulty, that actions often or always *are* productions and productions often or always *are* actions. . . . The brave man's action *is* fighting uphill to relieve the garrison, and the just man is paying off his debt *by* mending his neighbor's fence.' He proposes that an action must involve some such moral intention but also that the performing of the action involves producing some such result, and that 'it does not seem natural to say in such a case that the agent has done two things at the same time' (Ackrill 1997a: 213–14). What seems unnatural to Ackrill is precisely what is proposed by David Charles in Aristotle's defence. Whereas Ackrill denies that Aristotle referred to a single exercise of intentional agency by 'various act descriptions' (ibid.: 217), Charles argues that Aristotle paid 'sufficient attention to questions of action-individuation' to maintain 'the praxis/production distinction' whilst acknowledging that a moral activity and a productive process can 'co-occur' in *'one action-episode'* or 'basic act' (Charles 1986: 120–1; 1984: 62–6). On Charles's account of Aristotle's 'ontological theory', *praxeis* are 'a subset of [human] activities' comprising those 'chosen for no further goal', whereas productions are a subset of processes comprising those that involve skill and occur 'in an object other than the agent' (Charles 1986: 129). Activities and processes 'form mutually exclusive classes of entity' (Charles 1984: 35). Although the 'individuation conditions' of processes 'are context-free', processes are not 'a fundamental ontological category' (ibid.: 30–1) but exemplifications of the properties of fundamental substances. For example, it is a potential (even if not the natural or essential capacity) of wood that it may become the timber to make or repair a fence, but the process of it forming a fence should be understood as distinct from the intentional action of a neighbour repaying a debt even when the two co-occur, because the fence and the human are two absolutely separate beings.

Charles intends his 'philosophical scholarship' to demonstrate the 'continuing philosophical value' of Aristotle's ontology by advancing 'an *Aristotelian* account' of action against positions in contemporary analytic philosophy (Charles 1984: ix–x). His principal target is 'Davidson's account of events as an irreducible category', because this conflicts with Aristotle's distinction 'between processes and activities' and identification of both as properties of substantive beings (Charles 1984: 35; despite revisions, Davidson continued to maintain that actions are 'a species of event': e.g. Davidson 2005: 285). However, he also opposes what Anscombe and others advanced as an Aristotelian account of action as issuing from, and sufficiently explained by, syllogistic reasoning. In opposition to this, he differentiates between efficiently 'causal explanation' of intentional action, in terms of motive desires, and its 'teleological explanation', in terms of goods internal to the action (Charles 1984: 197–202), and his claim that desire informs not just the premises of deliberation but also the decision whether to act on what reason proposes (ibid.: 96) has been criticized by other interpreters as instrumentalist or quasi-Humean (see chapter 4 below). What he regards as more elemental is Aristotelianism's ontology. Once this is understood, it is possible to say that a production (such as mending a neighbour's fence) 'may be chosen as a means to acting justly right now, and acting justly right now chosen for its own sake without contradiction' (Charles 1986: 130). He avoids saying of *praxis* what Ackrill says of it in his case for an inclusivist reading of 'Aristotle on *eudaimonia*' (Ackrill 1997b): that action is both a means and an end, or an 'internal means', in that a *praxis* is performed both for its own sake and for the sake of something else.

Charles's ontological position – that actions and productions are distinct and irreducible one to the other, and yet that they can 'co-occur' in the same 'basic action' – is a fine analytic and exegetical solution to perplexities in Aristotle's attempt to distinguish *praxis* from *poiesis*, and yet it has persuaded few Anglophone scholars of any 'continuing philosophical value' in this elemental Aristotelian distinction. It has been better received in Europe, where such Aristotelians as Carlo Natali are happier to cross subdisciplinary boundaries and philosophize about action ontologically. In Germany (as we will see in chapter 3), a series of theorists have insisted that syllogistic logic as such is unimportant in practical reasoning because this is concerned not with demonstrable knowledge about necessary universals but with the pursuit of particular aims under contingent conditions, and that such practical judgement shares less with universalizable techniques than does *theoria*. In America, too, Germans like Hannah Arendt (1958), Leo Strauss (1964) and Nicholas Lobkowicz (1967) have vigorously argued that practice should be distinguished entirely from theory and from production, both in our interpretation of Aristotle and for us now. What is most important in human life, on their account, is ethical and political action, and this is neither the application of theory nor the production of things. Back in Oxford, Anthony Kenny (1979) differentiated 'ethical syllogisms' from the 'means-ends' logic of 'technical' syllogisms, whilst a permanent Oxford exile, John McDowell, has followed a temporary one, David Wiggins, in rejecting any idea that practical syllogisms involve the application of universal rules to particular cases (McDowell 1998a; Wiggins 2002), and has outdone him in arguing for the independence of Aristotelian ethics from both theoretical and technical reasoning (McDowell 1996a; cf. Charles 1995).

Technical Reasoning

Mure's complaint about the implausibility of Aristotle's concept of craft has been echoed by Sarah Broadie. She objects to the way in which Aristotle depsychologizes craft into 'a false abstraction' of 'end-directed automation' (Broadie 1990: 402–3). The craftsman is reduced to the status of a function of his craft in Aristotle's anxiety to deny to him the status of an actor and to his craft the status of *praxis* or of a characteristically human *energeia*. Perhaps it would therefore be truer to Aristotle to translate *techne* as 'technique' or even 'technology' than 'craft'. *Techne* is the excellence of production. It is the excellence of an artefact coming-into-being rather than of a human being-at-work. The process, like its product, is indeed abstracted – alienated – from the producer. The excellence of the craftsman or technician (*technites*) qua producer consists only in her perceptual apprehension of some form to reproduce and of the habituation of the movements of her hands into that reproductive process. Such habituation, says Aristotle, is contemptible. He denies that it shares anything further with the habituation of character into ethically excellent action.

Charles does not consider Aristotle's conception of craft to be so alien. On the contrary, he argues that Aristotle's account is more insightfully appreciative of the cognitive status of productive 'practices' than is the famous account advanced by Ludwig Wittgenstein, the philosopher with perhaps more proven artisanal ability than any other. Unlike the builders in Wittgenstein's exposition of a language-game (Wittgenstein 1958: 3–10 [§§2–21]), the master craftsman (*architekton*) of Charles's Aristotle acts not on the bases of habit or mere experience but through real knowledge of the natural substances that are his raw materials. This is why the master craftsman can teach his craft. Technical knowledge and judgement is not tacit, as asserted by conservatives like Michael Polanyi, but fully rational. There might seem to be, as Aristotle often suggests, an impassably wide gulf between the mechanical craftsman (*banausos technites*) and the excellence of the *architekton*. But to whom does the *architekton* teach his knowledge? Presumably, as Charles suggests, he must teach it to the low-level artisan. This trainee is, then, a potential master craftsman of their shared practice.

Charles makes still bolder claims for *techne* in arguing that Aristotle's theoretical idea of the causation of natural, universal kinds is 'rooted in the judgements of the master craftsman' and 'is best seen as an extension of the type of understanding already achieved (in limited measure) by the master craftsman' (Charles 2000: 358, 359). Aristotle's 'idea of a biological common nature is grounded in our ordinary dealings with the world, the ones exemplified in our activities as farmers or fishermen, breeders or hunters' (ibid.: 368). *Technai* are more than just ways of imitating nature; they are activities giving rise to the knowledge of universals that comprises our highest intellectual achievement. Drawing on *Metaphysics* Alpha: 1 (see also *Posterior Analytics* II. 19), Charles differentiates between three 'varieties of craftsman': the 'low-level artisan [who] has been trained to carry out a few techniques by his instructor'; the 'empirical doctor' who has learnt to make independent judgements informed by experience of particulars; and finally the master craftsman who understands the natural kinds, the real universals, with which he is dealing and can explicate, communicate and teach that understanding (Charles 2003: 111–12). On Aristotle's account, Charles argues, the master craftsman is able to advance both his craft and human knowledge as such. Even if it remains for the philosopher of nature to explain fully the scientific essence of natural kinds, it is the master builder who knows most and judges best about roof beams and fences, in part because he, too, knows something of the nature of the different kinds of wood used in their manufacture. Although, like Plato and Augustine, 'defending some of the claims of classical realism', Charles's Aristotle agrees with Wittgenstein 'in seeing conceptual thought and meaning as arising out of lower levels of activity' (ibid.: 126), including productive activities. What Charles does not say is how such agreement constitutes the problem with which Aristotle's Aristotle grappled in Book Six of the *Ethics* of decisively differentiating *techne* from *sophia*, and not just from *phronesis*. Nor does Charles tell us how his account of craft might be related to his own rigorous distinction of productions from specifically moral actions.

A more integrated account of Aristotle's conceptual distinctions is presented by C. D. C. Reeve. He agrees with Charles (Reeve 2000: 146; cf. Reeve 1992: 105) that Aristotle may be understood as implying that a person can act simultaneously for the sake of acting well and for the sake of some production over and above the action itself. He describes a process as something that has an 'external end', whereas a genuine activity has an 'internal end' (Reeve 2000: 144–6; 1992: 101–6). The product is that for the sake of which production is undertaken, but it is external to the process. *Praxeis*, too, are undertaken for the sake of distinct results (*erga*). These results may be internal ends which we might call events (a blow that is struck through the act of striking, a note that is sung through the act of singing; Reeve 2000: 146), but the real goal of *praxis* is *eudaimonia*. Here Reeve assimilates both the intellectualist and the inclusivist accounts of *eudaimonia* into his account of Aristotle's practical philosophy. *Theoria* constitutes *eudaimonia* in the primary sense, and this is the external end of *praxis*, but, rather like Kraut, Reeve says that *praxis* comprises a 'secondary *eudaimonia*', and action can indeed therefore be its own internal end (Reeve 1992: 106).

Poiesis, for Aristotle, comprises no type or part of *eudaimonia*, while *techne*, as a mere capacity or potential, requires external direction. However, the *technites* may also possess *phronesis*. Insofar as she does, Reeve observes, her deliberative and decisive virtue of *phronesis* will 'control' her *techne*, and she will therefore exercise her *techne* in a way that promotes her *eudaimonia* (ibid.: 166, 186–7). For example, 'a doctor's medical skill is expressed in productions, but if that skill is also controlled by *phronesis*, those productions . . . involve an activation of *phronesis* that is a *praxis*. . . . And that *praxis* is valuable or desirable independent of the value that attaches to the product of the underlying craft' (ibid.: 187). Here Reeve goes far further than Charles in allowing the identity of *poieseis* and *praxeis*. However, before we infer that this conceptual distinction between activities aiming at 'external' and 'internal ends' can be so easily dissolved, we should first explore the implications of a similar conceptual distinction.

Internal Goods, External Goods and the Best Humans

Aristotle follows Plato in drawing a distinction between 'internal' and 'external goods'. He uses this distinction to argue, against Plato, for the homonymy of good (*NE* I: 6; cf. *EE* I: 8) in a way that parallels his argument in the *Categories* and *Metaphysics* about the homonymy of being (Shields 1999). If we consider that his argument distances the teleological subject of his practical philosophy – the specifically human good – from his own as well as Plato's theoretical philosophy, this consideration should be tempered by appreciation of how very different is his account of the relation between internality and externality from that of a Descartes or Kant. On Aristotle's account, internal goods are those excellences of intellect and character (*ethos*; *EE* I: 2, *NE* II: 1) that are internal to the psyche and activity of some actor. Such virtues as justice and courage are analogous to *technai* in that they are practiced and habituated. Although he considers the psyche to be inseparable from the body, and although the distinction of internal from external goods is what is crucial, Aristotle again follows Plato's Socrates in sometimes adding an intermediate category comprising such 'goods of the body' as health, beauty and strength, but more usually includes such goods of the body amongst external goods. Goods of the body are external to the human psyche and *energeia*. Therefore, although also called good, and although attributes of the same being, their goodness is different in kind from that of internal goods. Aristotle argues that their goodness, like that of other external goods, is derivative from that of internal goods and that they should be regarded as good because they are necessary to 'produce' (*Topics* 106a8; *NE* 1096b11), preserve or protect internal goods. Their true goodness is only instrumental, and therefore to be assessed in the light of reflection upon the good specific and internal to human beings and their activity.

Besides goods of the body, external goods include 'good birth [*eugeneia*]', education, wealth and material goods, slaves, political power, honour, leisure, friends, and one's own children. If one is to cultivate the virtues and enjoy a good life, one requires more external goods than are necessary to merely sustain life. They are required because humans are incapable of *autarkeia* and, like other terrestrial beings, can only flourish and actualize their full potential under optimal conditions. External goods are necessary conditions for a good life, but they are certainly not sufficient ones. As internal goods are states of *energeia*, they cannot be simple products. Whilst no quantity of external goods can be sufficient to produce internal goodness, prior possession of internal excellences is necessary to ensure that external goods are indeed instrumentally good rather than corruptive. Like craft skill, and like the intellectual attribute of cleverness, external goods can be used for good or ill.

Whether an individual enjoys *eudaimonia* is explained by Aristotle in terms not of efficient or final causation but of luck. We should here note what might be misleading in translation of *eudaimonia* as flourishing and in its description as the actualization of a being's potential. On Aristotle's account, *eudaimonia* is a quality of an entire life. Good birth is its first requirement. It is therefore a possibility open only to those born into the 'best' class, of aristocrats. They inherit the wealth required for *eudaimonia*, because a life spent making one's own money is, for Aristotle, a life that is vulgar and corrupt. As has often been remarked by communitarian commentators, and even though he attributes ontological priority to individuals, Aristotle is no moral individualist of the modern kind. He considers a good life to be an attribute and achievement of individuals, but not something that is achievable solely through an individual's own efforts. A life of labour is a life incapable of excellence, devoted to the pursuit of external rather than internal goods. In this, it is similar to a life of *pleonexia*, of acquisitiveness or greed.

Aristotle commends 'household management' (*oikonomia*, root of our 'economy') as natural, because it concerns the acquisition and use of wealth for the good of one's family. In contrast, he condemns commerce as unnatural because it aims not at the acquisition of material goods to consume but at the accumulation of wealth for its own sake. Commerce is incompatible with any kind of excellence because it is premised on the intellectual error of mistaking things that are only good instrumentally as good in themselves, and therefore of adopting as an aim something that has no limit or possibility of actualization. Aristotle's aristocratic *phronimos* is someone who is not tempted to accumulate further wealth because he has never had to work to accumulate the abundance of external goods that he has always enjoyed. In this, he differs from Hesiod's industrious farmer and perhaps also from Charles's master builder. Of him, Aristotle might observe that he builds not in order to make buildings but in order to make money, and that he strives to become a better builder not in order to become a better person but in order to accumulate yet more money. As has often been remarked, Aristotle's critique of commerce reflects the disdain for tradesmen that may be assumed to be typical of his aristocratic audience.

Aristocracy (*aristokratia*) denotes at once what is loosely called a type of *politeia* and its group of ruling citizens. The aristocracy are those to whom *arete* is traditionally attributed (Adkins 1960: 156–62, 332–43), the gentlemanly successors of Homer's heroes (*arete*, like the Latin *virtus*, having originally denoted such characteristically masculine qualities as martial courage and a propensity to violence). However, the quality that specifies these 'best' humans is denoted less by the terms *arete* or *agathon*, which for Aristotle pertain to a range of moral and intellectual qualities, than by the common (Dover 1974: 69–73, 41–5) terms *kalon* and *kalokagathia*, which are most revealingly translated as 'noble' and 'noble-and-good' or 'nobility' (Woods 1992: 172–9). This concept of nobility is one that McDowell has attempted to place at the centre of an Aristotelian ethics which makes the properly habituated individual the highest criterion and judge of what it is to do and live well (e.g. McDowell 1996b: 23, 28, 30–1).

For Aristotle, '*kalokagathia* is complete virtue' (*EE* 1249a16). This most excellent quality of magnanimity can only be exercised by those who already possess wealth, power and status, and whose nature it is to know how to use such possessions without being corrupted by them. Thoroughly habituated in virtue and enjoying self-mastery (*enkrateia*), these men (they cannot be women) are fully fit to be the masters of others. They do not have the souls of ordinary humans; rather, they have 'greatness of soul [*megalopsychia*]' (*NE* IV: 3 (*EE* III: 5)). Just as a man should be ruled by the most sovereign part of his soul, so the *polis* should be ruled by such *megalopsychoi* (*Politics* 1327b38–1328a15).

Aristotle speaks to the aristocracy when he says that it is nobler and, even, more divine to promote the political good than the good only of an individual, because the good of a *polis* is more complete (*NE* 1094b8–10).

Although such a noble man would not (to return to Ackrill's example) stoop to mending his neighbour's fence and would be perturbed by being in anyone's debt, he would seize an opportunity to lead others in fighting uphill to save his *polis*. If he were to die a glorious death in such a cause, then that would only confirm his nobility. Such an ethics differs from the moral reflections of Ackrill and Charles in being political.

Politics and Nature

A *polis*, unlike an individual human, admits of *autarkeia*. According to Aristotle, the dignity of even the grandest man is diminished by his dependence upon others for the satisfaction of his needs, but a *polis* may be self-sufficient and independent. The good of a political community may therefore be a final or complete good. It would seem to be in part because of this possibility of a completion subserving no external beneficiary that Aristotle considers himself justified in theorizing the *polis* as 'natural'. Given his sophistic dichotomy of nature and artifice, activity and production, *phronesis* and *techne*, he wishes to accommodate the political community of citizens on the side of that which he celebrates rather than of that which he denigrates as base, servile and incomplete.

In his *Politics* Aristotle often proposes that the *polis* is a substantial being. In drawing an analogy between *polis* and individual he is, of course, once again following Plato, but he once again puts Plato's ideal into his own language in calling the *polis* a composite and natural being. The proposition that a political being (a *res publica*, as it was later called) is natural has been a target for some of the most influential anti-Aristotelian polemicists. Thomas Hobbes argued against Aristotle (on the basis of a thoroughly materialist metaphysic) that the state is not natural but artificial (Hobbes 1994: 106–18, 456–76), and this argument is repeated by David Keyt (1991) and assimilated to that of Aristotle by Andrés Rosler (2005). In contrast, Friedrich von Hayek argued that our extended order is neither natural nor artificial but 'spontaneous' (1973: 35–54; 1988: 45–7) in a way that James Murphy attempts to read back into Aristotle (Murphy 1994; we should note, with regard to discussion of McDowell in chapter 4, that Hayek's use of 'spontaneous' owes nothing to Aristotle's naturalism but something to Kant's epistemology). More affirmatively, W. L. Newman called the *polis* 'a Natural Whole' to be studied in the light of 'the Science of Being and Becoming' (1887: 64–5). Keyt calls Book One's argument that humans and households are constituents of the polis 'organic' (1991: 135–40), whilst Reeve consistently translates Aristotle's *taxis* as 'organization' (Aristotle

1998). Reeve also says that the *polis* 'meets all of Aristotle's conditions for existing by nature' (Reeve 1998: lvi). Aristotle suggests that all four causes of being can be attributed to a *polis*: its final cause will be discussed below; its formal cause is its *politeia* or, in the standard translation, 'constitution'; its material cause is its citizenry; and he sometimes indicates that its generative cause is some such historical founder as Sparta's Lycurgus or even Athens's Solon. He does not entertain the thought that the *polis* may be the consequence of the aggregated reasoning of self-interested individuals, either through a historical or hypothetical event in the way postulated by Hobbes or through an evolutionary process in the way postulated by Hayek. He does describe the *polis* as an organized structure of offices (*archai*) that is analytically separable from its citizens (even if he did not anticipate our modern abstraction of bureaucratic offices from the personality of their officials), sometimes presenting these *archai* as the productively causal sources of the *polis* as a distinct being. But the good order (*eunomia*), which he sometimes calls politics' product, is not analogous to an artefact because, with the completion of a product, the process of production terminates. In contrast, political order has not only to be produced; it must also be conserved over time.

As the activity of sustaining political order is ongoing, it is not capable of completion in the atemporal sense that Aristotle attributes to such activities as seeing or contemplating. But the life of *theoria* is the final good subserved by political order. There are no external beneficiaries of political order, but there are internal beneficiaries. Even if the activity of *theoria* is atemporal and self-sufficient, its specifically human practitioners cannot be.

Politics is only capable of completion in a secondary sense, as noted by Kraut and Reeve. This completion is not that of the 'dominant good' of *theoria* but of an inclusive good. It is inclusive of a plurality of different aims and activities, hierarchically ordered into a coherent whole by politics. 'The good and the best' within the active whole of a *polis*, like that of an army or household (*Metaphysics* 1075a11–23), is to be found in its rulers. This sovereign activity exemplifies *phronesis*, but Aristotle follows Plato in regarding political rule as a *techne*. Rulers' exercise of directive oversight he regards as akin to the skill of a master craftsman, an *architekton*, in directing his subordinates.

There is an obvious disanalogy between the activity of, say, a master builder directing other builders and their direction by a politician. The master builder's skill is as a builder, and he exercises authority over other builders because of his proven competence and superiority as a builder. The politician as such has no skill as a builder, and his authority (or power) over builders must be of another kind. Aristotle regards *politike techne* as the activity of managing other activities. In this, it resembles *oikonomia* or household management, and the term 'management' may direct us to what Aristotle calls craft's completion of nature. When wood is turned into timber to form a roof beam or fence, we might say that its nature is changed. What is exploited is not its capacity to flourish as a tree, but other of its potentials. Our term 'management' has a similar rationale. Originally it meant the 'handling' (from *manus*, the Latin for hand) or training of horses, not qua horses but qua steeds, as Alexander tamed, 'broke', trained and rode Bucephalus. Unsurprisingly, the greatest Greek writer on *oikonomia*, the aristocrat Xenophon, is also the greatest Greek writer on managing horses. Aristotle himself recounts the story of a free horse that allowed itself to be bridled and controlled by a human, comparing it to citizens who allow themselves to be similarly bridled and ruled by a tyrant (*Rhetoric* 1393b8–23). We might say that a horse that is a steed, a vehicle, ceases to act for its own sake and becomes a means, an external good, subserving others' ends and good. It becomes an artefact and an instrument, a managed and manipulated tool.

Politics and Craft

The *Nicomachean Ethics* begins by proposing that 'every *techne* and every discipline, and likewise every *praxis* and decision, seems to seek some good'. It immediately differentiates between such goods. Some, Aristotle says, are activities (*energeiai*), whilst others are works (*erga*) or products apart from the activities. Wherever there are goods or products apart from the *praxeis*, the product is by nature better than the action because the action is undertaken for the sake of the product. He illustrates this by saying that bridle-making is subordinate to horsemanship, which is subordinate to generalship, which is subordinate to politics. What is here illustrated is not any clear distinction (either semantic or conceptual) between productive and unproductive activities but, rather, a hierarchy of activities in which some are undertaken for the sake of others. Each subordinate activity in the hierarchy produces some good that is external to, but a necessary condition of, the activity which is superordinate to it. Each superordinate activity is described as *architektonikos*, or architectonic. Actions are performed within this hierarchical ordering of particular crafts (or activities) according to their that-for-the-sake-of relations. This rationale of architectonic ordering extends that of internal and external goods, according to which the goodness of an external good is relative and instrumental to that of an internal good. This is a logic of ends and means.

Such a hierarchical logic is, in one sense, thoroughly teleological. All the way through the hierarchy, that for the sake of which particular activities are practised may be specified in terms of productive aim and superordinate beneficiary. Practitioners need only be aware of that for the sake of which they act in terms of the aim, or product, of their activity (indeed, the *Metaphysics* says that a mere technician does not even need to know that much, producing by habit just as lifeless things do by nature; 981b2–5). The beneficiary of the product at which those practitioners have aimed is its consumer. We may recall Aristotle's teleological injunction that the order of nature is the reverse of the order of generation; the goal of consumption or use is naturally prior to the process of production, and the good of the beneficiary is naturally prior to that of the product and, therefore, of the producer.

The beneficiary of a medical process is the patient, but this is a peculiarly simple example of benefit because it describes a process that occurs within the body of an individual. What it well illustrates is the distinction between a process culminating in a product and, on the other hand, the application of techniques that efficiently cause that productive process to occur. Aristotle's addendum that a doctor may cure herself emphasizes the analytic nature of this distinction. An extended example of benefit is that of a carpenter whose aim is to produce a rudder that will be used by a helmsman (*Physics* 194a33–194b8). The proximate beneficiary here is the *energeia* of the helmsman qua helmsman, but his steering of a ship is of course done for the sake of yet further aims and beneficiaries. Interestingly, in this passage, within a treatise of theoretical philosophy, Aristotle allows that the activities of both carpenter and helmsman are in a sense 'architectonic [*architektonikos*]', the one because it involves knowledge of the material from which to make a good rudder (or roof beam, or fence) and the other because it involves knowledge about a good rudder's form and function, and this Aristotle allows even though he notes that the material is made to subserve the form and its work. Little such allowance is evident in his works of practical philosophy, where the bridle-maker's reasoning is subordinated to that of others. In Book Seven of the *Politics* (which begins by gently repeating the intellectualist message of *NE* X: 6–8), he draws an analogy with literal *architektones*, and a related distinction between what he calls 'external actions [*exoterikai praxeis*]' and actions of a type which, by implication, we may call 'internal', such as those between the parts of a *polis*. Even in the case of external actions (which correspond to what he normally describes in terms of *poieseis*), what is most active is the sovereign reasoning of master craftsmen (*Politics* 1325b14–30). How much truer must this be, he implies, with regard to actions internal to such a self-sufficient being as a *polis*. In writing on politics, he moves from analogy to the direct description of real relations of authority and power. His hope is to account for those relations in a way that imbues them with point and purpose, and to do so in a way that is consistent with his teleological conception of the good. Here he is concerned with much more than the role of architectonic authority within a particular craft, and with more even than such directive authority over subordinate crafts and processes as is exercised by, for example, an architect in the completion of a building (cf. *NE* 1174a19–29). His concern, rather, is with all such relations, and with how they together form a single hierarchical order culminating in the political authority of those officials who should, therefore, be understood as responsible for (and are, in this sense, the causes and sources of) the good of the political community as a whole.

Aristotle traces a hierarchy of wisdom from one who has only perception, through one with experience, on through an ordinary artisan, and up to an *architekton*, but he also insists that this hierarchy then extends well beyond those who produce to those who contemplate (*Metaphysics* 981b30–2). This would appear to entail that the ruling science, which explains what good each thing subserves within the naturally best order of the *polis*, cannot be one that is merely productive (*Metaphysics* 982b4–12). Explanation trumps action, and this is argued in the *Metaphysics* after Aristotle has explicitly referred back to his discussion of intellectual virtues in Book Six of the *Nicomachean Ethics*. However, if we look back to this, we find him emphasizing that *phronesis* concerns action and therefore acknowledging the importance of experience of particulars as well as of knowledge of universals, and he acknowledges the same of *techne* even whilst making the case for *theoria* (*NE* 1141b14–22; *Metaphysics* 881a1–23). It follows from this necessity of reasoning about contingent particulars that a purely theoretical science is ill-suited to rule over actors and producers. It is therefore unsurprising when Aristotle acknowledges that what is architectonic within *poleis* is the craft of laying down laws (*nomothetike*), whilst contingencies are dealt with by what alone is popularly called politics (*politike*), the energetic execution of which still more obviously resembles the activity of artisans (*NE* 1141b22–9). In saying this, Aristotle is no doubt reflecting the reality of most fourth-century *poleis*. He is also, again, reflecting his moral psychology, according to which it is the task of habituated virtues to ensure the goodness of aims pursued and the task of deliberative *phronesis* to ensure the success of their pursuit. If we understand law-making as the activity of determining the aims of the *polis*, then this sovereign political activity should be the preserve of the wisest and most virtuous. The laws they craft help to ethically habituate their subordinates.

Craft and Virtue

We have seen that Charles, exploring the relation of ontology to moral reasoning and setting aside politics, proposes that what he calls a single basic action may exemplify both a moral action and a productive process. From this intentionally limited perspective, what Aristotle says of the ethics of action relates only to the 'internal' benefits of actions for their actors and, sometimes, also 'externally' for other individuals towards whom the actor may 'choose' to act justly or (in Charles's own example: 1986: 123ff.) 'generously'. On the basis of this exegesis, Charles goes on to criticize Anscombe's critique of modern moral 'consequentialism' (see chapter 4) for the ambiguity of her term. The teleology of Aristotle's moral reasoning may itself, he claims, be understood as consequentialist in another sense than that of utilitarianism. Aristotelian consequentialism resembles utilitarianism in identifying the goods at which it aims as 'objects of enjoyment' and 'state[s] of affairs'; it differs in admitting of other than productive or efficiently 'causal' consequences. The consequences that may make actions 'right' are not only welfarist ones benefiting others (such as Ackrill's 'neighbour', whose fence has been mended) but also ones benefiting the actor; not only 'external results' but also results 'internal' to the actor and her action (ibid.: 142–4). On this account, although a basic action has a single aim, it may benefit both the actor herself and others.

We have also seen that Reeve agrees that Aristotle should be understood as claiming that an individual can act simultaneously for the sake of acting well and for the sake of some production over and above the action, thereby benefiting both herself and others. This happens when a producer's *techne* is 'controlled' by her own *phronesis*. When, for example, a doctor's skill is directed by her own practical wisdom, then her action is valuable to herself independently of the value of the health she produces in her patient. What Reeve says of the possible coincidence of what he calls internal and external ends agrees with what Charles says of the probable co-occurence of what *he* calls internal and external results. Each gives us reason to assume that production *can* be a path to virtue, rather as reproduction can benefit both parent and offspring.

But surely we have reason to suspect that Charles and Reeve are both too sanguine in their interpretations, given what Aristotle says of the political logic of the architectonic control of crafts by superordinate activities and

actors. And indeed, Reeve (whose interpretive concerns are more comprehensive than those of Charles) acknowledges that what Aristotle says of
political order implies that productive activity should not be controlled by
the producer but by her superior. In his prepolitical case, the doctor was also
a *phronimos*, an excellent person, virtuously directing her own production.
In contrast, we might suppose that when the activity of the *technites* is
controlled by another she is demoralized and deprived of any share in
eudaimonia. Reeve suggests that such political control of production might
be sufficient to warrant calling a *poiesis* a *praxis*, as in the first case (its
'intrapersonal analogue': Reeve 1992: 186). However, in the second case
phronesis is presumably an attribute of the controlling politician alone and
not at all of the controlled producer, and for Aristotle this control is normally justified by the claim that a *technites* lacks the virtue necessary to
direct her work to good ends. Her activity is a sub-rational process of production, the excellence of which inheres not in her but in the product.
Although Aristotle acknowledges that craft activity admits of rational
judgement, deliberation and decision, he also insists that such rationality,
even of a literal (rather than metaphorical and political) *architekton*, has
nothing in common with human excellence as such, and this because it is
expended on the product. Therefore, even if we allow that Reeve's first, isolated and prepolitical case may be considered to be one both of *poiesis* and
praxis, it does not follow that a *poiesis* may be elevated to the status also of
(or co-occur with) a *praxis* when it is under the control of a superordinate.
Aristotle's aristocratic politicians are alone *phronimoi*, possessors of a kind
of knowledge which, even though inferior to that of philosophers, is vastly
superior to that of ordinary artisans. The interpretive reflections of contemporary analytic philosophers such as Ackrill and Charles can render
many of Aristotle's arguments consistent with modern moral sensibilities,
but only so long as his ethics is not understood in the context of his metaphysics or politics.

Exclusion

Charles's disregard of what Aristotle says of politics is intentional. Even if
he would not go so far as Johnson in declaring the 'fact that Aristotle's
extension of teleology to the social and political sphere is unsuccessful'
(Johnson 2005: 246), he cautions Martha Nussbaum against discounting
Aristotle's and others' reasons not to advance an egalitarian perfectionism.
This she has proposed in the name of both Aristotle and Marx (e.g.
Nussbaum 1988a), and latterly (perhaps on Charles's suggestion at Charles

1988: 187, 203; cf. Nussbaum 1988b: 212f.) of Green (e.g. in Nussbaum 2000, where she also responds to a similar caution from Richard Mulgan). Charles objects interpretively not to the teleological perfectionism but to the egalitarianism, because Aristotle 'failed to provide even the basis of an acceptable theory of the distribution of goods and advantages' (Charles 1988: 206). Unable to accept what Aristotle does say on the subject, Charles himself says nothing more about any 'utilitarian consequentialism' regarding the distribution of 'external' products even whilst commending naturalistic perfectionism in what he says about action's 'internal results'. Perhaps, insofar as 'Aristotle's extension of teleology to the social and political sphere' *is* successful, it provides the basis for a 'theory of the distribution of goods and advantages' which we should consider unacceptable on other grounds.

Nussbaum considers her 'Aristotelian' case for 'political distribution' to be consistent with Aristotle's essentialist distinction between internal and external goods, between the good of exercising essential human functions and the necessary conditions of such exercise (e.g. Nussbaum 1992). In so doing, she easily – too easily – moves from the universalism of what Aristotle says of natural kinds and an inferred commonality of human beings to what he says of political community and the good of its members. This is, of course, a move refused by many of Aristotle's feminist critics, mindful of his insistence on women's natural incapacity and that women should be confined to the *oikos* and excluded from the *polis*. Some of these scholars are creating and deepening debate by relating what Aristotle said of women's biology and psychology to what he said of metaphysics and *energeia*. Aristotle afforded an inferior virtue – 'love of work' (*philergia*) (*Rhetoric* 1361a9; cited in Cole 1994: 131) – to women as household managers, and acknowledged their technical and productive role – 'technopoietike' (*Politics* 1253b10) – in the rearing of children. He nonetheless assured posterity that women, like most slaves and manual workers, are incapable of practical, let alone theoretical, reasoning. All they are capable of doing is listening to the reasoning and acting on the instructions of their male superiors. It is those superiors who have the practical wisdom to ensure that the amoral production upon which they spend their time and energy is beneficial, in subserving the action and freedom of those superiors. In this way, Aristotle lent his theoretical as well as practical philosophy to the legitimation of oppressive institutions. The greatest of these was the *polis* itself, an exclusive community of citizens united in their enforcement of non-citizens' subservience. For Aristotle, it no more followed from the fact that women and workers are necessary to the political community that they should be included within it than it followed from the fact that a human being needs material goods that those goods should be regarded as constituents of their consumer. A well-ordered political community is one that keeps women, slaves and workers in their separate place of absolute subordination, producing external goods for the sake of the good of perfection internal to citizens. Workers and women are external to Aristotle's political community, just as the goods they produce and provide are external to consumers. The best life can be actualized by a few, but only if a good life is denied to the many.

Aristotle posits a good at the apex of the architectonic structure of the *polis*, to which all *poieseis* and *praxeis* are supposed to be ordered by the *phronesis* of its aristocratic rulers. This good is the political analogue of that *eudaimonia* which is the unifying good posited as the *telos* of those individual human beings capable of such natural completion; a single activity of the soul which has no aim or beneficiary beyond itself, for the sake of which all lesser activities are ordered. To call its political analogue *eunomia*, or good order, could invite charges of vacuity or circularity, but Aristotle clearly intends that a political order is good when it facilitates the perfection of the best human beings through their own free action and, more especially, through their own free contemplation. The analogy of *eunomia* to *eudaimonia* is, therefore, only partial, as is the analogy of the constitution of a *polis* to a composite natural being.

If Aristotle's practical and theoretical philosophies were entirely separated, then politics would, on his account, have no final end. Its aim would only be *eunomia* or the temporal preservation of what we might call its own, internally functioning order. But Aristotle's practical and theoretical philosophies are not separate. His understanding of politics is of an architectonic art reproducing or conserving order in a way analogous to the reproduction of artificial forms, and he refers to *theoria* in providing *praxis* with its further, final end. This *telos* is the completion of the very best human beings through contemplation of the divine. It is true that, for Aristotle, theoretical wisdom prescribes no moral rules to *praxis*, and this because *theoria* imitates the self-sufficiency, perfection and self-absorption of his God. Just as Aristotle's God is entirely unconcerned with human affairs, so too is *theoria* unconcerned with temporal actions. But Aristotle's politics is concerned with *theoria* because, unlike gods, theorists need external goods. Aristotle's ethics should be understood in the context of his politics, and – not least because *theoria* requires *eunomia* – his politics should be understood in the context of his theoretical philosophy.

Teleology

The logic of postulating any single, unifying end of action has been famously rebutted by Anscombe. Aristotle, she alleges, is in error in moving from the claim (itself questionable) that all action aims at some good to the claimed corollary that all actions must aim at some final end (Anscombe 1971: 15–16; 1963: 33–4; cf. MacDonald 1991 and Richardson 1994, who both argue that the rebuttal is not a refutation, MacDonald on Thomist grounds). Aristotle's allegedly fallacious inference is presumably motivated by the thought that if we are to imitate the perfectly rational order of divine activity, then we must assume some unifying end. Without the possibility of actualizing some state of temporal completion, all our activities will be empty and vain, caught in an infinite regress of means to contingent and provisional ends that themselves become means to yet further ends. The logic of his inference is therefore opposed to a logic that we may call pragmatist. A *pragma* is a concrete act, understood in its immediacy and the immediacy of its aim and beneficiary. In this sense, Aristotle's ethical and political conception of *praxis* is unpragmatic. But it is not impracticable, and that this is so he intends to demonstrate in what he says of architectonic reasoning. As indicated by our modern term 'teleology', he intends the logic of explanation in terms of that-for-the-sake-of-which to limit, structure and order our chains of theoretical and practical reasoning. A *telos* is the terminus of such a chain, but this is not to be understood in a purely temporal sense like the finishing of a product. As a final end and good, a *telos* is also a ('final') cause, and it is in this sense that Aristotle postulates that a *telos*, though subsequent in time, is prior in nature. A being's *entelecheia* is its atemporal completion.

Charles has pursued the specifically Aristotelian logic of teleological explanation since differentiating it from efficiently 'causal' explanations of intentional action, and in so doing he has charged that logic with another error: of confusing what he distinguishes as an 'agency model' of teleological explanation with a 'functional model' of non-intentionalist teleological explanation, by reference to the benefit to some organic whole of its parts (Charles 1991). This resembles the distinction drawn by Johnson between two senses of 'for the sake of which': those of aim and of beneficiary. Their positions differ in that, whereas Johnson unifies these two senses into a single model which he considers successful when applied to 'nature' but not to human society or politics, Charles elaborates them into two different models of explanation. Charles's motivating concern remains that of elaborating an Aristotelian approach to intentional action (and, more broadly, to human intentionality) and, again, he offers a way through some perplexities in Aristotle's philosophy. What is crucial to his agency model is that aims be intentional and purposive. He, unlike Aristotle, would have us distinguish between agency and structure, and between work as something purposive and work as something functional. Here we may again note that his distinction of *praxis* from *poiesis* entirely disregards those perplexities raised by Aristotle's politics, and especially by the politics of Aristotle's *Ethics*. Aristotle intended what Charles differentiates as a functional model to explain not only the internal order of natural organisms but also the order internal to a political community.

Many twentieth-century social scientists argued that a functional model explained much about order, norms and actions within different societies, without any reference to actors' conscious aims or reasons for action. Some explained the 'teleological' or 'functionalist' rationale of a 'social system' (together with 'social facts' and 'social action') by analogy with the motions of organisms and cybernetic artefacts. Such sociological and anthropological theories reduced human action to the level of what Aristotle differentiates from action as process. In this, they differed from Aristotle's practical philosophy. And yet they also shared much with Aristotle's functional explanations of nature, of production, of the activity of those human beings to whom he denied a capacity for practical reasoning, and also of the Athenian *polis* as a being explicable apart from the reasoning of, at least, those whom he insisted should be excluded from it but whom we might insist should be regarded as members of Athenian society. A good order, Aristotle sometimes seems to imply, should work independently of the practical reasoning of its members, and a task of politics is to lay down and enforce constitutional laws to safeguard such operation. In *this* functionalist sense, we might call sociological Aristotle's ontology of political causation. Where the latter differs from recent social scientific functionalism is in its hierarchy. Whereas functionalists explain a social system in terms of the interdependence of its various parts, Aristotle argues that some parts work non-reciprocally for the sake of others.

The image of an Aristotelian polity that has proven so attractive for so long has been informed by an idea of teleology as at once an organic and an organizing principle. Aristotelianism's traditional political idea has usually prioritized agency over functionality. It is an idea, primarily, of intellectually and morally excellent rulers acting in intentional pursuit of a common good and, secondarily, of their subordinates working in their own different ways for that same good. This idea has been at once an ideal to be actively promoted and institutionalized and a model with which to explain what already exists (naturally, providentially, anthropologically, or historically and progressively). For example, in the hands of Green's numerous followers it informed the political programme of 'New Liberalism', whilst other of his followers reversed the priority of functionality to agency in helping to found the new academic discipline of sociology (Otter 1996). Too often, however, this image of political community has served as an explanation of how oppressive and exploitative social relations supposedly benefit even those who are oppressed and exploited. In other words, it has served as a legitimatory ideology. Only very recently has an attempt been made to combine the teleological logics of practical agency and of sociological explanation with one another in explicit and sustained opposition to institutionalized oppression, or so I shall argue in chapter 4.

Like Kraut, I have argued that Aristotle's practical philosophy (warranted, I have argued, by aspects of his theoretical philosophy) makes the best the enemy of the good. One response is to accept the implications of that practical philosophy and to renounce any egalitarianism or concern for the welfare of others as a false doctrine of slave morality, of Christianity, or of Enlightenment. Another is to set aside Aristotle's practical concern with the acquisition, exercise and nobility of supposedly superlative attributes, rejecting his idea of excellence along with his elitism. This approach has been taken most notably by Nussbaum, who underpins it with an account of Aristotle's naturalistic essentialism that also sets aside his accounts of production and of teleological causation. However, any such emptying of teleology from Aristotle's theoretical philosophy and of excellence from his practical philosophy empties from Aristotelianism what is distinctive of its tradition.

But there is a third possibility in response to the contradiction of the particularity of the best with the universality of the good, and this possibility may be extrapolated from Aristotle's idea of teleology. If the concept is temporalized, then a *telos* becomes something to work towards. Truth is neither something given and already unchanging, nor yet something as pragmatic as might be inferred from what Charles says of craft and knowledge. Rather, truth is the *telos* of enquiry. Further, if the idea of teleology is also socialized, then a *telos* becomes something that may be worked towards with others. That this is a thought that occurred to Aristotle is evinced by what he said of friendship and politics, even if it is a thought that more clearly occurred to Hegel. Alasdair MacIntyre has been a critic of both. Aristotle was once accused by MacIntyre of modelling a universal human *telos* on the prejudices and practices of Athenian gentlemen. He still accuses Hegel of postulating truth as something finally achieved in his own philosophical system, even whilst agreeing with Hegel that we are social as well as political beings. For MacIntyre, truth remains the atemporal goal of our temporally structured enquiries. These enquiries have issued no final truth about human completion. What they have told us is that, just as individuals are incapable of finally becoming self-sufficient, so too are humans incapable of actualizing their good apart from others. The best need the rest. But past enquiries have also told us to be sceptical of claims made by our rulers that it is they who are the best. Here, we need to differentiate philosophy from ideology, truth from power. With Charles, and with Wittgenstein, MacIntyre notes that our knowledge is a product of our social practices. What he adds, elaborating upon Aristotle, and upon Aquinas, is that goods to be actualized can be imputed to such shared practices and not just to individual beings. Practices, rather than institutionalized powers, are authoritative sources of truths and of standards of excellence. If we do not possess any single, objective and indubitable measure of truth or goodness, then we can nonetheless look to philosophical tradition and to our ordinary social practices for knowledge of the human *telos*.

2

Christian Practice and
Medieval Philosophy

Aristotelianism became a philosophical tradition in classical Athens, but scarcely in the ancient world. Hellenistic and Roman Stoics and Platonists often paid due respect to their greatest philosophical predecessor, but his influence was fragmentary. His work only informed a specifically Aristotelian philosophical tradition in what we call the Middle Ages, between the classical era and our own modernity.

That Aristotelianism could ever become a philosophical tradition at all is due to Aristotle's own action in founding a school in Athens, the Lyceum or Peripatos. This continued after his death but, under the direction of his student Theophrastus, its concern was much less to develop Aristotle's ideas than to engage in teaching and in empirical and historical research. The truth in Stocks's comment that Aristotle did 'not found a school' (Stocks 1925: 155) is that no doctrinal or canonic tradition was here established. Had it not been for the efforts of Andronicus of Rhodes, almost three centuries after the Lyceum's foundation, we might have lost most of the treatises which have been traditionally regarded as Aristotle's most important works, and these works might not have been regarded so readily as they were in the Middle Ages to comprise a single body of argument. It was Andronicus who 'established the form and canon of Aristotle's writings' and 'initiated a way of doing philosophy which was to predominate among Aristotelians to the end of antiquity and to spread to the adherents of other schools' (Gottschalk 1990: 64–5). This was the way of commentary, and it was this that established the canonic authority of Aristotle's texts.

It is one of the greatest ironies in the history of philosophy that the specifically political order which made possible Aristotle's philosophizing, and which he legitimated, was suppressed by his own student, Alexander. The Athenian *polis* continued to exist, but only under Macedonian and then Roman rule. Theophrastus may have edited Aristotle's *Politics*, but after this the *Politics* was neglected because of its lack of correspondence to the new political reality. Hellenistic and Roman practical philosophy was not that of

Aristotelian but of apolitical Epicureanism or cosmopolitan Stoicism. The Lyceum's institutional existence probably ended when Athens was sacked after rebelling against Rome, shortly before Andronicus' achievement.

Even if political order changed, the social and economic order celebrated by Aristotle continued. Manual labour continued to be denigrated and oppressed. Nonetheless, Aristotle's philosophical justifications for such oppression were little elaborated and of little practical import. When Aristotelianism was revived, centuries later, it would be under very different political, economic and intellectual conditions.

When Aristotelianism was revived, it was combined with monotheistic faith: Byzantine Christianity, Islam, Judaism and, then, Roman Christianity. Its combination with Catholicism was to prove the most thoroughgoing, widespread and enduring. We might well say – with Alasdair MacIntyre and many others – that this combination was a synthesis of two previously distinct traditions. But, if so, we should acknowledge how unequal were these two traditions prior to that synthesis. What is now Western Europe was dominated intellectually by Christianity. From the Roman Pope and Holy Roman Emperor downwards, action was constrained by the dos and don'ts of the Church. Christianity was an immensely stronger tradition than Aristotelianism, and in many respects Christian Aristotelianism is less a synthesis than an annexation. In this combination, metaphysics is happily understood as 'first philosophy' and, therefore, as providing premises for philosophizing about practice.

Christian Theory and Practice

Early Christianity provides a vast intellectual contrast with Aristotle, having developed out of the very different intellectual culture of Judaism. And yet the language of the New Testament is Greek and, through the action of Paul, its message rapidly spread to major *poleis* of the wider world. For Paul, Christianity is neither Jewish nor Greek. As he told Corinthians, the Christian is 'a new creature [*ktisis*]' (2 Corinthians 5: 17; biblical quotations are from the *English Revised Version* of 1881, and the Greek is from the parallel text of the New Testament published by Oxford University Press in 1923) and Christian community is a new kind of community. Early Christianity was consciously new and intentionally different. Christians, Paul warned, should not allow themselves to be spoilt by 'philosophy [*philosophias*] and vain deceit, after the tradition of men' (Colossians 2: 8), a point he rammed home in argument with Athenian Stoics and Epicureans. He intended faith to absolve us from any need for philosophy (Gilson 1936: 21).

Paul's *theoria* contrasts with that of Aristotle. Aristotle's *theos* may be the prime mover of the universe but it is not its creator, as is the personal God of Judaeo-Christian, theistic tradition. For Aristotle, natural kinds are eternal. For Christianity, God alone is eternal; He created the world, will end the world and intervenes in the world supernaturally. What Aristotle called natural, Christians came to call Creation, *Genesis*. The Christian conception of human beings as themselves creatures, made or created beings, beings essentially generated by God, differs fundamentally from Aristotle's account of human nature. Aristotle's mature philosophy identifies the *psyche* with the form of the body and that form as substantially unified with, and inseparable from, the body's growing and decaying matter. For Aristotle, the human soul is no more supernatural than the body, and in this he differs even more than Plato from the Christian doctrine of resurrection. What was to become the orthodox message of Christian theology is that human beings are capable of completion only in the next life, not this. True goodness belongs to another realm, and insofar as it can be actualized on Earth, this can only be through participation in, or imitation of, what is divine and otherworldly. For such reasons, Aristotle's influence upon Christian faith's gradual elaboration into theology was only felt through the medium of neo-Platonism.

For Christians, goodness is something much more than a being's actualization of its inherent potential through its own activity. Goodness is the attribute of God, infused throughout Creation by God's love or charity (*agape*); by, that is, His very act of Creation. This idea of charity – of the goodness of God, or of any agent, being manifest in his generating or producing something for its own good, or for the good of others – is something utterly alien to Aristotle. Whereas Aristotle posited the theoretical identity of particulars of a specific natural kind alongside a practical philosophy of human inequality, Christianity posits an equality of all created human beings that is formally prior to their material and temporal inequality. Christianity preached not a practical philosophy but active imitation of the divine. 'Be ye therefore perfect [*teleioi*], even as your Father which is in heaven is perfect' (Matthew 5: 48). The Christian virtues are those of faith in God, hope for salvation, and charitable action for the good of others.

In taking upon himself the task of spreading the Gospel to Greeks and Romans, Paul prescribed how they should, as Christians looking forward to the next life, live practically in this one. He told them to organize themselves into local communities. The principal word he used to describe such a community was *ekklesia*, a word often used to describe that traditional kind of Greek political community which subsisted and, indeed, spread

under Hellenistic and, then, Roman rule. The Greek *polis* was an *ekklesia* –
literally an assembly of people 'called' together by a herald – and Aristotle
said that a *polis* should not exceed the range of a herald's call (*Politics*
1326b2–7). Members of Christian communities were said to have had 'a
calling', and Paul pronounced himself 'called [*kletos*] to be an apostle'
(Romans 1: 1; 1 Corinthians 1: 1).

Paul declared that 'the *powers* that be are ordained of God. Therefore he
that resisteth the power, withstandeth the ordinance of God' (Romans 13:
1–2). It was, therefore, Paul who prepared the way for Christianity's accom-
modation with temporal power. Nevertheless, he, like Jesus (and James and
Peter), was to be executed by such power. What was more important for
Paul was not the relation of Christians to temporal power but their relations amongst themselves. He told them that they should, so far as possible, disregard temporal power, relating to one another charitably rather
than, for example, appealing to legal institutions. The purpose of his apostolic activity was 'the perfecting of the saints, unto the work of ministering
[*ergon diakonias*; literally the work of service], unto the building up of the
body of Christ' so that it be 'fitly framed and knit together through that
which every joint supplieth, according to the working [*energeian*] in *due*
measure of each several part, maketh [*poieitai*] the increase of the body
unto the building up of itself in love' (Ephesians 4: 12, 16). In elaborating
the idea of sharing in the body of Christ into an idea of active participation
in that body, Paul developed a conception of community that is both inclusive and substantive. For Christianity's community, unlike Aristotle's, all
may share in the human good. Women participated alongside men, aliens
alongside indigenes, slaves alongside slave-owners, artisans alongside the
leisured rich. Their shared community was to be sustained by their own
activity of mutual service.

In his work constructing Christian communities, the authority Paul
claimed for himself was that of 'a wise master builder [*sophos architekton*]'
(1 Corinthians 3: 10). He no more claimed a classically philosophical
warrant for his practice than for his Christian *theoria*, noting that 'it is
written, I will destroy the wisdom [*sophian*] of the wise, and the prudence
of the prudent will I reject' (1 Corinthians 1: 19). Nonetheless, he pitted the
'wisdom' and 'completion' of faith against those of traditional philosophy.
He told Greek Christians that theirs is a 'wisdom among the perfect
[*teleiois*]', a spiritual wisdom that appears foolish to 'the natural man' (1
Corinthians 2: 6, 14), and that love 'is the bond of perfectness [*teleiotetos*]'
(Colossians 3: 14). Different people have different callings, different spiritual
gifts and abilities to act, but these temporal differences make no difference

to their common ability to participate actively in the community of the faithful. Not all members have 'the same office [*praxin*]' (Romans 12: 4), but each of their different activities can be an expression of the same provisional completion or excellence. What matters is the charitable spirit in which they are conducted. Paul lists the activities of 'apostles', 'prophets', 'teachers [*didaskalous*]', 'miracles, then gifts of healings, helps, governments ['or, *wise counsels*'; *English Revised Version* marginalia], *divers* kinds of tongues', comparing these different activities to those of 'the foot', 'the hand', 'the eye', 'the hearing', 'the smelling', and noting that 'the body is not one member, but many' (1 Corinthians 12: 28, 15–17, 14). His point is that all of the different gifts contribute to the life of the community, and that none can substitute for any of the others.

Such *praxeis* are good, but Paul emphatically denies the goodness of free human action as such. Action is good only if done for the sake of God or, through love of God, for the sake of other people. He tells the Galatians to 'bear ye one another's burdens, and so fulfil the law of Christ' to love your neighbour (Galatians 6: 2), and the Ephesians that 'labouring ye ought to help the weak' (Acts 20: 35). The Christian must renounce 'the old man with his doings [*praxesin*]' (Colossians 3: 9), understanding that pride is always mistaken because one's achievements are only possible by God's grace. He warns against being a *phronimos* 'in your own conceits' (Romans 11: 25; 12: 16). Pride should be replaced by humility, and power by service. Where the old man may have stolen, the new man should 'labour, working with his hands the thing that is good, that he may have whereof to give to him that hath need' (Ephesians 4: 28). Paul repeatedly adverts to how he himself continues to work as a tent-maker, so as not to be a burden on others. 'Work with your hands', he instructed the Thessalonians, later adding that 'if any will not work [*ergazesthai*], neither let him eat' (1 Thessalonians 4: 11; 2 Thessalonians 3: 10). In a passage of which Luther was to make much, he seems to tell the Corinthians that all just temporal occupations may be spiritualized as occupational callings: 'Brethren, let each man, wherein he was called [*eklethe*], therein abide with God' (1 Corinthians 7: 24). Work, for Paul, includes both Aristotle's *poiesis* and *praxis*, and he places no higher value in non-productive than in productive work. Indeed, one may easily infer from Paul a contrast of honest labour with the corruptiveness of wealth and power. Manual work usually benefits others. However, his overriding concern is with things spiritual rather than material, and what renders work *dikaios* – 'righteous' or just – is the faith and motivation of the worker. Whereas Aristotle praises self-cultivation and condemns what is servile, Paul commends the service of others.

Self-sufficiency is something of which human beings are utterly incapable, and for self-sufficiency to be an ethical ideal is the sin of philosophical pride. The temporal perfection that marks out some is due to their faith, not to any habitual excellence gained through personal practice.

Augustinian Theology and the Institutionalization of Christianity

In spreading the spiritual message of Jerusalem to the heart of the classical world, Paul refused any compromise with its institutions, its philosophy or its social order. After Paul, with the increasing conversion of that world to Christianity, compromises were inevitably made. The Church became an established institution, recognized and respected by temporal rulers. In coming to terms with temporality, due to diminishing anticipation of the imminence of a Second Coming, its official servants or 'ministers' assumed the task of transmitting doctrine, of administering 'tradition'. But when Tertullian launched his uncompromising attacks on the idolatries of Athenian wisdom and Roman order, the Church that he championed rejected not them but him. It was Augustine of Hippo who, whilst the Western Roman Empire was collapsing around him, most authoritatively restated the independent position of Pauline Christianity.

Augustine's Latin writings demonstrate little of Paul's antipathy to Greek *theoria*, even though, whilst engaging it, Augustine warns himself and others that its claims of intellectual excellence and achievement can corrupt the soul with pride. Paul established the radical otherness of Christianity from pagan philosophy, and when medieval philosophers later identified resemblances they usually explained these by Judaism's supposed influences upon the Greeks. In contrast, Augustine painfully acknowledges the diverse sources of his theology. Although emphasizing the uniqueness of divine grace, he acknowledges that his attraction to Christianity was not simply spiritual but also intellectual and philosophical. What might be called metaphysical themes in Paul become explicitly argued in Augustine's theology.

Following Paul (Romans 9: 21), Augustine, in his early adult Christianity, reasons about God's making of humankind by analogy with the craft of the potter. Differentiating divine creator from created humanity, his argument is that God is greater than humankind as He created us and ordained our purpose (Augustine 1953: 398–402). Nonetheless, this account remains consistent with an interpretation of Paul that holds even human creativity in high regard. For Paul, 'we are [God's] workmanship [*poiema*], created [*ktisthentes*] in Christ Jesus for good works [*ergois agathois*]' (Ephesians 2: 10). Paul pursued this line of thought to the extent of claiming that 'we are God's fellow-workers: ye are God's husbandry; God's building' (1 Corinthians 3: 9). In creating us, and in continuing to act through us in the world, God acts as a farmer or a builder acts. In labouring, farming or building through love of God for the sake of others, in acting for the love of God and neighbour, a person is actually participating in a creative process initiated by God.

Augustine's later position is incompatible with such an understanding of Paul's message, as he argues that God's Creation is something utterly different from the way in which a potter forms a pot out of clay. Creation was the original historical event, after which God rested, and not an ongoing or repeated process (although this implies that all individual souls were made at one time, and perhaps therefore also implies the traducian and almost Aristotelian view that the soul is passed on from parent to child). Most importantly, it was an act of initiation out of nothing, whereas manufacture can never be more than the making of new things from antecedent matter. In his *Confessions*, he renounces his earlier suggestion that God 'can have gone to work like a human craftsman, who forms a material object from some material in accordance with his imaginative decision' (Augustine 1997: 288–9 [11.5.7]). Here, then, Augustine repudiates any philosophical idea of Creation as the productive imposition of form on matter. If he concurs with Aristotle in conceptualizing Creation apart from production, *Genesis* apart from *genesis*, and therefore the object of theology apart from the objects of skill, he nonetheless disavows any exaltation of human action conceptualized in juxtaposition to a lowly imitation of *physis*, as well as a lofty imitation of *theos*, when he describes art in terms not of imitation but of imagination and decision. For example, in *The City of Man*, although again denying that we are to think of Creation 'as if God worked in the manner of craftsmen', he lists 'many great arts invented and exercised by human ingenuity' (Augustine 1998: 535, 1161 [XII: 24, XXII: 24]). That said, Augustine here denies to humbly charitable labour the possibility of any special sanctity, whereas we might think he grants to *theoria* and *praxis* a certain dignity denied by Paul.

In differentiating 'the city of God' from 'the city of man', Augustine elaborated what became the canonic account of how Christians should understand their relation to political order. For Augustine, our original equality as human beings has been irretrievably lost by Adam's Fall. Our highest temporal good is not something we may actualize as individuals but something lost to us all, and this because of the choice by human free will of evil in preference to good. Temporal power is therefore, like labour, a post-lapsarian necessity. Political power can, Augustine wrote (at a time of bloody Germanic invasion, when the *Pax Romana* seemed like a lost blessing), minimize evil by enforcing a sort of peace. What political institutions cannot do is enable us to actualize the human good, as proposed by Aristotle.

The end of Greek scholarship in the Latin West is symbolized by the death of Boethius in imperial, Roman and Arian captivity, accused of complicity with the Greek powers of his time. His death, unlike that of Socrates, provoked no revenge from philosophy. Separated from the Greek-speaking civilization of the bureaucratically centralized Byzantine Empire, Western Europe entered what has been called its Dark Ages. The originally spiritual authority of the Church was increasingly centralized in Rome and compromised with the temporal world. What it received in exchange was not only wealth and power but, above all, temporal authority. Secular and religious authorities were increasingly separated, but in a different way from that envisaged by Paul. They became two complementary authorities, 'two swords' (cf. Luke 22: 38) wielded in defence of the same social order of *Respublica Christiana*. Authority was claimed to be ordained by God, but it was also taken to be accorded by antiquity, the Church's being bolstered by the claim that secular dominion was donated to it by Constantine. Conversely, the imperial claim to temporal authority and coercive power was revived by Charlemagne in what came to be known as the Holy Roman Empire. These two successors to the classical past continued to claim and confer authority in uneasy alliance, and often in open rivalry, throughout the Middle Ages.

The compromises made by the Roman Church cannot be blamed on Paul, nor even on Augustine, although it was largely in their terms, together with those of the Old Testament, that compromises were made. No sound warrant can be found in Augustine for equating the rule of Christ with that of an emperor, king or baron. Nor can much warrant be found for attributing true excellence or *nobilitas* to the ruling class, nor even (as has been claimed) for the proposition that 'the poor exist for the sake of the rich' (Salzman 2002: 209); Augustinianism here differs from Aristotelianism. It is less to theology than to the ecclesiastical power structure that we should look for such warrants.

The medieval Church, headed by the Pope, increasingly imitated temporal monarchy and nobility. Just as a king had his court or *curia*, so too did the Pope. Although clerical offices were not hereditary, they were routinely filled by the younger, non-inheriting sons of the secular nobility. This, more than scriptural pronouncement or theological reasoning, is why those whose calling – or, in Latin, *vocatio* – it was to pray endorsed the domination of those whose vocation it was to fight over those whose vocation was to work. What was lost was the Pauline idea of churches as sustained by all of their members' diverse activities.

Religious Lives and Organization

In the eleventh century a Pauline idea of apostolic and ecclesiastical life informed a counter-hegemonic ethic of temporal excellence, rivalling that of secular and ecclesiastical nobility and, therefore, the spiritual authority of the established Church. The Church had long allowed that something like the apostolic life was still possible, but had denied this possibility to the laity. Instead, the possibility of such activity was confined to monasteries, clearly separated from the rest of society. Monks' principal occupation was prayer and contemplation, but Augustine argued that monks must also 'work by their own hands' in emulation of 'the Apostle' Paul (*Of the Work of Monks*, 35). The canonic prescription for the monastic life, the sixth-century Rule of St Benedict, followed Augustine in stating that true monks 'live by the work of their hands, as did . . . the Apostles' (rule 48). In contrast to Aristotle, who praised leisure as a necessary condition for the cultivation of virtue, Benedict condemned idleness as 'the enemy of the soul'. In this, too, he followed Augustine. Nevertheless, increasing evidence that not only priests but even monks (also often recruited from the nobility) could be corrupted by their communal wealth and prestige led to monastic reform and to the co-optation of religious groups of workers that had developed outside the Church.

In the face of what were denounced as heretical challenges, vocational orders of a new type were developed by the Church. These were not orders of monks who had withdrawn from the world but of propertyless and mendicant friars, dependent upon others' charity, whose job it was to enter into the world and claim it – especially the rapidly growing cities – for the Church. Both the Franciscans and Dominicans developed as official orders in the early thirteenth century. The Dominicans were especially active within the new universities. In such ways the Church attempted to maintain its intellectual dominance even as scholarship expanded beyond its monasteries and cathedral schools. In scholasticism's elevation of dialectic from a part of the traditional *trivium* into a genuinely critical form of intellectual enquiry, Aristotle's works and Aristotelian ideas – newly received from what, after the Arab conquests, remained of the

Graecophone East, and from such Arabic commentators as Averroes – became the new authorities against which scholars tested the Church's canonic texts.

Robert Grosseteste – Chancellor of Oxford University, Pauline scholar, Bishop of Lincoln and translator of Aristotle, most notably of the *Nicomachean Ethics* – compared the mendicant orders with co-opted groups and (according to Thomas of Eccleston, quoted in McEvoy 2000: 60) judged it to be the latter who 'have the most perfect and holy religious order, because they live by their own work'. He protested that his own work was obstructed by the very structure of the Church; by the corrupt agency of the Papal Curia and by its active imposition of the deadening hand of bureaucracy. He went to Rome to tell it that 'just as . . . an army [must be commanded] by a general who understands the art of war and not by a saddle-maker, so the . . . art of saving souls must be given to those who understand the Gospel . . . without the interference of those who understand only the subordinate arts of secular administration' (quoted in Southern 1986: 280–1). Here we have the opening of the *Ethics* paraphrased for apostolic purposes. In Grosseteste, then (and notwithstanding Aristotle's original intentions), we have an appreciation of both manual and intellectual practice that informs a philosophical critique of entrenched power.

A critique of ecclesiastical and noble corruption had been advanced in Aristotelian terms still earlier, by John of Salisbury. John became one of the most respected classical scholars of the twelfth century through such works as his *Metalogicon*, a celebration of those of Aristotle's writings on logic originally bequeathed to the Latin West in Boethius' translations and collectively called the *Organon*, the organ or instrument of right reasoning. Our concern, though, is with John's *Policraticus*, famous for discussing not only tyranny but also tyrannicide. Its subtitle is *Of the Frivolities of Courtiers and the Footprints of Philosophers*, and it argues that if 'virtue be unharmed, one must turn away from the life of the courtier' (John 1990: 90). The ideal of monarchy which John juxtaposes to the noble court has little to do with apostolic asceticism but it is one in which the institution of monarchy heads not just a feudal elite but also a fully inclusive body politic. The monarch is therefore charged with pursuing the common good of all of his subjects. In arguing this, John elaborates an analogy between bodily organs and social classes. He describes the function of each part, presenting a picture of a whole in which each is dependent on all. The king is the head and the central institutions of state are the guts, but peasants are the feet that transport the whole.

Communal Functionalism

Cary Nederman has attacked the old academic orthodoxy that medieval political and ethical theory was transformed after William of Moerbeke's translation of Aristotle's *Politics* and Grosseteste's translation of the *Ethics*. This was part of a broader orthodoxy, according to which there was a comprehensive philosophical revolution – a medieval Renaissance – in thirteenth-century Europe due to the formation of an Aristotelian canon in Latin. The orthodoxy presented medieval Aristotelianism as a doctrinal unity, in which practical philosophy was premised upon Aristotle's logic and theoretical philosophy. This was, Nederman suggests, a conception of Aristotelianism derived from a Whiggish approach to the history of ideas; an approach that presented Aristotelianism's medieval revival as the prelude to Aristotelianism's dissolution after a second Renaissance in the fifteenth and sixteenth centuries, and which presented that dissolution as a necessary condition of the modern intellectual progress initiated by the Enlightenment.

Nederman's rival conception of medieval Aristotelianism is of a specifically practical philosophy, propounded then and apprehensible now in terms independent of Aristotle's theoretical philosophy. A central idea of this practical philosophy, giving its arguments a considerable independence from those of Aristotle's natural philosophy, is that of *habitus* (Nederman 1989), or ethical habituation. This idea could be assimilated to an idea of 'second nature', whether that authored by Cicero (the importance of whose medieval reception, distinct from either Aristotelianism or Augustinianism, Nederman has argued for in a series of papers) or by Augustine, of fallenness. This and other concerns of Aristotelian practical philosophy were, Nederman argues, already apparent in such twelfth-century Aristotelians as John of Salisbury. These concerns differed from Aristotle's temporal perfectionism. As Nederman notes, medieval Aristotelians' concern with politics was often more 'with the physical than the moral or spiritual well-being of citizens' (Nederman 1996: 568), more with human life as such than with the best life alone. John 'intended the organic metaphor specifically to be an institutionalized expression of political rule based on *cooperation* between diverse elements of society in order to realize . . . a collective end which is greater than any of its members and which is equivalent to the good of the whole society' (Nederman 1987a: 215). Nederman presents John as the exemplar of a type of political theorizing that he terms 'communal functionalism'. This 'paradigm, within which much creative theoretical discussion occurred during the Middle Ages', conceptualizes the body politic:

[as composed] of functional groupings, arranged according to the nature of their contribution to the communal whole. This . . . defines membership in the community as a direct result of one's contribution, through the performance of a given function, to the well-being or health of the whole. Yet although types of contribution to the community are distinguished – and specialization of function (or division of labour) thereby posited – there is no attempt to postulate a hierarchy of functions in order to exclude some part or parts from a place in public life or to cast aspersions on the qualifications of certain groups to exercise a basic role in government. On the contrary, any person from any segment of society that contributes in any way to the welfare of the communal unit is thereby accorded an equal capacity to gage the needs of the community and to perform one's function accordingly. (Nederman 1992: 978)

Communal functionalism is more surely Christian than Aristotelian (Nederman 1998). It 'does not transform ruling into a specialized art' (Nederman 1992: 978), and therefore differs from Aristotle's account of politics as *architechne*. What it takes from Aristotle is an understanding of politics as *praxis*, as action, and as citizenship; so long, that is, as labour is understood as a kind of action and as citizenship is understood to include all of those who contribute to the good of the community:

> [Communal functionalists] declined to disavow the competence of artisans . . . for public life merely by reason of their occupation. Not only did such writers simply ignore Aristotle's remarks on the subject, at times they distorted or entirely misrepresented Aristotle's own clearly stated positions and ascribed to The Philosopher ideas manifestly at odds with his explicit statements . . . because of a very prominent predilection in favor of the mechanical arts that became evident among philosophers from the middle of the twelfth century onward. In other words, the positive valorization of labor and artisanship that had been endorsed by thinkers well before the recovery of Aristotle's corpus helps to account for the readiness of certain theorists to promote a more inclusive vision of citizenship than one finds in the *Politics*. (Nederman 2002a: 77)

Nederman long described Aristotelian practical philosophy as a tradition, understanding it 'as a systematic position in distinction to other frameworks' (Nederman 1996: 573). It is systematic because based in an 'epistemic model' and 'epistemic principles' (ibid.: 582, 573). These principles were taken from Aristotle's proposals 'that ethics and politics were interrelated modes of *practical* knowledge' and that 'the study of these fields was not valuable *for its own sake* but for the sake of something else, namely, the improvement of human action in both individual and public spheres' (ibid.: 573).

So understood, the antecedents of twelfth-century Aristotelianism are to be found in accounts of the ordering of knowledge that distinguish practical from theoretical knowledge. The medieval world knew of two modes of ordering knowledge, observes Nederman. One of these modes 'derived from St Augustine's reading of Plato'. This Augustinian mode isolated ethics but construed it narrowly and, further, failed to recognize political knowledge at all. The alternative mode of ordering knowledge was Aristotelian. This mode differentiates 'between "contemplative" inquiry. . . and "active" or "practical" disciplines', allowing the equation of 'practical' with ' "productive" ' sciences (Nederman 1991: 183–4; 1996: 574; both citing *Eudemian Ethics* 1216b).

Nederman's main referent for the twelfth-century Aristotelian ordering of knowledge is Hugh of St Victor. However, we should be cautious here. This is because, as we are told by his translator, Hugh was 'famous in his own time for his fidelity to Augustine' and 'his true originality . . . appears to lie in the adaptation of an already current Aristotelian division of philosophy within a system of thought and action radically Augustinian, attentively orthodox, and mystically oriented' (Taylor 1961: 8). Hugh was no scholastic dialectician, like Abelard. Later identified as one of the authoritative *moderni*, Hugh was nonetheless a member of the old school rather than of the new scholasticism (Hugh 1961: 94–7). His *Didascalion* took its name from *didaskalia*, (Pauline) Greek for what is taught authoritatively and didactically. He cited many classical authorities, but did not pit them against those of the Church. His ethics is less a matter of judgement than of obedience.

Hugh wrote repeatedly of 'virtue', but cited only Socrates, Plato and Cicero as founders of ethics, not Aristotle (ibid.: 84). He differed from Augustine in repeatedly stating that art imitates nature, and he explained what he meant by this (ibid.: 56), but he derived the idea from Plato rather than Aristotle. He also differentiated practical from contemplative sciences, and from logical and productive or mechanical sciences (*scientiae mechanicae*), and he is often cited for his recognition of the latter. This is why he is Nederman's only named forerunner to John in having a 'predilection' for 'the mechanical arts', but it has been argued that Hugh's predilection for these crafts can be easily exaggerated (Hoven 1996: 162–77). Hugh says that the manual arts are part of philosophy, but certainly not that this makes philosophers of artisans. For example, 'the theory of agriculture belongs to the philosopher, but the execution of it to the farmer' (Hugh 1961: 51).

In this, his disparagement of artisans' rationality exceeds that of Aristotle, who at the end of the *Nicomachean Ethics* criticizes sophists for pretending to teach practitioners about their own practice. Hugh's conception of mechanical science is of something that 'supervises the occupations of this life' (ibid.: 60). His mechanical scientist is a manager. Even so, and although a part of philosophy, mechanics occupies the lowest place within the hierarchy of the sciences. It is valuable not for its own sake but for the sake of improving human action, which is the subject of practical science. It is *this* science that is valued for the sake of restoring us to our nature as intended by God, which is, in turn, for the sake of that salvation which is the concern of contemplative science. 'Contemplation of truth and the practice of virtue' both 'restore the divine likeness in man'. Here, also, Hugh appears innovative in his didactic transmission of Augustinian tradition. When 'we strive after the restoration of our nature, we perform a divine action, but when we provide the necessaries required by our infirm part [resulting from the Fall, what we perform is merely] a human action' (ibid.: 54–5). In this hierarchy of for-the-sake-of's Hugh may be consistent with Aristotle, but, in his specification of the highest end for the sake of which we should seek 'the improvement of human action', he still follows Augustine. Although the claims made for Hugh's 'predilection' by Nederman and many others may be exaggerated, his inclusion of producers in pursuit of a commonly human good at least contravenes their conceptual exclusion by Aristotle.

Thomistic Aristotelianism

Nederman has also opposed a new, genealogical orthodoxy about medieval thought. He has done so in insisting that we 'retain elements of an intellectual standard for judging the meaning of Aristotelianism' (Nederman 1996: 572), so that it becomes possible to describe a figure like John of Salisbury as exemplifying aspects of both Aristotelian and rival traditions. That said, Nederman differentiates his account from any 'more philosophical understanding of Aristotelianism such as is proposed by Alasdair MacIntyre' (ibid.: 567). He criticizes MacIntyre for treating 'Christian Stoicism and Aristotelianism as closed, hermetically sealed, and perhaps incommensurable systems of thought' (Nederman 2005: 195). Nonetheless, whereas Nederman describes scholastic attempts at 'the reconciliation . . . of authorities' as a 'mania' (1996: 569), MacIntyre argues for their rationality and, more specifically, that a coherent reconciliation of Augustinian and Aristotelian traditions was uniquely achieved by Thomas Aquinas.

Aquinas was bound to place the revealed knowledge of God, grace and salvation above the truths learned from pagan philosophy in his ordering of wisdom. Theology is 'the architectonic wisdom which philosophy cannot be', because 'theology offers a present discourse about the things which remain always future for philosophy' (Jordan 1986: 200). Yet even theology, as a temporal discourse, is, on Aquinas' account, subordinate in the order of knowledge to that towards which it can only point: our future beatific vision and knowledge of God. Below this, he integrated all of the Aristotelian sciences into a single, hierarchical ordering of knowledge, an order which was institutionalized in his workplace, the University of Paris.

To what extent does Aquinas' ordering of knowledge – which excluded mechanics – corroborate Nederman's charge that Aquinas 'embraced wholeheartedly [Aristotle's] aristocratic and exclusivist doctrines, using them to authorize and reinforce [his] own distaste for the mechanical arts' (Nederman 2002a: 100)? Certainly Aquinas advanced no consistent argument against those doctrines. In his unfinished *On the Government of Rulers* he adopted the terminology of *aristocratia* from Moerbeke's recent translation of the *Politics*, and in this way the dominant ideal of nobility was given the imprimatur of Aristotle's practical philosophy and imprinted with the mark of *arete*, excellence. On the other hand – unlike, later, William of Ockham and the Spiritual Franciscans – Aquinas regarded poverty as a political matter, arguing that human law should accord with natural law in trumping any right to private property with the rightness of life. He also argued that Aristotelian justice should apply to the charging of prices and payment of wages. In this, he followed the first great medieval Christian commentator on Aristotle – his teacher Albertus.

Even in the earlier of his two commentaries on the *Ethics* (with Aquinas reputedly acting as scribe), Albertus follows Aristotle in incisively distinguishing internal from external goods. He insists that 'the poor can have all the virtues as to habit, but there are some that they cannot have in activity, in which is the perfection of such virtue, as is clear with regard to magnificence' (Albert 2001: 113). The importance of these commentaries (more precisely, those on *NE* V: 5) in the development of economic theory has been authoritatively described as 'enormous' (Langholm 1979: 61). Albertus commented that if craftsmen cannot cover their costs, their crafts will be destroyed; if shoemakers do not receive a just price for their shoes, there will be no shoes to wear (ibid,: 79ff.). He authored a labour theory of value out of his own 'labour interpretation of Aristotle'. In his first commentary he understood by 'labour' (*opus*) something social and undifferentiated, ' "communal toil and trouble" '. In his second commentary he conceptualized labour much more in terms of different crafts producing different goods with different values in exchange and, by combining a 'labour and cost theory' with a 'need or demand or market theory', approached the equilibrium theory of modern economics (Langholm 1998: 187–90, quoting Albertus). Certainly, we can detect considerable sympathy for the status of artisans here. For both Albertus and Aquinas, poverty is no bar to the attainment of a virtuous character. As Dominicans, they denied the necessity of external goods for contemplation, even though, as Aristotelians, they recognized the instrumental value of such goods for temporal, prudential action.

Aquinas echoes Aristotle in calling the craft rather than the craftsman a product's 'agent cause' (e.g. Aquinas 1999: 365 [728]). In his own commentary on the *Nicomachean Ethics*, he describes art as 'right reason applied to things to be made' (Aquinas 1993: 4 [8]) and as dealing 'with external goods'. Art's rightness is merely technical, not moral, and he observes that 'moral virtue, for instance, justice, causes a craftsman rightly to use his art'. Whereas Aristotle suggests that what Aquinas calls the 'moral virtue . . . necessary to regulate its use' inheres in whoever directs the craftsman, there is no such implication in Aquinas. What he clearly implies is that the regulatory virtue is in the 'will' of the artisan (ibid.: 372 [1172]). In this, too, Aquinas may be understood as more egalitarian than Aristotle.

Aquinas issues no charge of inconsistency or illogicality against Aristotle's fundamental distinction of *poiesis* from *praxis* (in his commentaries he hardly ever argues against a consistent position of Aristotle). He uniformly maintains Aristotle's metaphysical distinction between those movements that constitute productive processes and those that constitute actions. He also upholds Augustine's later position that God's act of Creation is unlike processes of either artificial production or natural generation. Aristotle is right that everything natural or artificial comes-to-be from pre-existing matter. However, revelation, which is higher knowledge than natural philosophy, tells us that the cosmos came-to-be from nothing. In his depiction of the hierarchy of being, Aquinas is more consistent than Aristotle in differentiating artefacts from the truer beings of nature. Natural kinds are not eternal but they are divinely created, whereas artefacts are only contingent 'accidents'. What his commentary on the *Ethics* adds is that production involves essential and vital human activity. 'Man's first *esse* [being] consists in the fact that he has the capacity for vital actions. And the handiwork that a man produces in the actual exercise of vital activity indicates the reduction of this potentiality to actuality.' For this reason,

Aquinas observes, 'the producer actually producing is in some way the work produced', by which he explains Aristotle's observation that crafts-men 'love their productions because they love their own existence' (Aquinas 1993: 561 [1847, 1846]). To this we should add that what Aquinas says of production is less clearly separated from his celebrated critique of commerce and usury – of profit without the activity of work – than is implied by much of the past century's apologetic Catholic commentary. If we want to find a clearer distinction between the two, we may look, instead, to the most influential of the jurisprudential Decretists, Huguccio, who insisted on distinguishing craft from commerce and on endorsing profit acquired not 'from commerce but from craftsmanship, as did Paul' (quoted in Langholm 1998: 122).

Aquinas embraced much in Aristotle's idea of 'aristocratic' excellence, but it is less clear that he embraced Aristotle's 'exclusivist doctrines'. Notwithstanding the allusions still often made to Aquinas as an incipient republican (see, e.g., below p. 60), his conception of political order was less that of the ordering of a distinct community than of a part of that cosmic order reflected in his ordering of knowledge. For Aquinas, we know through our rational apprehension of the natural law, which applies equally to us all as created beings, that human beings cannot be excluded from this natural order in the way that Aristotle excluded most from the *polis*. Within this providential order, 'a king can be said to be ordered towards a peasant because the peasant derives benefit from the king's peace' and the aim 'of the king's governance is the common good' (Kempshall 1999: 98). This is a thoroughly Aristotelian and teleological argument. The king's aim is the good order of the political whole, and the beneficiaries are its individual constituents.

Even if we judge that Aquinas' writings express no direct argument for communal functionalism, they may nonetheless be thought to articulate the Christian premises for such an argument (and in a way that is consis-tent with a Pauline and Augustinian acknowledgement of temporal power). In his commentary on the *Politics*, for example, Aquinas says that 'in any society we see that one person serves the society by performing one function, another by performing another function, and in this manner all live well together' (Aquinas 1963: 329). Whereas Western Christian thinkers had previously washed their hands of temporal power, Aquinas, as a convinced Aristotelian, was determined to find the good in it, and this common good had to be one consonant with Christianity. His theoretical annexation of Aristotelianism in the name of Christianity freed it from the fallacy of maintaining an unactualizable ideal of self-sufficiency. Human beings' individual completion is deferred to another life, and their highest temporal good must therefore be reconceptualized. Consequently, practical philosophy could be informed by an idea of the goodness of productive service. Such service is good not only for its external beneficiaries but also in a way internal to the productive actor insofar as it is motivated by a good will and, also, insofar as it educates and habituates the actor into the virtues, especially that of charity. So understood, the good of political order will be common to all of its mutually dependent members.

If Aquinas in this way opened up the possibility of an inclusive politics by abandoning Aristotle's intellectualist ideal, he did so also by retaining and reasserting Aristotle's robust philosophical realism and universalism of natural kinds. Their inability to reconcile such realism with revelation is what laid more Averroist or 'radical' Aristotelians open to the charge of belief in a contradictory and impious 'double truth'. Conversely, such pagan realism was rejected by Ockham as a constraint upon God's will. To Nederman's longstanding perplexity over 'difficulties . . . in reconciling [Ockham's] political thought with his nominalist philosophy' (Nederman 1986: 387; 2002b: 151), it may be responded that Ockham's nominalism or conceptualism more surely warrants a Hobbesian voluntarism (cf. Heidegger 1988: 183ff.) than a communal functionalism. Ockham did not 'found his conception of political institutions on a theory of the needs and fulfilments of human nature, as did St Thomas and his followers' (McGrade 1974: 109), and it is in such a realist theory that communal functionalism has its surest theoretical foundation.

There is a danger here of conflating the rational with the actual. To expand Aristotle's idea of an exclusive political community into an idea of an inclusive communal functionalism is one thing. It is quite another to assume that a given society should be understood and explained in terms of one or other idea. Just as Aristotle denied that Celts or Persians enjoyed any veritably political community, so we might deny that medieval peasants really enjoyed the benefits of a communal functionalism. Such a judgement depends on what we consider those benefits should be. If, with Augustine, we simply aim at peace, then the benefit may indeed be achieved by a successful monarchy. If, with Nederman (2000), we add toleration, or if we postulate some egalitarian principle of justice, or an inclusive conception of human actualization and functioning, then we set the bar higher. Accordingly, we might think that when Aquinas says that 'in *any* society we see that . . . all live well together' he sets the bar too low.

Dominican and Non-Dominican Politics

Aquinas' most important political follower was Ptolemy of Lucca. Whereas Aquinas predeceased his teacher, Ptolemy outlived his. Aquinas, we may suppose, wrote the first quarter of *On the Government of Rulers*, but it was completed by Ptolemy. That it was long attributed to Aquinas in its entirety may go some way towards explaining misapprehensions of Aquinas' political thought. This is because the part by Ptolemy differs considerably from that by Aquinas, and also from Aquinas' other reflections upon secular power. Nonetheless, Ptolemy may be understood as continuing Aquinas' project of assimilating and subordinating Aristotle's practical philosophy to Christian faith and Augustinian theology.

Ptolemy may be called a communal functionalist. Conjoining Aristotle's biology with Paul's account of the *ekklesia* as a mystical body, Ptolemy moves from description of 'an animate body', in which 'the various organs having various functions [are] united in the one substance of the spirit', to a supposedly Pauline warrant for claiming that 'the greater the diversity of arts and offices in a city, the more celebrated it is, because in it the sufficiency of human life can be found to a greater degree' (Ptolemy 1997: 228). Conjoining Paul with John of Salisbury, Ptolemy concludes that 'in a true civility or polity it is required that the members be conformed to the head and not mutually discordant' (ibid.: 272–3). He accords artisans and farmers a place in his functionalist polity, supplanting Aristotle's concern that politics subserve the best life of a few with an Augustinian presumption that politics should instead be concerned with the subsistence of all.

Ptolemy's translator, James Blythe, tells us, to the contrary, that Ptolemy 'tried to make Augustine into an Aristotelian' (Blythe 1997: 50). On Blythe's account, Ptolemy thought a properly constituted polity could enable its citizens to overcome original sin (ibid.: 26–9; 2000: 57) and is 'almost necessary . . . to salvation' (Blythe 2002: 116). We have seen Hugh postulate restoration of our prelapsarian nature as the goal of moral practice and theoretical contemplation, and Ptolemy similarly assimilated 'political virtue and ends to theological ones' (ibid.: 115). Nonetheless, Blythe's attribution to Ptolemy of a conception of politics as the path to perfection may be exaggerated. Ptolemy denies to political community the perfection of the apostolic life; communism was fine for the apostles, whose 'polity was . . . ordained . . . to the celestial city' (Ptolemy 1997: 228–9), but the city for which he writes is ordained only to temporal sufficiency. Blythe writes of Ptolemy's 'teleological approach' to history (Blythe 1997: 37; 2000: 46–8), in the sense that 'the "end" of Aristotelian teleology is . . . united with the eschatological "end" of prophetic time' (Pocock 1975: 374), but of a genuine teleology of human completion we find less trace in Ptolemy than we might expect in a student of Aquinas.

For Blythe, Ptolemy is 'the earliest of the radical Aristotelian proponents of republicanism' (Blythe 1997: 29), having 'built upon and transformed the rudimentary republican arguments that he found in Thomas's writing' (La Salle and Blythe 2005: 265). The greatest of these Aristotelian political radicals was another native of northern Italy, where city-states, like Athens before them, were growing rich through commerce. Marsiglio of Padua's primary concern in his *Defender of the Peace* (Marsilius 1956) was ecclesiastical and Pauline. It was that the Church should return to its original ideals by practising apostolic poverty, and that if the 'Roman Bishop' and episcopate would not do so willingly, then they should be forced to do so by temporal rulers. The ecclesiastical hierarchy should be levelled and the Church subjected to temporal law in just the same way as are other parts of society. Indeed, as 'the whole body of the faithful' is presumed to be identical with the citizenry, they are granted authority over the Church in just the same way that he proposes they exercise it over institutions of coercive power.

Although, in siding with Emperor against Pope, Marsiglio became a political ally of Ockham, he was a philosophical opponent of nominalism, and his political radicalism, we may suppose (along with Marsiglio's translator Alan Gewirth: see Gewirth 1951; cf. Gewirth 1956), was informed by his radical, Averroist Aristotelianism. Aquinas had postulated a single, harmonious ordering of knowledge in which theological contemplation stood above human practice and, accordingly, had placed the spiritual authority of the Church above the temporal authority of monarchs. Ptolemy had maintained this hierarchy of authority, even whilst proposing that the authority of monarchs be replaced where possible by that of the people. In contrast, Marsiglio refused to assimilate philosophy and faith into a single order of knowledge. Like other radical Aristotelians, he followed Averroes' commentary upon Aristotle's *Peri Psyches* to propose that, besides our substantial form as physically separate individuals, we share in one or more unitary and purely intellectual forms. Aquinas famously argued, at papal request, against this monopsychism in *On the Unity of the Intellect Against the Averroists*, but did little to diminish the idea's popularity at Paris or at the University of Padua. We may reasonably assume that this strong conception of human commonality, in the form of something like a general will, did much to underpin Marsiglio's politics. In the first, political part of *Defender of the Peace* he makes much of an organic analogy. This may evince the influence of John of Salisbury, perhaps mediated through Ptolemy, but it may also be understood as giving graphic expression to his own Averroist conception of our metaphysical unity.

For Nederman, Marsiglio stands alongside John of Salisbury as one of the two paradigmatic exponents of communal functionalism (Nederman 1992: 981–5) and in having a predilection for the mechanical arts (Nederman 2002a: 94–102). However, Marsiglio also provides the limit case for Nederman's account of Aristotelianism as a specifically practical philosophy. 'Marsiglio's basic precepts stand outside of the domain of medieval Aristotelianism' because they do not relate political order to 'any deeper conception of a human good construed in ethical' rather than 'biological and material terms' (Nederman 1996: 583). Nederman rejects the idea that an Aristotelian conception of the human good is of a 'biological' *telos* requiring material goods to enable individuals to pursue their internal good. To Nederman's observation that 'Marsiglio is far more naturalistic than Aristotle in the sense that he relies on the direct determination by nature of individual human characteristics', it might be objected that Aristotle is no less naturalistic than Marsiglio even though, as Nederman observes, he has a very different conception of nature. For Aristotle, natural determination is primarily teleological, whereas for Marsiglio it is that of 'productive' causation. Marsiglio's type of naturalism 'constitutes a rejection of the cornerstones both of the Aristotelian conception of *habitus* and of the doctrine of teleology: the former, because nature fixes personal dispositions; the latter, because nature is regarded mainly in terms of efficient causation' (Nederman 1995: 60).

Marsiglio's temporal realm of productively or efficiently causal determination suffers none of the *fortuna* that so frightened Machiavelli, with whom he is often compared. Nor does he share Aristotle's underlying political concern with the contingent provision of external goods necessary for actualizing humans' internal good, or with the contingencies that make a 'practical' ethics of personal judgement so important. Marsiglio's properly formed polity is one positively determined by unconditional human law, and in this he shares something with Ockham. For theologically similar but philosophically dissimilar reasons, both Marsiglio and Ockham wish to separate the highest human good from the good of politics; and both wish to do so even more radically than Ptolemy or Aquinas.

Republicans versus Artisans

What is now widely called the tradition of civic humanist republicanism inherited from Aristotle an ontological ambivalence about the nature of the *res publica*, the public being. Assisted by the indigenous heritage of Roman law, much of the rhetoric of which civic humanists were so proud was used to identify the republic with the citizenry; that is, with individuals in their compartmentalized status as public rather than private actors. At the same time, the republic was held to be something with a 'constitution' apart from and greater than those of its physically constituted citizens. Unlike Machiavelli, Aristotelians regarded this constitution to be natural.

Ambivalence about nature haunts the much-vaunted Aristotelianism of the Renaissance, which spread from northern Italian universities in the fifteenth century. Aristotle provided a conceptual scheme that was used to explain terrestrial and celestial affairs. However, Paduan Aristotelianism of the fifteenth and sixteenth centuries, like that of Marsiglio, reduced the significance and distinctiveness of the idea of teleology within its explanatory scheme. Accordingly, civic virtue was increasingly understood as little more than loyalty to an institutionally distinct state, and to its rulers. As one contemporary champion of republicanism has admitted, its story is that of a descent from the concept of politics to a legitimatory rhetoric of 'reason of state' (Viroli 1992).

We may trace the idea of Aristotelianism as a specifically practical philosophy, shorn of any teleological metaphysics, back to this civic humanism. Increasingly, civic humanists took their ideal of personality not from philosophy, nor from Christianity, but from the appearance and activities of the ruling men of their city states. Rhetoric was employed to praise these men and to educate others into admiring them and emulating their actions. When Leonardo Bruni retranslated the *Politics* and the *Nicomachean Ethics*, along with the pseudo-Aristotelian *Economics*, he was far less concerned than had been Grosseteste or Moerbeke with representing Aristotle's precise concepts and conceptual distinctions. Instead, his concern was with presenting works of elegant Latin that flattered his Florentine compatriots into imagining themselves paragons of Aristotelian virtue. In this, he seems to have succeeded. Indeed, these much-republished works seem to have had a similar effect upon many members of early modern Europe's ruling classes.

Contrary to the impression it has successfully conveyed of virtuous civic activity, John Najemy (1982), on the bases of careful study of early Florentine politics, describes civic humanism as an ideology of mass passivity and of obsequiousness towards the rich and powerful by those wishing to become their official underlings. He contrasts 'two very different' and mutually antagonistic kinds of republicanism. One is civic humanism, the other the far less familiar 'popular guild republicanism that

periodically surfaced to challenge the hegemony of the elite'. This 'republicanism of the guilds envisioned a society of separate . . . interests, in
which difference and division were acknowledged as legitimate', and in
which organic unity was considered as much a political aim as a gift of providence. 'The guild republic was . . . a federation of autonomously constituted parts, each with a voice of its own' (Najemy 2000: 81). The story
Najemy tells is one in which the members of 'major', and mostly commercial, guilds were bought off by the urban plutocrats and divided from
'minor', mostly artisanal, guilds. The ideology of civic aristocracy that
legitimated this political transaction depoliticized the guilds. Civic humanists theorized an anti-collectivist kind of republicanism, in which people
could participate only as individuals and not as members or representatives
of society's functional parts. To act as a worker producing material goods
was to act for the private good of oneself, one's family or one's client, and
not for the common good. Any overtly sectional interest was condemned
as a conspiracy against the harmonious public interest, an alleged source of
corruption in the body politic. To be civically virtuous was to refrain from
acting with one's fellows and to await instruction from one's rulers.

The individualist republicanism self-servingly promoted by civic aristoc-
racies owed much of its success in Florence, and then in that transatlantic
tradition embraced by non-metropolitan gentries (and traced by J. G. A.
Pocock), to the authoritative appeal of its theorization. This Aristotelian
theorization equated ethical excellence with the good birth, education,
power and unproductiveness of gentlemen enjoying the political exclusivity of their 'polite' society. This is another of the many uses to which
Nederman tells us Aristotle was put, even if the least philosophical.

Republicanism legitimated the sovereign state by reference to
Aristotelianism's ethical idea of self-sufficient political community. This use
of that idea is very different from that which Nederman has termed communal functionalism. The modern state is supposedly separated from
private capital and commerce so as to safeguard a public sphere from selfish
interests. Republicanism's ideal described that public sphere in terms of citizenship and virtue, as though it could be constituted by one aspect of individuals and compartmentalized from another, 'private' and amoral aspect
of those same individuals. However, the story of the legitimation of the
modern state involves the replacement this republican ideology of civic
virtue with a procedural norm of official impersonality. Republicanism's
real legacy is the freeing of capital and commerce from any ethic of political accountability or social justice.

3

Aristotle in Germany

The revival of Aristotelianism in mediaeval Christendom may have been led by a German, Albertus Magnus, Albert of Cologne, but so too was the most incisive assault upon that scholastic Aristotelianism. Martin Luther's theological and ecclesiastical reformation focused German minds upon issues of religious theory and practice in a way that was to delay Germany's experience of what we know as the Enlightenment, and even when Germany belatedly underwent that experience it was still under Luther's influence. But, once Germany, in the person of Immanuel Kant, had taken hold of Europe's philosophical lead, it was not to relinquish its grip for a century and a half. During that time, it dragged the European intellect from rationalism, through revolution, to irrationalism and war. At the end of this adventure, understandably chastened, many German philosophers returned to Aristotelianism, albeit an Aristotelianism that was determinedly non-scholastic, anti-metaphysical and explicitly 'practical'. It is therefore not only for reasons of space that my discussion of modern practical philosophy will be confined to Germany; it is also because it is here, more than anywhere else, that, until recently, we find practical philosophy's leaders.

The Lutheran Ethic

The appeal and success of Luther's assault upon the Roman and 'Thomist, or Aristotelian church' (Luther 1961a: 265) owed much to popular and princely resentment at the Church's interference in local, German affairs, as well as to a popular, spiritual religiosity, and to the spread from Italy of civic, literary and philosophical humanism. Luther himself was certainly influenced by the way in which humanists challenged tradition and reread texts – not only classical but also biblical. Nonetheless, Luther's greatest philosophical debt was to Ockhamite nominalism.

After serving as Ockham's refuge from papal persecution, Germany had become a stronghold of nominalism. The central figure of German nominalism, Gabriel Biel, continued its association with temporal emulation of the apostolic life in his engagement with an educative *devotio moderna* that paralleled nominalism's philosophical *via moderna*. Both 'modern' intellectual trends influenced Luther, the Augustinian friar and Wittenberg academic. Nonetheless, Luther rejected the philosophy of Ockhamite nominalism along with that of Thomist realism. What he retained was nominalism's concern with the 'will' and the biblical 'Word' of God. God's Word he juxtaposes to the words of all philosophers, decisively separating reason from faith, philosophy from theology.

Luther differentiates between the Word of the revealed God and the will of the hidden God. Biel had taken the Word of God to say that God had bound His own will in a covenant with humankind, according to which voluntary and penitent submission to the sacraments of the Church guaranteed salvation. Luther rejects this formulation, as it allowed far more freedom to the will of 'Man' and far less to that of God than he can countenance. God's will, he protests, is entirely beyond the scrutiny of human reason, whilst fallen Man has no genuine power of free will. Rereading Paul, he reinterprets *dikaiosis*, one's righteousness or justification before God, as due only to an act of mercy by God and not at all as something that one might merit through good works. One cannot earn salvation, but one can have faith in God's forgiveness of one's own sins. Such divine grace is not extended to all, but if one has the gift of faith that one is saved then one can enjoy the inner freedom of a Christian, a freedom from fear of divine law and a freedom to do genuinely good works.

Luther also rejects Biel's formulation because it attributed far too much authority to the Church. For Luther, as the power of salvation is God's, any claim to that power by the Church is an outrage against God. The early sixteenth-century Church had come a long way since its formation by Paul and, in Rome, by Peter. So too had its idea of works. The works regarded as important for Christians had come to be those institutionalized in the procedures of the Church. The laity had been separated from and subordinated to the official body of the Church, and individual believers were obliged to act in accordance with its increasingly arcane rituals. They could earn salvation by willingly subjecting themselves to its formal and material sacraments. All that a believer had to do was place her faith in the Church and act as it prescribed.

For Luther, obedience to divinely ordained law and the performance of good works are 'a condition, but not a cause, of salvation' (McGrath 1998: 214). As the only cause of salvation is the grace by which God chooses to bestow faith upon individuals, the only thing that is important is the individual believer's direct relation to God. The success of Luther's rebellion against papal authority therefore entailed dismantling the Church's institutional apparatus of mediation between believers and their God. Such dismantling brought into direct relation to God the everyday activities of ordinary Christians. In preaching this, Luther embraced and affirmed ordinary, temporal life. Mendicancy he condemned. Without upholding any Aristotelian ideal of self-sufficiency, he preached that a Christian should work and serve others but should not expect to be served by them. Faithful Christians should be dependent only upon God and themselves. Luther therefore repudiated his own previous monkishness, advocated the dissolution of monastic and mendicant orders, married, and baptized secular work.

Luther, the scholar and the German rebel, did much to form both the German language and (as Romantics later adverted) a specifically German mentality in his translation of God's recorded Word into the vernacular. He did so directly from the original Hebrew and Greek. In omitting the epistles to the Hebrews and of James, he eliminated scriptures that suggested the possibility of justification through works. However, the aspect of Luther's translation that has been most famous over the past century, and that has arguably proven most momentous, is his use of the term *Beruf* to denote a temporal vocation to which the faithful are 'called' by God.

Max Weber was to claim that the specifically modern idea of a calling, vocation or profession derives from the spirit of Luther rather than from that of the texts he translated (Weber 2002: 39). In the time since Paul had written of his calling as an apostle and of the different callings of those called together as a church (see chapter 2), the Catholic Church had assumed exclusive ownership of this term so that only those who withdrew from the world and into its institutions were said to have been summoned by God to a vocation. With Luther, however, all the faithful are said to have been so called. Whereas Paul sanctified only the various gifts that individuals bring to a church that separates itself from the world, Luther, writing when the Church vied for worldly power and when even secular powers were supposed to be exercised by Christians, emphatically extends that sanctification to worldly activities. All Christians are called both to preach the Word in the world and to praise God through working in some particular worldly vocation.

For Weber and Ernst Troeltsch, 'the Protestant ethic of the "calling"' was to prove revolutionary in its eventual social and economic effects. It induced 'the bourgeois capitalistic spirit . . . of labour and . . . of industry for its own sake, a process of objectifying work and the results of work, which was only possible where work was exalted by means of an ascetic vocational ethic' (Troeltsch 1931: 645–6). Their historical account of this Protestant work ethic and ascetic ethos of early capitalism may be crudely adapted as follows. Medieval Christendom had two distinct conceptions of work. One was of work as earthly toil. This was the conception of work that John of Salisbury and others attempted to rescue from aristocratic disdain by explicating its contribution to the common, temporal good. The other conception was of religious works. This was the conception of works as monopolized and ritualized by the Church and dispensed by it to the faithful as their path to salvation. The distinction between these two conceptions represented Christianity's elemental distinction between temporal and spiritual realms, a distinction that was greatly radicalized by Luther's theology. For Luther, 'the first wall' protecting the Roman Church was that separating their own spiritual estate from 'the secular estate' comprising 'princes, lords, artizans [*sic*], and farm-workers' (Luther 1961b: 407). In demolishing this wall, he redrew the line between what is spiritual and what is temporal, rejecting any suggestion that temporal works could merit salvation. By clearly differentiating the concept of spiritual faith from that of earthly works, and by making one's faith a precondition of the goodness of one's works, Luther deradicalized the medieval distinction between the concepts of works and of toil. Work, of either kind, belongs solely to the temporal realm. It is a religious duty, a calling. *Good* works are a function of true faith. The faithful individual is motivated to participate in the Church, to work well and to do good in this world out of love for God and gratitude for His grace. By so making the individual's God-given faith the criterion of the goodness of work in a calling, Luther necessarily undermined the idea that the goodness of work derives from its contribution to a common good. One is called by God, not by one's society, and the believer knows that the goodness of her work derives from God, not from her self or her share in humanity. Responsible only to her God and her self, it is up to the individual to order her own life and work rationally and methodically. In this way, Protestantism entered decisively into a historical process of Western rationalization by introducing the absolute imperative of individual self-discipline.

Notoriously, there is much that is paradoxical in 'the Weber thesis' about the importance of the 'elective affinity' between Protestant theology and the 'spirit' of economic individualism implicated in capitalism's historical take-off (for an appreciation of MacIntyre's critique, see Marshall 1982: 66–7). Clearer is the influence of Luther and the Reformation in the development of state sovereignty and of a reciprocal political individualism – even if, as with economic individualism, an adequate account of this would have to extend beyond Germany to Calvinism's further radicalization of Protestantism. What is less clear about this development than about what Luther said of works is how it derives from his theological innovations. Indeed, we might well suppose that Luther's political pronouncements owed less to his theology than to the precariousness of his personal situation and his need for princely protection from Pope and Emperor alike, and to his desire to employ temporal power to enforce his particular vision of ecclesiastical and doctrinal reformation against those who would have combined religious reform with social revolution.

A Conservative Aristotelianism

Many of these would-be revolutionaries wished to bring the temporal realm closer to the eternal by applying 'Godly law'. 'The revolution of 1525' (Blickle 1981) may be understood as a result of many of the same grievances, combined with the same sense of lay religiosity, that accounts for much of the appeal and success of Martin Luther's own rebellion against papal and imperial authority. Now, though, Luther, the grandson of a peasant and son of a miner turned mine-owner and burgher, felt threatened by the people below him as well as by temporal powers above. The scholarly theologian suddenly tempered his own temporal rebelliousness. His theological revolution was intended to provoke no political revolution against aristocratic power. God has provided Man with princely powers to rule over him in order to keep his sinful rapaciousness in check. The inner conviction of the individual believer therefore properly concerns only his own salvation by God and can never extend to any reordering of the external world through his own self-righteous actions. Unlike Luther's theology, the lay religiosity that helped motivate peasants, miners and other workers to revolt may be understood as a continuation of the long history of medieval apostolic movements and of their attempts to bring a communistic Kingdom of God down to Earth. For all their shared appeals to faith, grace and the gospels, Luther, citing *Romans* 13, endorsed the brutal repression of this popular religious movement, much as repression of Cathars and Hussites had been endorsed by the papacy. The revolt of 1525 was the greatest in a long line of popular revolts in Germany, and the last.

Luther's vindication of princely power was consistent with Augustine's non-Aristotelian politics, in that it depended upon no attribution of virtue to the prince. More even than Machiavelli, his contemporary, Luther considered politics in terms only of instrumental power. In appealing to the hereditary aristocracy ('*Adel* ') of the German nation to lead ecclesiastical reformation (Luther 1961b), he reinforced that still recent (Morsel 2001) self-designation but, even so, he had no illusion that those he addressed were morally superior to their subjects. What they monopolized was not excellence but only the legitimate use of coercion. His redrawing of the traditional line between a spiritual realm of individual faith and a temporal realm of ineradicable, institutionalized power effectively juxtaposed an ethic of industriousness internal to the individual actor with a fact of external, coercive power in a way that was to ramify through the development of German and European intellects. He therefore did much more than continue the history of occasional Catholic repression. In endorsing princely authority – even within the Church itself – in the name of a popular and spiritual theology, he did much to cultivate a peculiarly Germanic mentality and tradition of deference and subservience to local, temporal power. For Luther, theological radicalism was distinguished from political radicalism as surely as God from Man.

A part of Luther's theological radicalism was his famous assault upon scholastic Aristotelianism. It might therefore seem to be a second historical paradox concerning his influence that Aristotelianism was, nonetheless, to retain its academic dominance far longer in Germany than in Italy, England or France. However, this chapter in the history of ideas is more straightforward than that entitled 'the Weber thesis' in that its plot involves a change in Luther's mind. The incisiveness of his initial assault is indubitable. In his 'Appeal' to the German aristocracy, he told them that 'the universities need a sound and thorough reformation' because in them:

> the blind pagan teacher, Aristotle, is of more consequence than Christ. . . . Aristotle's writings on *Physics*, *Metaphysics*, *On the Soul*, and *Ethics* . . . along with all others that boast they treat of natural objects . . . have nothing to teach about things natural or spiritual. . . . [A] potter has more understanding of the things of nature than is written down in those books. It pains me to the heart that this damnable, arrogant, pagan rascal has seduced and fooled so many of the best Christians with his misleading writings. God has made him a plague to us on account of our sins . . .
>
> His book on *Ethics* is worse than any other book, being the direct opposite of God's grace [and of] the Christian virtues. . . . I have read him and studied him with more understanding than did St Thomas Aquinas. (Luther 1961b: 470–1)

Like Paul, Luther wished 'to destroy the wisdom of the wise'. He had a special animus towards Aristotle's *Ethics* because of what it says of practice, habit and justice or righteousness. For Luther, only God is righteous; Man cannot be. He identified Aristotle's claim that individuals can become just and virtuous through practice, so that such excellence becomes a habitual, personal attribute, as the source of scholastic arguments for justification through works, and he understood this idea of ethical activity to be informed by Aristotle's metaphysics of *energeia* and *entelecheia*.

But Luther was to prove less uncompromising than Paul. When he appealed to the German aristocracy in 1520, Luther had already been working for a couple years with the young Aristotelian humanist and Professor of Greek, Philip Melanchthon, who became his lieutenant and, after his death, for a short while, the undisputed leader of Lutheranism. Initially, Luther did much to temper Melanchthon's Aristotelianism, whilst Melanchthon did little to temper Luther's animosity. Conditions changed in 1525. If theologically radical ideas could be transformed into revolutionary political demands, then something was needed to distinguish and to underpin Lutheran orthodoxy. Luther and Melanchthon therefore looked, again, to Aristotle. If Aristotelianism could reinforce Catholic doctrine, then it could reinforce Lutheran doctrine too.

Princely power might be the instrument of temporal law and even of ecclesiastical reformation, but the 'sound and thorough reformation' of the universities and their curricula and textbooks was entrusted instead to Melanchthon, who thereby became *Praeceptor Germaniae*, the teacher of Germany. Even in 1520 Luther had admitted that he 'would gladly grant the retention of Aristotle's books on *Logic*, *Rhetoric*, and *Poetics* . . . to train young men to speak and preach well' (Luther 1961b: 471). Now Melanchthon rehabilitates the *Ethics*, and especially what it says of a specifically human justice that may inform temporal law. What Melanchthon stresses is Aristotle's praise of moderation rather than fanaticism, of order rather than revolution, of communal functionalism (e.g. Melanchthon 1999a: 10) rather than either tyranny or communism, of hierarchy rather than democracy, and of method rather than sophistry. Moral philosophy is good, but only if it is Aristotelian; Melanchthon censures the spreading enthusiasms for Stoicism, for Epicureanism, and for a Platonism newly contrasted to Aristotelianism. His Aristotelian ethics aims not at temporal happiness but at virtuously self-disciplined action in performance of divinely sanctioned works. Far from being the God-given plague denounced by Luther, Melanchthon now presents Aristotle as our divinely provided guide to philosophy (Melanchthon 1999b: 206, 210), rather as Luther perceived divine providence in princely rule. For Melanchthon, then, almost as much as for Aquinas, Aristotle was *the* philosopher, and Melanchthon made much of Aristotle's teleological natural science and psychology (and of his supposedly nominalist logic). Philosophy, though, remains distinct from theology, and therefore Melanchthon usually passed over the *Metaphysics* in silence. Albertus, he said, had confused the two. In re-establishing theology's integrity, Luther had given Melanchthon both a theology to codify and the opportunity to re-establish philosophy's proper status as one of the arts and as theology's handmaiden. It was questions of theology rather than of either practical or natural philosophy that continued to excite German minds for decades after Luther's death, and it was disputes about works' significance for salvation that were to divide Lutherans from one another and, more deeply, from Calvinists and Catholics.

From Reformation to Enlightenment

Devastated by the Thirty Years War, Germany was barred by the Treaty of Westphalia from the path of centralized state and nation-building taken by England and France. Numerous princely courts imitated the baroque elegance, polite tastes and conspicuous consumption of Versailles whilst lording it over their localities, much of the governance of which was effected through local churches. The old medieval distinction between those who prayed, fought and produced was legally formalized as that between the three estates (*Stände*) of clergy, nobility and burghers, with the great mass of the population excluded from these constituents of the particularistic *Ständestaat*.

These are the conditions to which is attributed what is conventionally portrayed as early modern Germany's benighted intellectual condition, in contrast to France and Britain's scientific and cultural enlightenment. In Germany, old philosophical battles were refought within the terms of Melanchthon's Augsburg Confession. His theologically inspired exclusion of metaphysics from Aristotelianism was subverted, a new scholasticism was created (with borrowings from Catholic Iberia) and, once again, philosophical theory furnished premises for an orthodox theology. The eventual challenge to this came from Pietism, a popular movement that aimed to return Lutheranism to what was understood as its original concern with individual faith and conduct. This was a consciously 'practical' rather than doctrinal Christianity, and its adherents preached a toleration that permitted Prussian enlightenment.

The claims of theoretical philosophy were pressed in Germany by Baron Gottfried Wilhelm von Leibniz and by Christian Wolff, who was ennobled for his philosophical services. Leibniz intended to combine Lutheranism with the Catholic Church and a providentialist theism with the new science of matter in motion, this latter ambition being known more generally as 'natural theology'. The substances or 'monads' of his metaphysics occupy a harmonious universe in which all are ordered for the best. Wolff attempted to fulfil Leibniz's ambition to construct a 'universal science' by elaborating Leibniz's philosophy into a comprehensive and highly formalized schema, enunciated in both Latin and a specifically philosophical German that he did more than anyone else to shape. Within this system, 'universal practical philosophy' – which tells individuals of the means to their natural end of happiness and includes ethics, economics and politics – is clearly preceded by a theoretical or metaphysical first philosophy that claimed to enunciate truths about God without reference to revelation. What eventually tested Pietists beyond endurance was Wolff's claim that the systematically providential nature of the universe is such that even the Chinese may rationally base their practical philosophy upon natural law, obviating the relevance to practice of revelation and perhaps even of free will. In Wolff's system, function entirely displaces agency.

Aristotle's various hierarchies of for-the-sake-ofs in natural beings and in human practice are ordered by Wolff into a single account of a world and a universe providentially designed for the benefit of humankind. Amongst his many neologisms is one that describes the logic of accounting for everything in terms of such an anthropocentric but autopoietic purposiveness: *teleologia* or *Teleologie*. The most distinctive component of Aristotle's conceptual scheme, already long freed from the tradition of commentary upon his texts, is now freed even from its original meaning within that scheme to begin a new and adventurous life of its own.

A Metaphysics of Practice

One of the greatest ironies in the history of practical philosophy is that the decisive blow against Germany's aristocratic Aristotelianism was struck by the son of a bridle-maker (cf. above pp. 30–1, 50). The entirety of Immanuel Kant's crushingly 'critical' philosophy, but especially his moral theory, is influenced by his austere, Pietist upbringing. In his 'Copernican Revolution', claims to objective truth regarding external beings are replaced by the methodically disciplined practice of individual judgement. Although there may be no limits to our desire to know, there are limits to our ability to do so because we are constrained by the categorial limits to that conceptual scheme which is particular to no philosopher but universal for reason as such. Even if all empirical particularities were to exemplify the functioning of a universal and providential system, our perceptual and intellectual capacities would not be adequate to its recognition. What is knowable with certainty is our own free will, and what is most architectonic for us is a rationality that is universalizable by being purified of any empirical concerns.

In his desire for a comprehensive system of knowledge, Kant nonetheless remains something of a Wolffian. As he says in his *Critique of Pure Reason*, the metaphysical philosopher is not – as are the natural scientist, logician and mathematician – a merely imitative 'artist of reason but the legislator of human reason', using each of those others 'as instruments' and assigning to them their tasks in pursuit of 'the essential purposes of human reason (*teleologia rationis humanae*)'. 'The final purpose [*Endzweck*]' of human reason, to which lesser purposes 'necessarily belong . . . as means . . . is none other then the whole vocation of the human being' (Kant 1996: 760–1 [A839/B867–A840/B868]; Kant's Latin). This vocation comprises active, voluntary and virtuous obedience to the deductive rationality of the moral law. Accordingly, Kant sets himself the task, given his own more particular vocation as philosopher, of drafting a pure moral law that rational wills ought to legislate for themselves. Like Wolff, he grounds his philosophy of practice explicitly and systematically in metaphysics, albeit that Kant's metaphysics is epistemologically chastened. Self-sufficiency is found not in any empirical object but only in reason itself. Humans are capable of a rational self-sufficiency or 'autonomy', but this can only be actualized if they nullify their passions and unconditionally obey only their own pure reason. Whereas Aristotle's architectonic was practical and his final end vocationally theoretical, Kant's architectonic is theoretical and his final end practical.

Kant's purely rational architectonic system requires some single good at its apex as its final end. This final good is that of the individual's good will. In his *Critique of Practical Reason* Kant provides the terms in which have been conducted more recent arguments over Aristotle's idea of the highest good. 'The highest can mean either the supreme . . . or the complete. . . . The first is that condition which is . . . not subordinate to any other condition . . . ; the second is that whole which is not part of a still greater whole of the same kind (*perfectissimum*)'. Virtue is 'the *supreme* good', and virtue in combination with the happiness it deserves is the complete and highest good (Kant 2002: 141–2 [110]; Kant's Latin). The conclusion to which Kant moves is that the supreme good can be surely achieved by the autonomous and conscientious individual in this life, but that the complete good cannot be so guaranteed. Empirical anthropology tells us that evil often goes unpunished and the good often suffer, even whilst practical reason tells us that virtue must have some reward beyond itself. At this point, Kant, leaping backwards across the conceptual chasm hewn by Hume to prevent deductions from *'is'* to *'ought'* (Hume 2000: 302 [3.1.1]), proposes God as saviour of the virtuous and guarantor of the complete good. In so doing, he elaborates a still more metaphysical argument than those of Leibniz or Wolff for divine providence. He also elaborates a position closer to some previously condemned as heretical than to Augustinian orthodoxy; the individual can achieve a kind of otherworldly perfection voluntarily, even in our fallen and imperfect world. He advances the very claim with which Luther charged scholasticism: that works warrant salvation – works, that is, of the will, evaluable in isolation from any particular effects or empirical conditions. What Kant denotes by 'practical reason' is therefore different from what was meant by Aristotle. For Aristotle, what is practically right is often particular to and conditional upon circumstances; for Kant, it is something unconditional and universalizable. Where Aristotle attempted to draw a line separating the internality of action from the externality of production, Kant drew one separating the internality of an individual's will from the externality of any consequences of her actions. With far greater rigour and consistency than Aristotle, Kant argued that moral excellence must be conceptualized in isolation from temporal effectiveness.

Kant's system culminates in his third Critique. Having addressed the good and the true in his second and first Critiques, the first half of the *Critique of Judgement* concerns the beautiful. In this 'Critique of Aesthetic Judgement' (following a Wolffian lead), he casts *aisthesis*, perception, as a crucial aspect of our power of judgement. In discussing such 'taste', he briefly but influentially turns his attention to human creativity. He had acknowledged technical 'skill' as an aspect of practice (*praxis*) in his previous Critiques, allocating it to the empirical world of efficient causality and hypothetical imperatives and describing it as an effective means to one's ends. Now – reflecting upon the cultivated 'culture' of refined aristocratic taste and 'sensibility' he partially inhabits, in which certain commodities are celebrated in the polite 'communication' that they facilitate – he draws a radical distinction between craft skill and individual genius. He begins by distinguishing artistic from natural production, 'the first being a work (*opus*), the second an effect (*effectus*)'. Then, in contrast to *'mercenary art'* which can only be a means to other ends, he identifies *'free art'* which 'could only turn out purposive (i.e., succeed) if it is play, in other words, an occupation that is agreeable on its own account; mercenary art we regard as labor, i.e., as an occupation that . . . is disagreeable (burdensome) and that attracts us only through its effect (e.g., pay), so that people can be coerced into it' (Kant 1987: 170–1 [303–4]; Kant's Latin). The individuality of artists is conceptually separated from the standard practices of artisans because the original products of genius's 'free' or 'fine art', being constrained by no universal rules, are ends in themselves. Although genius, like technical skill, is judged by its products, and although it differs from moral excellence both in this and in its freedom from rules, it nonetheless constitutes another kind of personal excellence and of untaught, almost atemporal, virtuosity. Rather as Augustine differentiated divine creativity from human production, so Kant differentiates mere production from a newly recognized power of individual human creativity.

The third *Critique's* second half, the 'Critique of Teleological Judgement', concerns reflective judgement about nature's apparent purposiveness. As in its first half, Kant here attempts to bridge the chasm dividing our practical reasoning about our own free action from our deterministic understanding of natural causation, here through analysis of our power to reflect upon and to judge natural phenomena in the same terms in which we reason about our own and others' actions: those of means and of ends. He recognizes that, in exercising such teleological judgement about nature and about ourselves as natural beings, the world around us appears less alien to our purposive wills than is suggested by his antinomy of freedom and determinism. Like Aristotle, he brings 'nature under principles of observation and investigation by *analogy* with the causality in terms of purposes' that is involved in our production of artefacts. For Kant, 'we adduce a teleological basis when we attribute to the concept of an object' a causality concerning that concrete object's eventual and actual production (ibid.: 236–7 [360]). A concept, for Kant, only exists within individuals' minds. In contrast to this, a form, for Aristotle, is a real universal that is instantiated in particular substances that are external to, but may be apprehended by, the human mind. When Aristotle described artefacts as forms, he could attribute the causality that Kant attributes to human imagination, conceptualization and purposiveness instead to the extant form, which it is then up to the artisan to imitate as best he can. We might well consider Kant's conceptualization of artefactual production more plausible than Aristotle's, were it not complicated by his absolute separation of a supposedly rare and inexplicable genius from technical skill which, in a way redolent of Aristotle, he compares (in the *Critique's* original introduction) with the 'technic [*Technik*] of nature' and our 'technical power' that judges 'objects of nature *as if* they were made possible through art' as the actualization of some concept (ibid.: 390 [200'–1']).

Central to Kant's analysis of teleological judgement is his juxtaposition of 'internal' to 'external purposiveness'. What he intends by 'internal purposiveness' resembles what Aristotle denoted by *entelecheia*. It describes in functional terms the constitution, or formation, of discretely organized beings as living wholes. This, he proposes, is a necessary type of judgement, in that it is the only way in which we can understand such 'systems' as 'the inner structure of plants and animals' (ibid.: 405–6 [217']). It is a regulative ideal of subjective reason apprehending such readily identifiable wholes as if they were purposively designed, without any assumption that this ideal corresponds to anything that is really constitutive of the things in themselves. In contrast, 'external purposiveness' denotes the way in which some things serve others as – or, rather, '*as if* designed as – means to the latters' ends. It is this idea of external purposiveness (and not that of *internal* purposiveness, systematized by Hegel into 'the Idea') which underpins the Critique's concluding thoughts relating the theological argument that Kant developed from his practical philosophy to the theistic hypothesis of a hierarchical, architectonic and 'teleological system' of nature as a created whole, in which his critical philosophy still follows Wolff.

The chasm separating Kant's ideal kingdom of moral ends from his temporal kingdom of efficient causality and 'practical anthropology' was never bridged by the architectonic system that he premised upon that separation. It was, however, not merely bridged but filled in and ploughed over by those who have been called 'left Kantians' (Yack 1986: 102ff.). They differ from Kant in being less pietistic and much less politically quietistic, and also in being more philosophically anthropological or humanist. Friedrich Schiller was at the forefront of attempts to combine Kant's moral rigorism with an Aristotelian concern for the formation of character as a second nature (Beiser 2005a). Their political concerns were inspired by events abroad. In between the publication of Kant's second Critique, in 1788, and that of his third, in 1790, a republican revolution had erupted in France. The fissures that now excited philosophers were more political than epistemological. Everywhere, philosophers understood the French Revolution as the attempted application of enlightened ideals to political reality, or even as the instantiation of such ideals, however imperfectly, in that reality, a possibility that was precluded from Kant's system. In Germany, many young adherents of his system sought to reconstitute it in a way that could make sense of the Revolution as such a concretization. Where he had spoken of individuals' public use of reason and the rational universality of law, they called for a fully rational and veritably political community. Schiller again led the way in following Kant's suggestions about a rationally universalist history. Inspired also by the Graecophilia which Winckelmann had initiated and which Lessing, Herder, Wolf (teacher of Immanuel Bekker, Andronicus' modern successor) and, later, Schleiermacher and Hölderlin refined (and which, in a decreasingly aesthetic and increasingly philosophical form, was to remain a striking feature of German intellectual culture until well into the twentieth century), Schiller told a story beginning with free Hellenic harmony, moving on to Christian self-consciousness alienated from the world, and now concluding in a new era of self-conscious freedom and political virtue to be achieved through the aesthetic education of mankind.

A Historical Teleology

The most famous of the 'left Kantians' was G. W. F. Hegel, and this because he was the most single-minded in systematically elaborating the new conception of philosophical theory as progressively instantiated in historical and political practice. Hegel's system describes a universe that reaches its highest actualization in self-conscious human activity and, especially, the theoretical activity of reason's reflection upon its own power. As he acknowledges in both his *Logic* and the *Encyclopaedia Logic*, he adopts Kant's analysis of teleology in terms of 'internal' and 'external purposiveness'. External purposiveness was erroneously attributed to a pre-established and atemporal harmony of relations within Wolff's system, in which non-human objects serve naturally as means to human ends. For Hegel, in contrast, the subjection to human purposes of external objects with their own natures is what involves human actors in the very effort and conflict (the negation of negation) that develops their self-consciousness. The actor is driven to such efforts by an internal purposiveness that Hegel explicitly presents as the re-expression of Aristotle's account of teleology. (The best comparison of Hegel and Aristotle is now Ferrarin 2001, although Mure 1940 remains an important Anglophone monument.) Like Aristotle, Hegel attributes real, causal and constitutive ends to all living organisms. Aristotle's exposition of teleology was deficient only, according to Hegel, in limiting such internal purposiveness to individual beings and particular species and in not extending it to temporal actuality as a whole. Hegel therefore presents his conception of teleology in the *Encyclopaedia*, and more stridently in his lectures on the history of philosophy, as an extension and, indeed, completion of that of Aristotle. Against those, such as Goethe, who opposed Plato's idealism to Aristotelian scholasticism or empiricism, Hegel portrayed Aristotle as continuing and sublating Plato's philosophy. What remained was for Hegel to sublate Aristotle's speculative but relatively unsystematic philosophy within his own architectonic system.

Hegel's supposed rearticulation of Aristotle's account of 'internal' tele-ology is expressed in terms of ends and means. That it is expressed in these same terms as is his account of external teleology is unsurprising, given that external teleology describes one object's subjection to another's pur-poses. Conversely, it is in actively and purposively mastering external objects that an individual comes to understand herself as a subject, actual-izing her potential as a fully human and rational being. This temporal process of individual self-recognition is also a universal process of self-determination in which a human being comes to act in accordance with her concept, as a person. Subjective concept and universal form are actualized together in the self-conscious human actor.

Actuality is, for Hegel, a process of actualization. Being is becoming. As Manfred Riedel observes, Hegel effects a 'speculative dissolution of the relation [or 'demarcation'] of production (*poiesis*) and activity (*praxis*)' (Riedel 1984: 8–9). Everything is in movement, and therefore actuality cannot be what it was for Aristotle: an atemporal state of completion. If Hegel's *telos* is not the Prussian state, then this is perhaps because it is no achievable state of affairs at all. Although Hegel provides grounds for the-orizing a potential completion of history, he also provides grounds for thinking that history can have no such end. If we read him in the latter way, then his is a teleology that commits what for Aristotle is the cardinal error of recognizing no limit. Nonetheless, Hegel is more Aristotelian than Heraclitean. This is because he perceives movement as, actually, an ordered process. The task of reason is to apprehend the logic, the ratio-nale, of such order. In apprehending different kinds of change – mechani-cal, chemical, biological, intellectual and institutional – reason comes to understand itself. Humans' rational apprehension of, at least, mechanical and chemical processes allows their control and manipulation. Intellectual developments constitute reason's progressive apprehension of its own powers. Such is the case with regard to the history of religion and, indeed, of philosophy. The logic inherent in human history has, hitherto, been superior even to the rationality of individual human beings. Such histori-cally evolved institutions as the state and market are products of human action, and such action is sometimes represented by that of world-histori-cal individuals, but such institutions are never the products of individual genius. Rather, they are products of individuals' mutual interaction and of the development of society as a whole. Reason is not just an attribute of individual human beings; it is also an impersonal attribute of human history. Hegel's logic is a temporal and historical logic of society, a sociology.

Hegel's extension of teleology from individual beings to entire systems, and his extension of universality from atemporal and natural kinds to temporal and historical processes, has had vast influence on the modern understanding of teleology. Individuals are not, as they were for Aristotle, primary beings but, rather, parts of a universal whole which gives them their particular identity, role and function. In this, even though Hegel renounces any providentialist 'external teleology', he may be said to subordinate agency to functionality through his extension of actualization from the individual to the universal. Accordingly, it can still be said that 'all of Hegel's thinking essentially proceeds from an organic vision of the world, a view of the universe as a single vast living organism' (Beiser 2005b: 80).

Hegel's conceptual scheme differs crucially from that of Aristotle, in juxtaposing the universal not only to an infinity of particular instances of 'this' individual but in juxtaposing also concrete individuals to conditional particulars. The unconditioned realm of individuals can only be one of an unreal abstraction, such as the abstraction of Kantian moral imperatives. Real relations between human individuals are necessarily relations of historical, social and institutionalized particularity. Accordingly, the final end posited by Hegel is not that of individuals in some atemporal realm, as speculated in Kant's second Critique, but that of impersonal reason's onward progress towards its ever more integrated understanding of and identification with actuality as an ordered whole. So conceived, reason is not separated from a reality of which it can only have an incomplete, empirical knowledge, but, rather, is actualizing itself in the world. There is no unbridgeable chasm between facts and values; rather, rational activity progressively imbues reality with value. Such a metaphysics allows no juxtaposition of atemporal activities with temporal processes. Action objectifies mind in the world through its temporal effects, and salient amongst such effects are material products. 'For Hegel, the most visible manifestation of the necessary "mediation" between subjective end and objective world is "the tool"', which is 'a means' to that 'end' (Pippin 1989: 245).

Even though Hegel is still understood as bringing together what Kant had torn apart, he is now often interpreted as completing Kant's work. Like Kant, Hegel is concerned with our 'leaving nature behind' and 'legislating for ourselves' (McDowell 2002a: 276–7). This new Hegel is centrally concerned with the sociality of reason, apperception and intentionality, and perhaps even with how one finds 'oneself in one's formative activity' (McDowell 2003: 12) in a way that could be called therapeutic. In the former case, if not the latter, he remains a political thinker. Terry Pinkard has long been concerned with Hegel's constitutional state as a form of political community, and Robert Pippin understands Hegel's 'self-directed "purposive life"' as 'a necessarily collective agency' (Pippin 1997: 8). Knowledge, rationality, self-consciousness and freedom are, on Hegel's account, social achievements, the principal condition of possibility of their achievement by individuals being their progressive accomplishment by society. Rather as the self is objectified in its products, so relations between selves are objectified in institutions. As rationality and its concretization in the institutionalized actuality of ethical life progress hand in hand, so too do morality and productivity, freedom as an internal good and freedom from natural necessity through possession of external, material goods. A Hegelian society is one that is both ethical and efficient; such is an 'absolute ideal'. Human action upon external objects is the means to the human end of a self-determination that must be social and political as well as individual. The production of material goods and the satisfaction and transcendence of natural needs is neither an achievement of lone individuals nor of merely reciprocal relations between master and slave or buyer and seller. Rather, its attainment is actually and rationally social and systemic. For Hegel, it is not just impersonal law that should be understood as an objectification of universal reason, but all of those particular social institutions that have been actualized in history and that individuals feel as constraints upon their wills. If Hegel has an ideal of human life, it comprises neither contemplation of the divine nor entirely autonomous action, but an actor happily reconciled to the rational constraints of social actuality.

Riedel anticipated the interpretive subordination of Hegel's grand metaphysical construction by the likes of Pippin, Pinkard, Brandom and McDowell when he proposed that it is Hegel's 'inclusion of modern political economy in the design of practical philosophy' which entails his 'speculative dissolution' of the traditional division of production from action, and not vice versa (Riedel 1984: 8–9). It might well be thought that such a speculative reconciliation of the concepts of production and action would be accompanied by a dissolution of any conceptual division of economy from polity (Baum 2004: 147), but this is not what occurs with Hegel. What Riedel has long argued is that Hegel distinguished so radically between state and civil society that it is he, rather than Hobbes, who made the decisive break from an Aristotelian to a modern understanding of the state and politics. I shall argue that this interpretive judgement misapprehends Hegel, both because of the way in which he draws his distinction between state and civil society and because of the way in which the distinction is sublated within the broader conception of ethical life he elaborates in his theoretically informed practical philosophy.

The Ethical Life of Modern Society

Humans are, for Hegel, 'social' beings. *Civilis societas*, Bruni's Latin for Aristotle's *koinonia politike*, was adopted by the likes of Melanchthon to denote a political community. With the translation of philosophy into vernacular tongues, the concept was denoted by '*bürgerliche Gesellschaft*' and 'civil society'. The latter term was used by such Scottish protagonists of Enlightenment as Hume, Adam Ferguson and, above all, Adam Smith (more than the similarly influential but less innovative James Steuart) in reference to the ordering effects of custom and commerce, in addition to the effects of the English state. Influential upon Kant and many others in Germany, this usage helped inspire Hegel to conceptualize civil society in juxtaposition to the state (Waszek 1988). Basic to his account of civil society is what he calls 'the system of needs'. This is what Marx was to call the capitalist mode of social production. It is what is now called 'the economy', understood as something entirely separate from the *oikos* or household. What so impressed Hegel about this was precisely that, as Smith had shown, it could be understood as an ordered, functioning system operating apart from any directing intelligence, whether of the head of a household or of a state. As Hayek was to argue, this is in effect an order of human 'cooperation'. Production is not to be understood in terms only of an asocial relation between producer and product, but also of social relations between producers and needy consumers. In showing how such social relations are ordered, says Hegel, the science of 'political economy . . . does credit to thought because it finds the laws underlying a mass of contingent occurrences' (Hegel 1991: 228 [§189]). Smith, like Newton, has demonstrated that laws apply in the relation between what Aristotle would have regarded only as particular beings constrained by their inner natures and external chance. For Hegel, this demonstrated a rationality greater than that of the individual participants within it; a 'cunning' and providential reason 'which, while seeming to abstain from activity', watches whilst concrete purposiveness, pursuing what it considers only its 'particular interest, is in fact doing the very opposite and makes itself a moment of the whole' (Hegel 1977: 33 [§54]) through the unintentionally beneficial effects of individuals' actions for society. The operation of such impersonal rationality makes of selfish individuals fully social beings, serving as means to society's ends by satisfying each other's material needs. Nonetheless, Hegel emphasizes that this market system cannot be self-sufficient. He emphasizes this in including alongside the system of needs what we would surely call, first, the judicial and, secondly, the regulatory and welfare functions of the state

as aspects of civil society. As an extension of those explicitly political functions (and not as a part of the system of needs), he adds 'the corporation'
to which individuals belong 'in accordance with their objective
qualifications of skill and rectitude'. A corporation 'is itself a member [or
part] of society', and as a member of such a guild-like organization an individual 'has *his honour in his estate*'. Without such membership, an individual's 'isolation reduces him to the selfish aspect of his trade'. Within it, skill
'is freed from personal opinion and contingency . . . and is recognized,
guaranteed, and at the same time raised to a conscious activity for a
common end'. The corporation is therefore the '*ethical* root of the state'
within civil society. It is 'a *second* family for its members', supplementing the
first's ethical socialization of individuals. Unfortunately, complains Hegel,
having recently abolished the guilds, and having not replaced them with
any more integrated corporate structure, 'modern states' now fail to offer
ordinary individuals any such ethical or 'universal activity' (Hegel 1991:
271–3 [§§252–255]).

If a subject's action upon external objects is an educative means to her
self-determination, then does Hegel think that this is true of the activity of
production? In his lectures on aesthetics, Hegel steers a middle course
between Aristotle's account of the production of fine art as *techne* and the
account of it as a creation of genius advanced by Kant and the Romantics,
but in so doing he draws his own distinction between such production and
that undertaken by labour. Even if he does not use the term *Entfremdung*
before the *Phenomenology of Spirit* (Inwood 1992: 36), he argues earlier that
labour is alienated (Hegel 1979). Political economy (and even speculative
history) may demonstrate theoretically how labour's effects are of universal significance, but this is not enough for production to be a means by
which the alienated producer can attain a consciousness of universality. As
Hegel makes amply clear in the *Philosophy of Right*, such means can only be
institutional and political. His theoretical philosophy is far more architectonic than Aristotle's but, as it sublates Kant's distinction between rationality and actuality, he can concur with Aristotle in drawing from it the lesson
that politics must be an architectonic activity. The state need not manage
the process of production, but it must, to be practically rational, impose an
institutional structure upon the social relations of the system of needs.

Although Hegel separates civil society's economic system of needs from
the family, conceiving the latter in far more romantic and less managerial
terms than did Aristotle, his conceptual separation of civil society from the
state can hardly be regarded as decisively modern, including as his civil
society does almost all of the state's managerial functions. Hegel's analysis

is not structured empirically but philosophically. Civil society is the sphere of particularity, the state the sphere of universality. Therefore, besides its central legislative function, the state includes only the 'universal estate' of army, central bureaucracy and, of course, professoriate, and its legislature must represent and reconcile the particular interests of civil estates. The reason for this is given in Hegel's account of ethical life.

The significance of Hegel's analytical distinction between the state and civil society is given in his synthetic conceptualization of 'ethical life' as a totality. That totalizing concept is an explicit attempt to theorize the modern world in terms of political community. As Karl-Heinz Ilting has argued, this attempt owes much to Hegel's reading of Aristotle's *Politics*, *Ethics* and *Metaphysics* (see, for example, Ilting 1971: 98–102; 1984: 109). Hegel describes ethical life as more determinate than are natural individuals because it is the historical actualization of the universal 'idea'. The *polis* had been a part of that history but, whereas it was a community premised on the identity of its members, modern ethical life is premised on their differentiation. Such a conception is indeed modern but, as Hegel made clear in his lectures on the philosophy of history, modernity begins with the Reformation and, more generally, our 'German' age is that of Christianity, of individual self-consciousness, and of spiritual freedom, equality and universality. If modern ethical life is about difference rather than identity, that is because it must include not just the leisured few but the activities of all. If he is impressed with modern commercial and bureaucratic practices of mutual and 'civil' service, this is for reasons that may be more fully understood in Pauline than in Smithian terms. His idea of ethical life as an internally differentiated social totality, in which individuality and universality are reconciled by corporate particularity, is a more sophisticated conception than that of a simple organic analogy, but what it is a more sophisticated conception of is a politically organized community and one which he, too, was happy to call 'organic'. As he had learnt from both Kant and Aristotle, an organized whole is one composed of functioning parts. On Hegel's account, it is only through understanding themselves as such parts that individuals can really come to consciousness of the universal, and it is only through rationally participative activity that individuals may be educated into an ethical understanding of themselves.

Actuality and Rationality

Hegel's tripartite division of the *Philosophy of Right* into the pristine individuality of 'abstract right', the particularity of 'morality' and the universality of 'ethical life' (like the tripartite division of the latter between family, civil society and state) represents the trinitarian and particularist theology by which his God enters history, reflecting the trinitarian structure of his dialectical logic. If it also resembles the tripartite division into morality, economics and politics of scholastic and Wolffian practical philosophy, this is not what Hegel most shares with Wolff. Although the totality he postulates differs from that of Wolff in lacking any pre-established and atemporal harmony, it nonetheless includes a kind of providentialist necessity in its temporal development that has no parallel in Kant. The same kind of impersonally rational necessity is evident in the social order described by the *Philosophy of Right*. We noted the danger of conflating rationality with actuality in what Nederman calls communal functionalism, but Hegel considers their conflation to be the great virtue of his philosophy. Nederman (1987b) notes that Hegel considers the particularity of corporations within modern states to be a historical advance from that of the medieval guild, and this advance is from the semblance of a functionally integrated whole to what he declares to be its progressive actualization.

Hegel's account of ethical life did much to inspire that politics of both left and right in twentieth-century Europe which attempted to create those corporatist structures of mediation between individual and state for which he had argued. His solution to the problem of social particularism and civil conflict was very different from republicanism's rigid separation of public institutions from private interests. Hegel argued that if individuals are to become fully self-conscious of themselves and others as moral beings, then they must not be compartmentalized into public and private selves but instead related to the universal through their concrete particularity. The descent of the French Revolution into Terror and Empire demonstrated the dangers of attempting to apply ideals of public virtue in the modern world, but Hegel thought that he could nonetheless detect the cunning of a teleological reason operating in history. A universal reason is not, and cannot be, instantiated by the state alone, but it is instantiated in the social totality. This is a totality constituted by the institutions of ethical life: families, courts, local governments, the central state with its bureaucracy and monarchy representing the unity of the whole and, crucially, legally sanctioned corporations bringing political order and ethical consciousness to the satisfaction of material needs. It is through recognition of the necessity of the constraints imposed by such institutions upon their wills that individuals become aware of their true freedom and of the content of morality, and it is by acting within their corporations and estates that they participate in political community. It is through the particular activities of such institutions and of individuals as participants in such institutions that universal reason is empirically instantiated in actuality. In more traditionally Aristotelian terms, it is through such institutionalized activity that the political community pursues the common good.

Whereas Kant's practical philosophy was limited to the dictates of individual conscience, Hegel's also encompassed political and economic norms and institutions. Where Kant proposed teleology as a way in which we can comprehend unknowable objects in themselves, Hegel postulated a dialectic by which our reason can conform to such objects by apprehending both them and ourselves as parts of the temporal actualization of a universal *telos*. Even if his teleological understanding of our relation to social institutions seemed conservative at a time of Prussian reaction, the revolutionary aspirations of his philosophy were nonetheless continued after his death by such Left Hegelians as Ludwig Feuerbach and, despite their often intemperate critiques of their fellows, Friedrich Engels and Karl Marx.

A Revolutionary Teleology

For Marx, even more crucially than for other Left Hegelians, human beings are alienated from a true understanding of themselves and of their powers and potentialities. For Feuerbach, alienation consists in the attribution of what are really human powers to a product of human consciousness, God. The real human good cannot be to imitate some such other being but to actualize our own 'species essence'. For Marx, alienation consists in our attribution of an independent form to *all* human products, especially to those material products exemplifying our most crucial capacity to change the natural conditions of our own consciousness. Human production indeed differs from the notion of God's Creation, and it does so in that it is the activity of social and historically progressive beings rather than of some notionally self-sufficient individual.

Marx's critique of Feuerbach and the others was that they saw the issue as one only of philosophy's correction of false consciousness. They, like Hegel, considered their task as merely educative; as, on the bases of their own superior understanding, helping others to see the world correctly. Theology apart, what Marx most shared with other Left Hegelians was their repudiation of Hegel's idea that individual universality could only be actualized through social particularity. Where they mostly understood this repudiation to entail only a radicalization of the republican ideal of citizenship, Marx understood it to entail abolition of the social division of labour.

In his famous *Theses on Feuerbach*, Marx follows Left Hegelian fashion in renaming his ideal of self-activity (*Selbstbetätigung*) *praxis*, and the idea is indeed redolent of Aristotle's idea of free action. Insofar as such self-activity is understood as actualizing the potential of human beings, it is also redolent of Aristotle's more elemental ideas of *energeia* and *entelecheia*. This is the primary reason why Marx is now often regarded as something of an Aristotelian (e.g. Rockmore 1980; Wood 1981; Meikle 1985 and 1995; McCarthy 1990; Booth 1993; Murphy 1993; Pike 1999; and several of the essays in McCarthy 1992 and Meikle 2002, which also includes an essay by George Kline debunking 'the myth of Marx's materialism' on which MacIntyre draws in MacIntyre 1998a). This interpretive development follows on from the earlier, anti-Stalinist, 'Western Marxist' reception of such texts of the early Marx as his *Economic and Philosophical Manuscripts* of 1844 in terms of a Hegelian and humanist Marxism. Certainly for Marx, as for Hegel, production is a social process, and is so in a way that it was not for Aristotle. Certainly Marx also allows that production may be creative and freely expressive of individuality in a way that Aristotle did not. It is this human potential that the young Marx sees denied by the capitalist division of labour. Capitalist labour he understands in terms similar to Aristotle, as something that passes into its product. He recasts its Smithian description in calling labour power *the* essential factor in production, either as immediately expended or as previously accumulated in capital, and as the ultimate source of all economic production and value. Workers are the means of capitalist production; its end is the usable commodity and, through the sale of commodities, the further accumulation of capital.

Workers are alienated not only from their product but also from their own labour power and labour time, as this too is commodified by capitalism's social relations of production. Their craft skill is simply value added to their labour, which is controlled by their employer – the individual or corporate owner. This proprietor has power over capital and over workers, whereas workers are denied power over themselves or their own products. Workers therefore have a real interest – whether they recognize it or not – in overthrowing this social system of alienation and exploitation. Their potential as human beings can only be actualized after the abolition of capitalism's division of those who produce useful goods from those who control such production.

If capitalism is the negation of human potential, then communism is the negation of that negation. The actualization of human potential is for Marx, as for Hegel, something social and historical. Marx follows Aristotle's speculation that slavery would be unnecessary if tools could move themselves and material goods be produced without labour but, whereas Aristotle regarded this as impossible, Marx saw such automation as a historical possibility. Communism is the *telos* of human history, the actualization of the necessary social conditions for the free self-activity of all individuals. Under communism, material scarcity, and therefore social conflict over the distribution of material goods, can be ended. Throughout history, labour has been necessary and necessarily oppressed, but in communism characteristically human work will finally be transformed into self-activity. 'In communist society, where nobody has one exclusive sphere of activity but each can become accomplished in any branch he wishes, society regulates the general production and thus makes it possible for me to do one thing today and another tomorrow, to hunt', fish, farm or philosophize 'without ever becoming hunter, fisherman, shepherd or critic' (Marx and Engels 1976: 47). To become identified with any such particular occupation would, it seems, be to alienate oneself and deny oneself the opportunity of universal activity.

Marx argues that under communism the 'alien force' of the state will disappear along with natural compulsion but, crucially, that producers' 'united power' will remain. What institutional form this united power will take remains unaddressed; as his followers said, one does not write blueprints for the future. Engels later made the similar prediction that under socialism 'the government of persons is replaced by the administration of things, and by the conduct of processes of production. The state is not "abolished". *It dies out* [or, more famously, '*withers away*']' (Engels 1987: 268). The implication is that management is a mere technical issue of distributing resources without directing people. The problem with capitalism is ownership, not management. Engels, himself a capitalist and a manager, made this implication evident when editing Marx's *Capital*. He welcomes the creation within a 'branch of industry' of '*one* big joint-stock company with a unified management', wherein 'technical management remains in the same hands as before, but financial control is concentrated in the hands of the general management'. Managers' elimination of mutual competition in order to safeguard their jobs is, for Engels, tantamount to 'socialization of production'. A monopolistic company is one 'preparing in the most pleasing fashion its future expropriation by society as a whole, by the nation'. (Engels, in Marx 1981: 569) Despite talking early of abolishing the division of labour between hand and brain, management is seen as a distinct function apart from production. It is this distinction that allows Marx and Engels to presume that the division of labour between productive workers could be abolished even whilst the function of management continued. However, as syndicalists and others predicted before 1917, if managers are freed even from the diminishing constraints of private owners or elected oversight, then they will claim absolute authority and exercise control over everything and everyone. That such absolute power corrupts absolutely has been proven by the subsequent history of Marxism.

Heidegger's Aristotle

Hegel stimulated a historicism that permeated much of the intellectual culture of nineteenth-century Germany and, in the twentieth, issued in Werner Jaeger's historical approach to Arsitotle's texts. He also provoked Adolf Trendelenburg's attempt to disprove his claim that, although there have been five Aristotelianisms, no further return to Aristotle is now possible (Hegel 1894: 129–30; 1892: 46). However, what Trendelenburg returned to is perhaps more the philosophy of pre-Kantian Germany than that of Aristotle himself. The same may be said of the more Thomistic and still more forthright Aristotelianism of Trendelenburg's student, Franz Brentano. Such an Aristotelianism had survived in Brentano's Catholic Austria, teaching a traditional theoretical and practical philosophy within an architectonic scheme that resisted Kant's antinomies and Hegel's dialectics. Famous for his faithful reconstruction of a metaphysically informed psychology of intentionality, which was formative for Edmund Husserl and phenomenology, Brentano's most single-mindedly metaphysical book was his first, *On the Several Senses of Being in Aristotle* (Brentano 1975), which is now most famous for its supposed influence upon the young Martin Heidegger.

Heidegger, raised a Catholic, may have initially followed Brentano's aim of reconstructing the tradition of scholastic Aristotelianism, but – through engagement with the writings of Paul and Augustine, with nominalism's assault on Thomism, and with Hegel's concerns with temporality, experience and self-consciousness – he converted to Luther's project of destroying or deconstructing, first, Christian philosophy and, then, the whole Western tradition of philosophy. Rejecting Hegel's rationalist reconstruction of metaphysical universalism, Heidegger instead attempted to 'encounter the object concretely and factically' (Heidegger 2001: 112). From a traditional perspective, such a rejection of universalism might be thought to entail a focus upon particularity or individuality but, along with his rejection of Platonic 'participation' and of Hegelian 'mediation', Heidegger rejected any veritable particularism and, given his claim that 'life is so constituted as to lack an "outside" and an "inside"' (ibid.: 88), he can hardly be understood as articulating an ontological individualism.

In seeking to destroy what he called 'the tradition', Heidegger sought a more authentic understanding of Aristotle than had Hegel or Brentano. Certainly, his understanding was more philologically informed than theirs, and more philologically speculative. (His influence on the interpretation of Aristotle, which has long been great in Germany, is still filtering into the Anglophone world, especially through the publishing programme of Indiana University Press and the translating programme of Joe Sachs.) He protested against the anachronism of characterizing Aristotle as an 'epistemologist' or 'realist' and against the 'presupposition that Aristotle has anything at all to do with the Middle Ages or with Kant' (ibid.: 5–6). Nonetheless, he recollected that it was, above all, Aristotle who set philosophy on its historical course. Like Hegel, and unlike Jaeger (or Goethe), he regarded Aristotle as advancing Plato's project. 'Life seeks to assure itself by looking away from itself' (ibid.: 81) and this, Heidegger increasingly argued, was where Plato and Aristotle had directed their gaze.

As many of Heidegger's students, including Gadamer and Hannah Arendt, have proposed (and has been agreed by too many recent commentators to mention), a crucially orientating step on Heidegger's path was his engagement with Aristotle. Indeed, we know that Heidegger's early intention was to write a book on Aristotle, a book for which it has often been suggested *Being and Time* should be understood as a stand-in. We can follow this engagement through his lectures. Especial significance is attached by those of his students who became practical philosophers (and even by some of those who instead became theoretical philosophers, such as Jacob Klein) to a few lectures in late 1924 on Book Six of the *Nicomachean Ethics*, in a course on Plato's *Sophist* (Heidegger 1997). What interests Heidegger here is Aristotle's juxtaposition of such intellectual virtues as *sophia, phronesis* and *techne*, which he presents as various modes of discovering or revealing being. Like medievals, even if more knowingly, Heidegger at first read the otherness of Greece through the text of Israel. What the Socratic quest for truth through reason had lost was the sense of truth as revelation. This, he suggests, is the proper meaning of the term standardly translated as 'truth', *aletheia*. In this, he attacks the traditional understanding of truth as propositional and, correspondingly, the traditional identification of logic with rules regulating such propositions. He wishes to destroy the traditional division between reason and revelation, theory and theology, and also to deconstruct the division of both from actual, living human being which he perceives in the tradition's privileging of *theoria* and *sophia*.

Heidegger's task is to get human beings to come to terms with their own activity, to gaze at themselves and to disclose philosophy as one way amongst others of revealing, conducting and being themselves. This is also what Aristotle should be understood as saying, argues Heidegger in his *Sophist* lectures. At the same time, he grapples with Aristotle's own privileging of *sophia* over *phronesis*. As *sophia* meant something like 'skill' in ordinary Greek, its orientation of us towards other things should be understood as similar to that of *techne*. Indeed, *sophia* turns out to be the completion or excellence of *techne*. *Phronesis*, in contrast, is an orientation to our own being. It is, as Heidegger famously and tendentiously puts it, 'conscience set into motion, making an action transparent' (Heidegger 1997: 39). We are always aware of our present activity, but we can forget other things, whether things that we make or that we merely contemplate or consider. *Techne* and *sophia* disclose such things, but in so doing they distract us from the significance of human being itself. 'Even if a doctor practices medicine in order to attain a higher degree of the *techne*' of medicine, her practice 'has as its end the state of health and this alone'; not truth, and not her own good (Heidegger 1996: 223; Greek transliterated). *Phronesis* is the only way of being human that is solely concerned with uncovering human being through its own action. Therefore, *phronesis* and the *praxis* it 'serves' disclose the most authentic mode of being human.

If Heidegger translated one of Brentano's several homonymous senses of being – 'being in the sense of being true', or *aletheia* – into his own isolation and celebration of *phronesis* and *praxis* as authentic being, *Dasein*, he later credited another of Brentano's senses – 'potential and actual being' – as 'the decisive, basic discovery of the entirety of Aristotelian philosophy' (Heidegger 1995: 42). Aristotle's discussion of *phronesis* constitutes no such discovery because *phronesis* is the everyday self-consciousness of being which Aristotelian philosophy has, traditionally, led us to forget. This would presumably, on Heidegger's account, have surprised Aristotle, given his thought that *phronesis* concerns what cannot be forgotten, and this indicates that Heidegger still understands himself to be attacking only the tradition, and not Aristotle, in subverting its canonic interpretations. After Hegel had completed Christianity's dissolution of Aristotle's distinction of *phronesis* from *techne*, *praxis* from *poiesis*, Heidegger determined to redraw the line. But even if he was not attacking Aristotle, Heidegger may still be said to have conceived potential and actual being in a way that is unAristotelian. 'A for-the-sake-of-which, a purposiveness, is only possible where there is a willing' (Heidegger 1984: 185). On Heidegger's account, there is no *telos* in nature apart from the exercise of human free will and intentionality. 'The existence of Dasein is determined by the for-the-sake-of' but 'this for-the-sake-of is to be understood as the metaphysical structure of Dasein', so that human 'freedom is itself the origin of the for-the-sake-of' and identical with it (ibid.: 186, 191). As he says in *Being and Time*, 'the call of conscience fails to give any . . . "practical" injunctions, *solely because* it summons Dasein to existence, to its ownmost potentiality-for-Being-its-Self' (Heidegger 1962: 340). Its 'ownmost potentiality' is a limitless array of possibilities between which Heidegger reveals no way of judging. It is not a potentiality for any specific actuality. *Dasein* is as *Dasein* does.

Heidegger detached Aristotle from later tradition in order to throw him back into the world of 'the Greeks'. If at first this was so as to understand better what Aristotle really meant, it increasingly led to a preoccupation with reconstructing that immediate 'factical' consciousness of being which Heidegger charged Plato and Aristotle with concealing. If the world to which Heidegger would have us return is not the pre-philosophical one of Nietzsche's Homer, it is at least the pre-Socratic one of Parmenides and Heraclitus. This radical turn in German Hellenism Heidegger shared with Jaeger. By 1933 it had become a concern to reconstruct what Jaeger called an 'aristocratic humanism' not only in theory but also, tragically, in German academic and political practice.

A Rehabilitation of Practical Philosophy

Defeated, divided and occupied, chastened by the experience of the National Socialist German Workers' Party's domestic 'totalitarianism', blamed for having caused a second world war, and threatened from the east by another, Marxist totalitarianism, Germany – even the Germany of what became the Federal Republic – was stripped of all its previous intellectual pre-eminence and confidence. Many of Heidegger's students and others whom he had directly influenced had fled Europe for America, and many of these – including Arendt, Klein, Leo Strauss, Herbert Marcuse and Paul Oskar Kristeller – chose (like Jaeger) to remain there. In Kristeller, the Aristotelian tradition found an influential champion prepared to do the scholarly work necessary to demonstrate its continuity from the Middle Ages through to the Renaissance. More faithful to Heidegger were Strauss and Arendt. Both believed that Heidegger's deconstruction of tradition had allowed them unmediated access to the political ideas of the Greeks. Strauss was thoroughly Heideggerian when he said that Aristotle's *Politics* articulates a 'political science [that] is nothing other than the fully conscious form of the common sense understanding of political things' (Strauss 1964: 12). Whereas he was a conservative, Arendt was a protagonist of what she called republicanism's 'revolutionary tradition' (Arendt 1965). Nonetheless, her *The Human Condition* (1958) is Heideggerian, Aristotelian and anti-Marxist in its celebration of *praxis* and denigration of *techne* and *poiesis*. Together, their impact on post-war American political thought was considerable, as recently has been Strauss's impact on American political practice.

Back in the Federal Republic, what were followed were better-established American models. The social sciences became ahistorical and value-free, and were applied technically by a newly utilitarian politics of the kind that appalled Arendt. It was only after she and Strauss had made their imprint upon the American academy that similar signs became evident in Germany. *The Human Condition* was translated into German in 1960, and the same year saw publication of the first edition of Gadamer's *Wahrheit und Methode*. Three years later there followed Wilhelm Hennis's *Politik und praktische Philosophie*, still considered by some the most remarkable single attempt to reconstruct an Aristotelian methodology for political science (Kullmann 1998: 332). A decade later Riedel assumed the leadership of what, in the title of two volumes comprising forty-three essays by thirty-seven authors, he called 'the rehabilitation of practical philosophy' (Riedel 1972a and 1974).

Riedel juxtaposes 'practical philosophy' to philosophy as *theoria*, the passive and value-free contemplation of 'objects'. Similar to such *theoria*, he proposes, is that positivism which attempted to annex ethics, aesthetics, natural law and the philosophy of state into empirical science. Against this attempt, the human sciences only maintained their independence in Germany by basing themselves in the discipline of history. Whether as positivism or historicism, what was lost by such explanatory science was 'the *unity of theory and practice*' basic to the old 'concept of "practical philosophy"'. He dismisses the types of unification detectable in 'technology', in 'political ideology' and in Heidegger. Those to which he is more sympathetic he collects together in the two volumes, including the work of what he called the 'Aristotle- and Hegel-renaissance after 1945' (Riedel 1972b: 9–11). Despite his sympathy for those – including Ilting, Strauss, Gadamer, Hennis and Joachim Ritter – whom he understands to be trying to renew practical philosophy within an Aristotelian paradigm (Riedel 1972c: 81–2), he argues that this scheme, unlike that of Hegelianism, is not adequate to the task. Aristotle's distinction of theoretical from practical reason, coupled with his 'ontological prejudice' for unchangeable objects, for theoretical disciplines and for ' "being" ' and ' "truth" ' (ibid.: 88), raises aporia insoluble by Aristotelianism. Other aporia arise from that division of *poiesis* from *praxis* which Hegel dissolved. Aristotle, Riedel adds, thought of action as sharing in something common but of production only as an individualizing

relation of the producer with his material. That production is a social relation is an insight of Hegel, not Aristotle, as is the insight that for a subject
to work on an object is a process that is dialectical, resulting not only in the
formation of the product but also in the self-formation of the producer as
a conscious actor.

Riedel champions Hegel, and therefore champions a teleological conception of history and modernity. As he has said since, the Greek 'origin of
the political theme' confirms 'an *entelechy* inborn in European history . . .
toward an ideal shape of *being political*' (Riedel 1996: 20). However, as suggested above, his teleological perspective justifies, for him, a retrospective
rationalization of Hegel – and still more of Aristotle – that may be Hegelian
in spirit but invites the accusation of anachronism. Riedel's ideal form of
'being political' is implicitly Weberian and explicitly Hobbesian. He accuses
Aristotle of an aporia in saying both that the *polis* forces citizens to be good
and that the best are already good by nature or upbringing; but Aristotle,
still more than Hegel, understands politics in terms that are primarily
ethical and not simply coercive. For Aristotle, the *polis* is an ethical community because of the excellence of its participants and because of the
exclusion of those he regards as unable to share their characteristic goodness. His teleology of the human good is a teleology internal to individual
human beings and not to human history. If there is an aporia in Aristotle's
politics, it is metaphysical and ontological rather than historical and institutional. It arises from his identification of a *telos* that is internal to the *polis*
as a distinct being, the 'good order' of which individuals should actively
pursue. However, this is an aporia that may be resolved in favour of the
goods internal to humans and their shared activities. For Hegel, the state is
the universalization of ethical life because of the impersonal goodness of
its institutions, but to this it may be objected that goodness is a property of
individuals and a function of their mutual relations. If the modern state,
which Hegel wished to legitimate in both ethical and metaphysical terms,
cannot subserve that common good of human beings, then perhaps this
good should be pursued apart from the state.

Ritter was involved in the 'renaissance' of both Aristotle and Hegel, but,
unlike Riedel, he did not oppose the two. Rather, Ritter's Hegel 'renews the
institutional ethics of the Aristotelian tradition', thereby passing from the
abstract ethics of Kantian 'morality to the ethics of "politics," which had
previously vanished with it' (Ritter 1982: 175, 166). His 'practical philosophy' is 'a theory of ethical orders and institutions' which 'takes up the
ethical determination of institutions in Aristotle's sense', according to
which institutions are identical with the 'reality' of individual action (ibid.:

171–2). Ritter does allow the possibility of 'unethical institutions', and therefore of 'the heroic possibility' of a conscientious individual clashing with institutional order. However, 'the reality and subsistence of a free ethical life cannot be founded upon' such conflict (ibid.: 175). For Ritter's 'Aristotle, ethics is the doctrine of "ethos," taken as the constitution of individual life and action in the household and the polis, a constitution developed in custom, use, and tradition', whilst ' "praxis" has reality not in the immediacy of action, but in its integration into the polis' ethical and institutional order' (ibid.: 165).

Such an ethics has 'hermeneutical foundations', says Ritter, in an essay (translated as Ritter 1983: 45) that was already famous when Riedel republished it in *Rehabilitierung der praktischen Philosophie* (and is cited by Nederman in his case that Aristotelianism is a specifically practical philosophy: 1996: 573). But Ritter acknowledges that Aristotle's practical philosophy has still deeper foundations in his biology. '*Praxis*', he proposes, is a 'synonym' of *bios*, 'the peculiar way of life' of a species. Accordingly, and equally tendentiously, he implies that *praxis* is equivalent to *entelecheia*. 'Praxis is identical with the actualized nature, that is, with a "way of life" that actualizes the potential nature of a living being.' Accordingly, 'practical philosophy' considers *praxis* 'not as mere action, but rather as actualized human nature' (Ritter 1983: 51–2). What nonetheless distinguishes practical philosophy from biological science is that 'man is the sole being that does not' actualize its 'potentialities "by nature" '. 'This is the fundamental principle: Man's nature as potentiality is not actualized by nature. Its actualization consists in the ethico-political order' (ibid.: 56). Human nature can only be actualized within the *polis*, which 'makes man free to actualize his own nature', and this, Ritter judges, is 'an insight of infinite importance' (ibid.: 55, 53). It was an insight lost by Kant, in whom morality 'breaks its connections with law, society, and the state and emigrates inwards, into subjectivity' and 'inner thoughts and convictions' (ibid.: 41). Hegel 'liberates this morality from [its] separation from reality' in uniting it with Aristotle's insight. Although, by effecting such a combination, 'ethical life in Hegel is no longer identical with the "ethos" of Aristotelian practical philosophy', what is most important in Ritter's account of Hegel's practical philosophy, and what stands in great contrast to that of Riedel, is his claim that Hegel regains Aristotle's insight and 'renews the institutional ethics belonging to the tradition of Aristotle's *Politics*' (Ritter 1982: 168). This, for Ritter, is a conservative tradition, investing existing political and social institutions with ethical legitimation.

Aristotelianism's Rehabilitation as Heideggerian Recovery

Heidegger's influence upon Ritter's understanding of Aristotle is significant but largely implicit. His influence is greater upon many others who were involved in the post-war German 'Aristotle-renaissance'. Most of these others agree with Ritter in perceiving an Aristotelian 'tradition' that expired sometime before the twentieth century, even if they are less keen to iden-tify it with scholasticism or to acknowledge Hegel as its rehabilitator. (That said, their concern with tradition makes most of them more sympathetic to Hegel's historicism than were either Strauss or Arendt.) Not Hegel but they are the real rehabilitators of Aristotle's specifically practical philoso-phy, their reconstruction presupposing Heidegger's deconstruction, if not of 'the tradition', then at least of neo-Kantianism. The historical story they tell of the tradition of practical philosophy is of its corruption by scientific or epistemological or natural law theory, or by a bourgeois or banausic concern with production, or by some combination of these.

Heidegger's mark upon these practical philosophers' Aristotelianism is a sharp distinction of *phronesis* from both *sophia* and *techne*, and of action from both theory and production. They take from Heidegger an antipathy to the theoretical tradition that has issued in the modern privileging of science and technology over *praxis*. Whereas Marxists see in technology the potential to free human activity, they see in it a constant danger. As with earlier German interpreters of Aristotle, they leave it to their Anglophone counterparts to make of him a progenitor of utilitarian hedonism or prag-matic productivism. But perhaps their own interpretation of Aristotle's practical philosophy independently of his theoretical philosophy is no less questionable, especially given his identification of *eudaimonia* with *theoria*. Their interpretive case resembles, in some ways, the so-called 'inclusivist' one advanced by such Anglophone commentators as J. L. Ackrill (see chap-ters 1 and 4). They differ from the likes of Ackrill in that their concern is less interpretive and analytic than fully philosophical and practical, and yet they differ also in understanding *theoria* not as a way of life but in terms of the kind of grand metaphysical theorizing against which Heidegger and history have warned them. Their characteristic ambition is to rehabilitate Aristotelianism as a modern philosophy of practice.

In themselves privileging practical wisdom and activity, such 'neo-Aristotelian' practical philosophers are, however silently, truer to Heidegger's own philosophy than to Heidegger's interpretation of Aristotle as the great theorist of ontology, potentiality and actuality. What they refuse in Heidegger is his identification of Aristotle as the source of theo-retical 'tradition' and his blaming of Aristotle for theory's covering over of practice. In place of the disreputable Heidegger's talk of *Dasein*, they use Aristotle's venerable vocabulary of *praxis* and *phronesis*.

Gadamer has most often and most fully acknowledged Heidegger's influence upon neo-Aristotelian practical philosophy. To Gadamer, Heidegger had appeared in the 1920s as '*Aristotle redivivus*' (Gadamer 1997a: 10). Even long after, he could still describe Heidegger, then, as 'an advocate of Aristotle who . . . far surpassed all of the traditional shadings of Aristotelianism, who surpassed Thomism and, yes, even Hegelianism' (Gadamer 1986a: 4). Heidegger's interpretation was superior because it made 'the decisive point' about 'the independence of practical knowledge, of *phronesis*' (Gadamer 1997b: 526). For Gadamer, practical philosophy is not preceded by Aristotle's 'first philosophy'. He writes of Aristotle's *Metaphysics* – which Heidegger called 'the basic book of antiquity' (Heidegger 1988: 80) – as a 'stack of papers', and writes it off as 'a collection of uncertainties that share th[e] character of being marginal' (Gadamer 1986a: 130; about the still larger stack of papers which Aristotle devoted to the study of non-human animals, Gadamer has nothing to say whatsoever). Told by Heidegger to study philology rather than philosophy, Gadamer made of it a philosophical hermeneutics. In so doing, he moved the furthest of any post-war German practical philosopher beyond 'Aristotle- and Hegel-renaissance' and onto new philosophical terrain.

In writing of 'The Hermeneutic Relevance of Aristotle' in *Truth and Method*, Gadamer describes Aristotle as 'the founder of ethics as a discipline independent of metaphysics', a discipline asking not what is 'the good' as an intellectual abstraction, but 'what is humanly good, what is good in terms of human action. . . . The very name "ethics" indicates that Aristotle bases *arete* on practice and "ethos"' (Gadamer 1989: 312). He elaborates on this in *The Idea of the Good in Platonic-Aristotelian Philosophy* (elaborating also upon Heidegger's account of Aristotle's continuity with Plato) and in his contri-bution to *Rehabilitierung der praktischen Philosophie* (translated as Gadamer 1981a). His own rehablitation of Aristotle's philosophy of practice attempts to merge its horizon with that of self-consciously modern theory. So under-stood, practical philosophy is independent of both metaphysical theory and technical knowledge. 'What separates it fundamentally from technical expertise is that it expressly asks the question of the good . . . for example, about the best way of life or about the best constitution of the state' (ibid.: 93). The idea here is the familiar one that technical reasoning is concerned only with means and not at all with ends. However, *phronesis* does not assume its interest for Gadamer because he is concerned with 'the good'. His primary interest is not in 'the best way of life', as in Aristotle's *Ethics*, nor in 'the best constitution of the state', as in Aristotle's *Politics*. Rather, his interest is in the significance of *phronesis* for his own philosophy of hermeneutics. His claim is that hermeneutics is a third 'example' of practical philosophy and that hermeneutics is a *praxis* of understanding, complementing ethical and political *praxeis*. This claim owes nothing to Aristotle's *On Interpretation* (*Peri hermeneias*), and little even to his *Topics*. Gadamer argues that hermeneutics was developed by Melanchthon out of rhetoric and then informed the human sciences, that rhetoric was regarded by Aristotle as a practical science, and therefore that we should, on Aristotelian grounds, regard hermeneutics as a practical science (Gadamer 1981b). One of these grounds is questionable: Aristotle regarded rhetoric as a teachable *techne*. Here we may agree with Heidegger's claim that *phronesis* is concerned with action in the strong sense that it results not simply in a judgement that one should act, but in a concrete action. This is not true of rhetoric, and still less is it true of interpretation.

Aristotelianism and Kantianism

Gadamer's last major (if short) work, his translation of and commentary upon Book Six of the *Nicomachean Ethics*, returned him to the original source of his practical philosophy. Here, close engagement with the text obliges him briefly to acknowledge economics as another example of *praxis* (Gadamer 1998a: 9) and, more importantly, that Aristotle prioritized what Gadamer calls 'the existential ideal of theoretical wisdom' (ibid.: 66). This opens a gap between Gadamer's exegesis of Aristotle and his own philosophical ambition. He attempts to close this from one side by applauding Heidegger's role in bringing out the meaning of practical rationality for contemporary philosophy (ibid.: 21) and, from the other side, by repeating his long-standing interpretive argument that Aristotle maintained the real, living priority of *phronesis* over *sophia*. Not even Plato offered a theoretical 'definition' of the good, and nor did Aristotle. The human good is a matter of taking the right decision at the right time, and this involves another sort of knowledge than the written formulations of scientific or mathematical theory. Both *phronesis* and *sophia* are, though, excellences that are 'inseparable aspects of the same spiritual being of Man' (ibid.: 63). This spiritual being is what Aristotle elsewhere calls the human *energeia*, intending the theoretical reflectiveness of his 'practical philosophy' to serve actual 'practical reason', despite the uncertain relation between the two. It therefore seems to Gadamer that Heidegger's *Sophist* lectures do not do Aristotle justice. Heidegger's concern is with Aristotle's theoretical philosophy and not with his practical philosophy, but Aristotle's central point in Book Six is, on Gadamer's account, to establish the reality of practical knowledge as a distinct intellectual excellence and, accordingly, to establish the distinctiveness of specifically practical philosophy (ibid.: 66–7).

If we agree that Heidegger is uninterested in doing justice to Aristotle's practical philosophy, we may add that Gadamer has little interest in doing justice to Aristotle's theoretical philosophy. He is close to Kant when he insists that philosophy cannot exceed the bounds of language to explain any extra-linguistic reality in itself. 'The difference between Greek *theoria* and modern science is based . . . on different orientations to *verbal experience of the world*' (Gadamer 1989: 455). He finds 'in Kant . . . the most rigorous concept of that nature thematised by the sciences', the Newtonian nature of 'the lawfulness of phenomena in space and time' (Gadamer 1986b: 41). That which is revealed by the sciences is theorized by Kant. Kant's concept of science is 'an explanatory principle'; Aristotle's is not.

Gadamer acknowledges his proximity to Kant when, like Arendt (1982), he assimilates the idea of aesthetic judgement in Kant's third Critique to Aristotle's account of *phronesis*. He goes beyond Arendt in embracing Kant's account of teleological judgement as 'the bridge between understanding and reason' (Gadamer 1989: 54), practical philosophy and practical rationality. It turns out that his practical philosophy has little to do directly with action, as he separates practical wisdom from any substantive conception of the human good or its actualization. Understood in Aristotle's terms, he observes, practice is not subject to any categorical imperative of right because it is instead grounded in a teleology of the good. Conversely, he employs Kant's critique of any realist metaphysics or teleological naturalism to argue that there can be no rational ground for any conception of the good apart from the ethos of some particular society and culture. Jürgen Habermas can therefore accuse Gadamer, Hennis and other neo-Aristotelians of conservatism not only for denying the political imperatives perceived in Kant's practical philosophy by his successors, but also for denying any practical implications of Aristotle's universalist metaphysical theory in the name of post-Kantian hermeneutic and linguistic philosophy (Habermas 1979: 201–4).

Another Conservative Aristotelianism

Gadamer's ethics and politics are bound to be conservative if they are to be consistent with his philosophical premises. *Phronesis* he grounds in *ethos* and culture. Despite this, when he writes of tradition he, like Heidegger, writes in the singular. His unitary tradition is less philosophical and more cultural then Heidegger's. The political implications of such a conception of tradition must (notwithstanding protestations to the contrary) be conservative. When Gadamer famously writes of the 'political incompetence of philosophy' (1998b), he is excusing not only Heidegger but also himself.

Hennis, who has become one of Germany's leading political commentators, lacks Gadamer's political reticence. He denies any influence from Heidegger but readily acknowledges that of Strauss (Hennis 2000: 230). Under Strauss's influence, he railed against Weber's value-free and 'technicist' definition of politics in terms of means rather than ends, which he opposed to practical philosophy's concern with 'the life conduct of Man' (Hennis 1963: 17, 84; 1959: 22, 5; cf. Strauss 1953: 35–80). His attempted 'reconstruction of political science' aimed to save its traditional 'teleological orientation towards the good' from the ravages of behaviouralism by bridging positivism's separation of facts from values. The influence of his particular account of the tradition is evident in, for example, Habermas's early account of practical philosophy; of how (contra Ritter) this 'tradition reaches even into the nineteenth century', of the centrality to it of 'the art of disputation – dialectics', of 'the logical force of . . . *topoi*', and of its contrast with 'an apodictic science' (Habermas 1974: 41, 79–80, 286, 291). Yet Hennis's interests were never merely academic. In saying that the academic discipline of politics should be a 'practical science', he meant that it should be one that informs political reasoning and political activity. He largely identifies the Aristotelian tradition of politics with republicanism, but his understanding of republicanism is unsentimental. Like Strauss (and Weber), he conceives of politics as an elite activity, an activity of leadership and of the responsible direction by individual politicians of instrumentally effective institutions. This responsibility is ethical but, because ethics is separated from *theoria*, it can have no bases other than the ethos of social norms as internalized by the individual statesman and instantiated in the state's constitution. The executive should be structured in an entirely instrumental way and fully subordinate to politicians' judgement, unhampered by ideology or by mass party. In this way, politics is to be reduced to practical reasoning separated from any concern with theory or with production, and therefore to a pragmatic conservatism. It is scarcely surprising that Hennis left the Social Democratic Party for the Christian Democrats. Nor is it surprising that he changed from being a critic of Max Weber to being his most controversial champion. He found Weber to be the greatest modern theorist of that very 'life conduct of Man' in the cause of which he had previously criticized him. At first, this change involved identifying Weber with a still Platonic and Aristotelian standpoint. Now, though, Hennis looks to the broader and earlier cultural spirit of Hellenism as the origin of Weber's political way of thinking. Hardly any mention is made of Aristotle, and none of any teleological orientation. Instead, Weber's way of thinking is identified with 'political *science* in the tradition of Thucydides', the earliest master of situational political analysis, in contrast to any 'political philosophy' (Hennis 2003: 51). This is not the same political tradition with which Hennis previously identified. Whereas Hobbes had been the most prominent opponent of that Aristotelian tradition, Hennis now presents Hobbes as the most prominent modern protagonist of this newly identified, Thucydidean tradition (ibid.: 46, 51). This turn from the philosophy of Aristotle to the culture of the Greeks is not Hennis's only resemblance to Heidegger. His concern with life conduct or comportment resembles that of Heidegger, as does his often repeated concern with the dangers of industrial technology and administrative technique. In his turn from Aristotelianism, he has proven more Heideggerian than Gadamer.

The exclusivity of the 'practical' perspective of German neo-Aristotelianism is triply conservative. It is conservative, most famously, in its exclusion of *theoria*, of theoretical access to any truth greater than prevailing convention. In this sense, it shares its conservatism with that broader postmodernism (Habermas's 'new conservatism') which has been influenced by Heidegger. This is the conservatism criticized from the perspective of Kantian practical reason, and especially of left Kantian attempts to apply moral ideals to sensuous reality, but also from the perspective of anyone else who aspires to a stronger conception of truth. According to our post-Heideggerians, there is no truth apart from simple existence, and therefore no true human interest, and therefore no cause to overthrow what exists.

Neo-Aristotelianism is conservative, secondly, in its institutionalism and its concomitant elitism. This elitism may take the celebratory, Hegelian approach of Ritter or the more resigned approach of Hennis, but, either way, it simply negates any negation of the constituted powers that be. Both the bureaucratic state and the capitalist corporation instantiate a supposedly ineliminable separation of judgement from execution, of leaders from led. The job of practical reason is not to challenge such institutionalized power but to inform and improve the actions of the powerful.

Thirdly, it is conservative in its exclusion of *poiesis* and *techne*, and therefore, again, in its exclusion of the working masses from the elite activity of politics. The characteristic activities of workers are not, under any actual or potential social conditions, to be considered properly human actions. Even Ritter can forget Hegel here, excluding work from 'the ethico-political order' and allocating it to mere nature. Although it is Arendt who has most famously warned of the danger of politics' corruption by economics, the most extended argument comes from Nicholas Lobkowicz, author of *Theory and Practice: History of a Concept from Aristotle to Marx* (1967), written in the United States by an aristocratic academic who has thrived since his return to Germany, the home of *Begriffsgeschichte*. To such a neo-Aristotelian, it is irritating that Marxists use the concept of *praxis* in a way that obfuscates its distinction from the concepts of theory and production. Lobkowicz's protest is that Marxist usages 'have almost nothing at all to do with praxis in the original sense but represent an enormous reduction of all human action to poiesis. Even at those points where praxis is understood as political action, it is always the production of a state of affairs' (Lobkowicz 1977: 25).

Two points could be made in response to Lobkowicz's charge. First, neo-Aristotelian practical philosophers inherit Aristotle's difficulty in differentiating *praxis* from activity that is productive, technical or instrumental (see chapter 1), and therefore it may be replied that Lobkowicz is mistaken in saying that *praxis* differs from *poiesis* in being unconcerned with 'the production of a state of affairs'. As Heidegger conceded, *praxis* is an *energeia* and *energeia* 'means to be at work . . . and this means engaged in the production of that for which it is a capability' (Heidegger 1995: 143). Even in those cases of action where no material or social effect is intended, it might be said (with Charles) that the actualization of excellence or *eudaimonia* is the production of a state of affairs 'internal' to the actor. In any case, political action involves the production of some effect external to the actor.

Secondly, most of those who might be called Aristotelian Marxists (including some of the contributors to Markovic and Petrovic 1979, as well as the interpreters of an Aristotelian Marx listed above, p. 86) themselves attempt to maintain a distinction between *praxis* and *poiesis* and, furthermore, use it as their main conceptual base from which to criticize capitalism. Their claim is that production *could be* an expression of *praxis*, of free and cooperative human action which is good in itself, but that what is morally wrong with capitalism is that it negates that potential, that it reduces work to manipulated labour, activity to process, and that it thereby alienates us from our human, creative nature. I shall argue below that this was the original position of Alasdair MacIntyre, and that he has since elaborated it into a coherent and powerful moral critique.

4

A Revolutionary Aristotelianism

MacIntyre's Aristotelianism is often compared with that of Gadamer because of the importance to both of a concept of tradition. 'Tradition' usually denotes something unitary and cultural, and this is the case with Gadamer's concept. When Gadamer criticized what he regarded as theoretical mistakes, he did not suppose that those mistakes affected everyday practice, because he supposed theory, unlike culture and tradition, to exist apart from practice. The sharpness of this separation of practice from theory is, MacIntyre suggests, due to Kant's influence. Gadamer's separation of practice from theory prevented him from seeing how 'the understanding of practice' itself informs practice so that a theoretical transformation of that understanding may itself become 'part of the transformation of practice' (1980: 178). What most distinguishes MacIntyre from such German practical philosophers as Gadamer is that he, unlike them, wants to help effect such a transformation. In this, his practical philosophy resembles less that of Gadamer than of Marx.

MacIntyre's own concept of tradition is very different from Gadamer's. It is of something plural, and at once practical and theoretical. Traditions he defines by their mutual rivalry. They are grounded in definite social relations but the social relations they express comprise rival interests, interests that are themselves partially constituted by those intellectual traditions. And yet MacIntyre is no more a relativist than he is a simple interpretivist. For example, he argues that 'to regard individuals as distinct and apart from their social relationships is . . . a theoretical mistake. . . . embodied in institutionalized social life' (1998a: 228–9).

An aim of this book is to establish how little MacIntyre shares with the likes of Gadamer and how much he shares with the likes of Marx. It does so by taking seriously MacIntyre's self-interpretation of his position as Aristotelian, and therefore taking seriously that in his work which might be thought to bind him most closely to Gadamer. Certainly what MacIntyre says in *After Virtue* of both Aristotle and practice shares something with what Gadamer had already said in *Truth and Method* and was yet to say in

The Idea of the Good in Platonic-Aristotelian Philosophy (cf. 1988a: 89–96;
1990a), two works that MacIntyre considers 'classics of twentieth-century
philosophy' (2002a: 157), and certainly what he said of Aristotelianism in
After Virtue owes something to Gadamer. But what he said there and has
said since of Aristotle's practical philosophy owes less to Gadamer than to
such analytic (and non-Cartesian) philosophers of mind and action as
Gilbert Ryle, John Austin, Elizabeth Anscombe, Peter Geach, Anthony
Kenny and Georg Henrik von Wright, and to such commentators
influenced by that Anglophone philosophy as Gwil Owen, John Cooper,
John Ackrill and, later, Richard Kraut. What the MacIntyre of *After Virtue*
shares most with Gadamer is a desire to separate what they consider to be
of lasting value in Aristotle's practical philosophy from what they both
dismiss as Aristotle's discredited theoretical philosophy. Nonetheless, the
nature of their dismissals is revealingly different. Gadamer interprets
Aristotle's *theoria* in the light of what Aristotle says of *praxis* and not vice
versa, whereas MacIntyre has always understood Aristotle as presupposing
what he said of metaphysics and biology in what he said of human practice. This difference of interpretation must be explained in part by further
differences in their philosophical and even theological commitments.
Whereas Gadamer is a hermeneutist through and through, MacIntyre is
fundamentally a realist. Therefore, when he identified himself with an
Aristotelian tradition, MacIntyre committed himself to thinking through
what that tradition has said of nature and of human being. When he was
at his closest to Gadamer's hermeneutics, he could say that 'reinterpretation is the most fundamental form of change' (1980: 178). Now that he has
thought through his Aristotelian commitments and 'metaphysical presuppositions', he understands himself to be in still more fundamental 'conflict
with both Gadamer and Heidegger' (2002a: 169, 171).

MacIntyre allows that 'Aristotle's text underdetermines its interpretation' but affirms that it provides 'genuinely conclusive grounds for rejecting some interpretations' (2006a: 40). Among these is Gadamer's.
MacIntyre believes that 'the concept of *phronesis* cannot after all be
detached from the theoretical framework of which it is an integral part, as
Gadamer detaches it' (2002a: 169). It will now be noticed that my interpretation of Aristotle in chapter 1 approximated more to that of MacIntyre
than of Gadamer, even though it attended to those conceptual distinctions
influentially highlighted by Heidegger. These distinctions raise difficulties
for MacIntyre's identification of his position with that of Aristotle but,
before addressing these, I shall lay the grounds for my interpretation of
MacIntyre's present position by contextualizing it within his Marxist past.

MacIntyre's Marxism

Communism

MacIntyre inhabited the Marxist tradition for more than twenty years, becoming one of the best known Marxist and Trotskyist theoreticians of Britain's post-Communist 'New Left'. The importance of his work was well recognized by the leading English Marxist of the time, E. P. Thompson, who wished 'that MacIntyre could complete his own thought' about the potential for 'socialist consciousness within capitalist society', a consciousness that Thompson perceived in the 'ways in which men and women seem to be more "realized" as rational or moral agents, when acting collectively in conscious rebellion (or resistance) against capitalist process' (1978a: 150–1).

By the time that Thompson expressed this 'wish' in writing, MacIntyre had already left behind both Britain and Marxism. Before then, Thompson had urged, even pestered, MacIntyre to complete his thought about workers' present moral and socialist consciousness. In his new home, the United States, he was free of such urgent demands. Like Marcuse, Arendt and Strauss before him, he thrived far from his political and philosophical roots. Distancing himself from the debates in which his ideas had developed enabled him to elaborate those ideas at leisure and in novel ways. That his ideas have appeared still more novel in these new surroundings seems never to have caused him regret, even though he rails against misunderstandings that have allowed his work to be assimilated to an alien 'liberal-communitarian debate'. The argument of this chapter is that MacIntyre, in elaborating those ideas, is rightly understood as having been doing just what his erstwhile comrade wished him to do, even if his practical philosophy of collective moral agency is still not yet 'complete'. His continuing opposition of properly human activity to institutionalized alienation originates in the position that

> the self-activity of the working class is revolutionary for it marks a total break with both the economic and the political systems of capitalism which rely upon the passive acceptance of their alienated role by the workers. And socialism is self-activity as a total form of life. (1961a: 22)

What Thompson and he then understood by 'socialism' was something very different both from capitalism and from the practice of what they called Stalinism, represented locally by the Communist Party of Great Britain. Disillusioned with Communist dogma, MacIntyre left the party well before it was traumatized by the events of 1956: Khrushchev's revelations about Stalin's purges, followed by his own suppression of Hungarian workers. Then, though, MacIntyre was followed out by Thompson and by thousands of others, many of whom were intent on forming a new, post-Stalinist left. Having just declared the death of Marxist philosophy (1956: 370), MacIntyre's own revolutionary hopes were now reinvigorated. Those who deserted not only the Communist Party but also Marxism, instead embracing liberal values in condemnation of Stalinist oppression, he scorned for what he has always regarded as the elemental error of separating values from facts, moral reason from social practice (1998b).

MacIntyre has always rejected such a separation of theory from practice, and of theoretical from practical philosophy. Morality is not something to be separated from sensuous reality and then theorized a priori in some pure, idealist form. It is not something that individuals, as social beings, can or should autonomously impose on their own practice in consistent defiance of social relations and pressures. Nor is it something that they should seek to impose upon themselves in resistance to their own desires. This was the young MacIntyre's most persistent moral theme; it was why he was interested in Hume, and why he was later drawn to the rival moral psychology which Aquinas fashioned from that of Augustine in combination with Aristotle's idea of identifiable goods as causes of action. Morality should not be opposed to human desires, wants and needs, but instead understood in terms of their proper satisfaction. What he was later to argue was that individuals' desires are educated by their social relationships, and that the human good should be identified not with the satisfaction of our untutored desires but of those desires acquired through our participation in social practices.

Thompson insightfully quoted MacIntyre's recognition 'that it is in virtue of what they can be and not of what they always are that men are called rational animals' (1971a: 210; Thompson 1978a: 156). They both understood socialism as the actualization of a potential to be what capitalism prevents most humans from becoming. Conversely, they denied that social conditions simply determine individual consciousness in what they termed a 'mechanistic' way. Such explanation they condemned as Stalinist, attempting to complement the contrast of Stalinist practice to socialism with a contrast of Stalinist theory to genuine Marxism. Because they did not consider socialism to be a simple function or mechanistic effect of state ownership of the means of production, they lacked what Thompson called 'an overly utopian notion of "revolution"'. And, because they were not deluded by such a utopian notion, they were not, as were those who believed that utopia already existed in the USSR and Hungary, intellectually 'disarmed' by the events of 1956 (Thompson 1978a: 160). Like Marx himself, they understood human consciousness as shaped in activity and, through such activity, and especially through material production, as historically shaping its own conditions. Thompson, articulating this conception of human agency, was already becoming the great historian of the self-making of the English working class. MacIntyre, further elaborating this same conception, was to become the great philosopher of cooperative self-making through social practice.

The truth of alienation

MacIntyre takes from Marxism, and not just from his Calvinist upbringing, his abiding commitment to a strong, non-relativist conception of truth. Marxists claim truth for their explanatory accounts of society, history and human potential and, therefore, impute falsity to rival accounts. Our consciousness is false insofar as it fails to recognize how we are constrained by our social relations and how our social relations are constrained by our material needs. We might say that our consciousness is therefore false theoretically insofar as we explain the effects of those constraints in other terms, and that it is false practically insofar as we misconstrue our own good or, as Marxists prefer to put it, our own interests. Marxists' materialist conception of history provides them with a way of explaining the content of rival conceptual schemes, and of rival explanatory and evaluative theories, by reference to particular modes of social production. For example, capitalist production, which requires the accumulation of capital through competition between individuals, promotes normative liberal theories of possessive individualism. MacIntyre has always been opposed to such theories, and he has also always been prepared to explain them by reference to the social and economic relations that they legitimate. To explain rival views in such a way is to impute to them not only falsity but also a certain purchase on social reality. 'False consciousness is essentially a matter of partial and limited insight rather than of simple mistake' (1963a: 16). The rationality of liberalism is institutionalized in capitalism, as is that of bourgeois political economy. Their rationalities are actualized in what they legitimate and the actuality that they legitimate is rationalized by them. They are not, as their protagonists often imagine them to be, heuristic or normative ideals existing apart from social actuality. Rather, they are parts of that actuality. They inform belief and motivate action, and therefore they inform and actualize the social relations that are constituted by and reproduced in human action. Theory and actuality are therefore mutually reinforcing. Liberal theory is nonetheless false insofar as it extrapolates from the historical particularity to which it corresponds in making universalistic claims, denying our potential to act in ways other than that of present actuality. Historical materialism can therefore concede the rationality of rival conceptual schemes whilst still contesting their explanatory adequacy and prescriptive authority.

The young MacIntyre saw much similarity in the two conceptual schemes to which he was committed: the Calvinism in which he was raised and the Marxism that he adopted. He explains their similarity historically and philosophically by reference to Hegel's concern with overcoming human alienation, which he reads as eschatological and Pauline (1953: 23, 29). For Paul, human beings after the Fall are estranged from God and from one another, but will overcome this alienation at the end of time. For Hegel, they will overcome their alienation at the end of history, and the end is nigh. Marx retained this concern but 'saw that philosophy was not enough' to overcome alienation and, also, 'that the situation of German philosophy after Hegel resembled strikingly the situation of Greek philosophy after Aristotle', in that, after Aristotle, Greek philosophy 'became practical' (1953: 38–9).

For Hegel, MacIntyre notes, 'alienation' was 'a word which described men's mistakes about their relation to society', and once they understood that relation correctly all would be well. For Marx, in contrast, alienation describes our 'real situation in capitalist society' (1960a: 6) and, therefore, what is required in order to overcome alienation is a new, revolutionary kind of activity. In elaborating his own 'philosophy of social practice' in the *Economic and Philosophical Manuscripts* of 1844, Marx takes from political economy a 'view of the centrality of labour'. He interprets the condition of the worker in Hegelian terms of being 'alienated, estranged from himself' in perceiving himself as a commodity and 'objectifying his life in the form of labour', and of being 'estranged from the product of his work . . . from the act of being, from his own essential nature', and therefore also from other men and from the economic powers that his labour helps to create but by which he is dominated (1953: 47, 49–51). Capital is not a power separate from humanity. Rather, it is accumulated, alienated labour. Under capitalism, labour is 'not a means to a truly human existence' but 'an end in itself, and has thus created an existence for man which is non-human'. Socialist consciousness is consciousness of what work might be: 'a means to a truly human existence, in which the non-human – nature – is made into the image of man by means of art and science' (ibid.: 53). Humanity contrasts with nature in a way that is true to what Marx took from German idealism. For MacIntyre, this 'view of labour derives not at root from economic theory but from moral insight'. And from religion, as Marx 'moves between the poles of man fallen, man redeemed'. The place of the Fall is taken by a historical division of labour. Estrangement is evil, whereas 'the poor, the proletarians, bear the sign of redemption'; the sign, that is, of a *future* redemption. 'We have to learn to understand our views as symptoms of our condition, as expressions of our place in history, rather than as judgments of an impartial reason.' This may be learnt by 'the proletarian and the thinker who stands beside him', for it is only from the vantage point of 'the dispossessed' that it is possible to develop a socialist consciousness of the potential to overcome human alienation (ibid.: 58–60). It is those whose actions are most immediately and constantly constrained by material need who most keenly understand self-estrangement and desire its end, and it is those who labour who are likely to have most insight into how best to reform society.

Saving revolutionary science

MacIntyre follows Marx's *Theses on Feuerbach* in arguing that 'truth resides not in contemplation but in action', in 'active discovery' and in simultaneously 'transforming ourselves' and 'transforming circumstances'. 'It is this conception of truth that enables Marx both to affirm a historical relativism where all philosophies are concerned and also to deny that his own philosophy is merely a product of the time, since it is in Marx's own thought that philosophy has for the first time become conscious of its historical basis in seeking to transform that basis' (ibid.: 61–2). For Marx, such transformation would end the division of labour and thereby enable the completion of 'man'. Overcoming the division of mental from physical work would enable a person to engage in both. The goal of communism is that of such completion.

MacIntyre identified the *Communist Manifesto* as not only 'the practical program of a political party', but also 'the first mature statement of historical materialism, where the attempt at social science has finally expelled the earlier Hegelian terminology' (ibid.: 74, 71–2). Marx, suggested the young MacIntyre, achieved a break from Hegelese that was epistemological, antimetaphysical, sociological and practical. And yet Marx retained Hegel's term 'alienation' (1970a: 36). 'The category of "alienation" was precisely that by which the young Marx passed from quasi-theological to quasi-sociological explanations' (1961b: 37); although he did not use it in *Capital*, he did there elaborate upon the concept in what he wrote on fetishism and on freedom (1968a: 77). Completing human nature will involve overcoming commodity fetishism and achieving freedom.

> Socialism, precisely because it is the overcoming of alienation, must be a self-consciously constructed society in which institutions transparently serve the human purposes of those who construct them. This is why the emancipation of the working class can only be the task of the working class itself; it cannot be accomplished for and on behalf of them by anyone else. Equally, this is why the form of society they will construct in the course of emancipating themselves cannot be prescribed to them by anyone else in advance of their own decisions, and hence cannot be predicted. (Ibid.: 91–2)

Predicting that alienation will be overcome is, MacIntyre continues, a matter of 'belief in the possibilities and resources of human nature', and this belief 'is a secularized version of [the] Christian virtue' of hope. In contrast, such predictions as those of a falling rate of profit and of increasing class polarization and proletarian immiserization are matters 'of social science' (ibid.: 92).

About the first kind of prediction, MacIntyre notes that Marx's liberated person would enjoy 'liberty to create his life in a way analogous to that in which an artist creates', given that 'in Marx's vocabulary there are many reminiscences of the terms in which Schiller had described the artist' (an insight into Marx's left Kantianism that MacIntyre, like Marcuse, owes to György Lukács). 'The ending of alienation will transform work into a creative activity to be judged by aesthetic standards' (ibid.: 92–3). It will allow full employment of 'the skills of hand and brain and eye, the exercise of which is part of man's true being' (1953: 98).

The second kind of prediction, unlike the first, should share nothing with prophecy. Social scientific prediction must be open to falsification, and MacIntyre already accepts that central claims of Marx's social science have indeed been empirically falsified by the subsequent historical development of capitalism. This he links to his critique of Stalinism. The systematically 'evil' practice of Stalinism was not warranted by Marx. On the contrary, Stalin's purges of 'principled and tough Old Bolsheviks . . . were necessary . . . so that the true nature of socialism could be forgotten . . . in a society where not the working class but the bureaucracy ruled' (1971b: 51, 50). Stalin's subsequent theoretical achievement was to turn 'Marxist-Leninist' social science into a closed dogma that systematically excluded any possibility of falsification, a dogma which MacIntyre repeatedly compares to that of Christian orthodoxy. As with capitalist practice and liberal theory, the practice and theory of Stalinism are mutually reinforcing.

Stalinist theory takes the form of 'a conceptual scheme which claims final and absolute truth'. Its central concepts are those of a 'mechanistic materialism'. Such 'mechanistic concepts are extremely tempting in an industrial society' where 'the industrial manager knows that . . . all specifiable tasks for human beings can be reduced to routine movements which a machine can perform' (1964a: 66–7), but such a managerialist conception of change is antithetical to Marx's idea of revolution as the self-activity and self-emancipation of the working class.

MacIntyre acknowledged that the characterization of Marxist social science as mechanistic promoted by both Stalinists and their liberal critics could indeed be attributed to Marx's nomological analyses of capitalism, to Engels's philosophical writings, and to the emulation of these texts by Karl Kautsky, by Mensheviks and even, on occasion, by Lenin and other Bolsheviks, including Trotsky. On the other hand, he agreed with much in the very different Marxism that was advanced by Thompson, by Christian and ethical socialists, by the young Lukács, by numerous East European revisionists and by almost any reading of Marx's own, long-neglected early writings. This latter Marxism is centrally concerned with human agency, whereas the former conceives of social structure as independent of particular human beliefs and intentions. MacIntyre was not alone in adverting to these two Marxisms, but he was unusual in his hope that their division could be mended through a better theory of practice and practice of theory.

For MacIntyre, the specific task facing Marxist intellectuals was to combine an account of self-activity with a non-dogmatic research programme, capable of analyzing, explaining and predicting social change. The research programme apprehends the efficient causes operative upon actors; the account of self-activity is intended to help those actors escape such external constraints. The final end is what he called freedom.

Towards Aristotle

Besides Protestantism, another early and formative influence upon MacIntyre was the Greece of Homer and Aeschylus, to which he was introduced (as he was introduced to R. G. Collingwood, as archaeologist and historian) long before his introduction to academic philosophy. This was primarily an effect of his 'public school' education into English bourgeois culture, but there was more to it than that. He had been enthused by the writings on Greece of the Communist George Thomson, in part because of the comparisons it enabled him to draw with the very different culture of rural Ulster in which the other part of his childhood was spent – an upbringing that allows us to understand him, as he tells us to understand Aquinas, as having inhabited a 'boundary situation' between conflicting conceptual schemes (1990b: 114; he reports having been 'an anti-Davidsonian from about five years old' (2004a)). That Thomson 'played a part' in his joining the Communist Party (1998c: 256) indicates a certain continuity between his early admiration for the moral agency of farmers and fishermen, his later admiration for the moral theories of Plato and Aristotle, and his Marxism, a continuity that will have made it difficult for him to understand Marxism in the same way as any Cockney comrade when he joined the Party as a Classics undergraduate living in London's East End. What he understood Marxism to share with those other influences was its antipathy to the dominant ideas of liberal and capitalist modernity.

This complexity of MacIntyre's intellectual formation is reflected in the complexity and provisionality of the argument of his first history of Western moralities and moral theories, *A Short History of Ethics* (1967a). The title of its final chapter, 'Modern Moral Philosophy', implicitly acknowledges his inspiration by Anscombe (Anscombe 1958). Nonetheless, he credits not her but Marx with the historical insight that morality, because it presupposed 'a communal framework' (rather than the theistic one stressed by her, and by Nietzsche; on this see 1967b) that 'no longer exists', can now 'only be an attempt to invoke an authority which no longer exists and to mask the sanctions of social coercion' (1967a: 267–8).

Anscombe differentiated intentions and reasons for action from causes. In making this distinction, she helped revive Aristotle's unKantian distinction between practical reasoning and theoretical reasoning. Wanting something provides a reason for action. Insofar as what is wanted is called 'good', we can say that practical reasoning aims at what is good in a way that parallels theoretical reasoning's aim at what is true. The deductive, abstract logic of a theoretical syllogism issues a proposition. Analogously, a *practical* syllogism – that is, a piece of deductive practical reasoning – issues in a concrete action. To reason about causes is to reason theoretically, as an observer. To reason practically is to reason as an actor (Anscombe 1963; first published 1957). If any of this is redolent of Heidegger, it is is nevertheless innocent of his influence.

MacIntyre was well prepared to receive these ideas. He acknowledged as a 'Kantian insight' (1958a: 51) the distinction between reasons and causes, knew Collingwood's post-Kantian explanation of events in terms of 'inside' thought and 'outside' action, was familiar with Wittgenstein's and Ryle's attacks on any elemental separation of 'internal' mind from 'external' matter, employed the concept of intentionality in criticizing Freud's idea of the unconscious as a cause, and perspicaciously reported the importance of Heidegger's development of the concept from Brentano into that 'most primitive mode of being-in-the-world, *"Dasein"* ', a development ensuring that 'two philosophical traditions . . . have to be disowned and not just one; not only is it wrong to start with consciousness and reach out to the world [Cartesianism], but it is also wrong to try and capture the primitive reality of *Dasein* through the derivative concepts which we apply to the world of things, such as the concepts of cause and substance [Aristotelianism]' (1964b: 517) But MacIntyre's philosophical allegiance was more analytic than continental, and he told Marxists that the importance cannot 'be [over]estimated' of *Wittgenstein*'s re-establishment of 'the connectedness of the inner life and the outer' (1958b: 73) This importance lay less in Wittgenstein's newly therapeutic approach to philosophy than in what its way around the aporia of modern philosophy made possible: the revival of such concepts as that 'of activity for its own sake' (1964c: 22) and the elaboration of new forms of social theory.

MacIntyre therefore happily adopted Anscombe's account of practical reasoning. 'The relation of belief to action is not external and contingent, but internal and conceptual. We can understand in the light of this Aristotle's view that the conclusion of a practical syllogism is an action.' In such a syllogism, 'the major premise is an assertion that something is good' whilst 'the minor premise is an assertion warranted by perception' that such a good is immediately available 'and the conclusion [is] an action' to secure that good. This action 'follows from the premises in just the way in which a proposition follows from the premises in a theoretical syllogism' (1964a: 52–3). We may crudely summarize the structure of such a syllogism as: rational end; empirical means; act (cf. MacIntyre 1967a: 71). To fail to act as required by a practical syllogism would be to behave as illogically and unintelligibly as it would be to deny the conclusion of a valid theoretical syllogism.

This contentious conception of practical reasoning and self-activity has remained elemental for MacIntyre ever since (see especially 1988a: 129–41). It may be contrasted with what Ritter presents as an Aristotelian account of action in accordance with 'the doctrine of "ethos" ', which maintains that action is constituted 'in custom, use, and tradition' and 'has reality not in . . . immediacy . . . but in its integration into the . . . institutional order'.

First we may note that, for MacIntyre too, ethics cannot be a private language; one's reasoned actions are most immediately intelligible to those with whom one shares most, and the greatest problem with the analytic philosophy of action is its concentration upon the individual actor's particular act and its neglect of social conditions and context. Conversely, MacIntyre shares Anscombe's conviction that our ends should be determined by reason, not custom, and that our institutional order now provides us with no ethically compelling reasons for action. At the time of *A Short History*, his only answer to this dilemma was for individuals to choose communities in which they can share some form of life. His own choice was then still a revolutionary organization.

Against instrumentalism

'History is a dialectic of contradictions, intelligible not as natural events are or as a machine is but rather as a conversation or an argument is' (1960b: 200). To understand history in such a way is, MacIntyre claims, to understand it in terms of 'the family of concepts which belong to what [Marx] called "practical consciousness": the concepts of intention, deliberation and desire' (ibid.: 217–18). Marx's aim was not to elaborate a science telling some elite how best to control society but to help workers to think in terms of simultaneously transforming their social conditions and themselves. Therefore, Marx conceived society not in mechanistic or technical terms, but in terms of human agency and of alienated human powers. In an observation that was to be elaborated by Thompson in his powerful critique of structuralist Marxism (Thompson 1978b), MacIntyre says that 'the machine model will do to explain how we come to be modelled and acted upon, but not how we act' (1960b: 212). Although 'success in explaining and predicting can never be divorced from success in manipulating and controlling' (1957a: 29), MacIntyre's increasing understanding of intentionality and action encouraged him to believe that such success could never be total.

If this seems to take MacIntyre far from any social science of causal explanation and prediction, it should also be noted that there were limits to how far he would go. These were delimited in vigorous intellectual engagement, not with Anscombe but with another Wittgensteinian: Peter Winch. Rather like Gadamer, Winch wished the social or human sciences to escape any requirement to explain and instead to address only the understanding of different conceptual schemes that give meaning to actions within different cultures. On this account, the rationality of actions (and the intelligibility and, to this extent, validity of truth claims) is relative to conceptual schemes, and the rationality of each conceptual scheme is *sui generis* (albeit constrained within biologically 'limiting conditions'). MacIntyre could never, as a Marxist, endorse Winch's non-historical, cultural relativism, because the practical implications of such a relativism are necessarily conservative. As a Marxist, what concerned him was the opposition of rival conceptual schemes *within* a single culture and social order. What he accepted from Winch was that, as understanding action requires understanding the actor's reasons for acting, it therefore requires understanding whatever conceptual scheme informs her beliefs (1971c: 254). What he argued against Winch was that social science should 'uncover' the partial 'mechanisms which blind agents to or enable them to ignore the irrationalities of their own social order', such as the contradiction between Americans' belief that theirs is a classless society and their actions which belie that belief (ibid.: 256).

MacIntyre's social scientific methodology may also be compared with that of von Wright, a co-executor with Anscombe of Wittgenstein's works, one of the seminal figures (like Geach) in the revival of virtue ethics, and a founder of deontic logic. While Anscombe employed the practical syllogism in understanding action, von Wright more strongly extended its logic and use to action's explanation. Drawing upon Charles Taylor's intentionalist explanation of action in terms of 'purpose and teleology' (Taylor 1964), he went on to identify this intentionalist and 'teleological' mode of 'explanation' with an 'aristotelian tradition' which rivalled the efficiently 'causal' mode of a 'galilean tradition' (Wright 1971). This historical juxtaposition is redolent of that drawn by some German practical philosophers, and anticipates the pluralism of MacIntyre's account of rival traditions.

MacIntyre agrees with Anscombe and von Wright that actions should be understood in terms of intentions and with Winch that intentions should be understood in the various terms of distinct conceptual schemes. He disagrees with Winch's supposition that all actors within a single society are to be understood as reasoning in terms of the same conceptual scheme and, also, that actions can always be sufficiently explained by reference to the actor's own concepts and purposes. There is no need to refer to such exotic beliefs as those of the Azande to illustrate this last point. Managers may effect a reduction in trade union activity by introducing incentive schemes, so that individual workers have reason to act in such a way as to undermine their collective strength (1971d: 225). Here the workers are, as MacIntyre says, 'manipulated' by their managers. That is, the workers' actions can only be adequately explained by reference to the motives of others acting upon them, as causes, for those others' own ends. If the workers are unaware of this manipulative effect upon them and upon their own actions, then they are suffering from false consciousness. Social science might, by explaining the effect of their own actions to workers, enable them collectively to resist manipulation, even if it cannot reduce the financial incentive to individuals, but it can also inform managers of new means of manipulation.

Manipulation, as MacIntyre was to put it in *After Virtue*, is in the 'character' of managers qua managers (and when he used the term 'characteristic' at that time, we should understand it to imply what he later denoted by 'essential', i.e. pertaining to something's very being). The terms 'manage' and 'manipulate', like 'manual', come from the Latin for hand. As noted in chapter 1, to manage originally meant to handle and train horses; that is, to treat something apart from its own nature and good and to use it instead as a means to one's own ends. That managers have such power over their fellow human beings is evident, but it is not evidently right or necessary. MacIntyre, as a Marxist, believed that workers' true interest is not to be managed, nor simply to earn more pay, nor even just to exercise some collective power within capitalism, but rather to enact a revolutionary transformation of their social conditions. This is why he was exercised by the issue of what Thompson called 'socialist consciousness'. The obverse of this issue is that of manipulation, of how managers manage not only to direct the labour of workers but also to prevent those workers from learning and acting in their own true interest, as workers and as human beings. As a Marxist and, now, as an Aristotelian, MacIntyre understands the good of human actors to comprise their individual and collective control of their own activity. This is what he once simply called freedom, and what he now calls the good of independent practical reasoning. To be managed is to have this elemental good denied and negated.

MacIntyre argued that 'in the Bomb the irrationality of capitalism' is 'permanently manifest' (1963b: 9), and in this he again shared something with Anscombe. Her articulation of the distinction of practical from theoretical reasoning was motivated by a profound abhorrence at the kind of abstractly calculative morality that could justify use of nuclear weapons as the most efficacious means to a desired end (e.g. Anscombe 1981). Their shared concern was to find some argued alternative to the ruling morality. Where MacIntyre was far more radical than her was in recognizing that in every epoch the ruling ideas have been the ideas of the ruling class, and he therefore confronted the issue which she did not of how to contest the fully social presuppositions of modern moral philosophy.

Orthodoxy and its limits

What Marxism 'really is', thought MacIntyre, is not 'an economics' or 'a politics', but 'a sociology of a peculiarly philosophical bent' (1961a: 20). Central to his conception of Marxism as such a sociology has always been his appreciation of Marx's *Theses on Feuerbach* and, more particularly still, of the third of those theses:

> The materialist doctrine concerning the changing of circumstances and upbringing forgets that circumstances are changed by men and that the educator must himself be educated. This doctrine must, therefore, divide society into two parts, one of which is superior to society.
>
> The coincidence of the changing of circumstances and of human activity or self-change can be conceived and rationally understood only as *revolutionary practice [Praxis]*. (Marx 1976: 4)

The materialist doctrine casts ordinary persons 'for the role of inert matter to be moulded into forms chosen by the elite' (1970a: 92). It distinguishes 'between those who are the causally manipulated and those who are somehow able to perform the manipulation'. From this perspective, all change is understood as caused by 'someone acting upon someone else' (1964a: 67–8). With such a doctrine, reformists and revolutionaries can justify elitist rule as much as do conservatives; not, though, in terms of superior birth but of superior knowledge. To such claims that privileged possession of some special theoretical reasoning justifies rule over ordinary actors and over their reasoning about their own practice, MacIntyre has always been utterly opposed.

MacIntyre was aware that a revolutionary elitism could also be justified in terms other than those of mechanistic theory. This awareness is most obvious in his criticisms of another revolutionary whose theory was opposed to materialism and whose practice was motivated by the hope of overcoming human alienation: Ernesto 'Che' Guevara. His elemental criticism of Guevara's 'Marxism of the will' is that it postulated the possibility of socialist revolution irrespective of empirical conditions, including the present consciousness of those amongst whom the revolution was to be made. He attributes such belief in the Promethean ability of a revolutionary elite to what he characterizes as a 'Kantian' conception of practical reason. In reality, Guevara was no more a philosophical Kantian than was Karl Liebknecht, to whom MacIntyre attributes the same combination of 'moral heroism' and 'Kantian moral theory', but MacIntyre's objection is less to theoretical eclecticism (if it were, he would have referred instead to the neo-Kantian Austro-Marxists) than to any separation of intentionally revolutionary practice from socialist theory. For a heroic voluntarist, revolutionary practice is a matter of acting on 'abstract' individual duty in a way redolent of Kant's metaphysics of morals but inconsistent with Marx's account of social *praxis*. It would seem that on Guevara's voluntarist view, what is important is less the likelihood of success than a categorical imperative to act. (1971e: 74–5). For MacIntyre, such individual heroism, if uninformed by social scientific analysis, is erroneous and elitist.

MacIntyre also objected to Guevara's disregard of the working class. For an orthodox Marxist, any attempt to make a socialist revolution in the absence of a large and class-conscious proletariat is utopian. As MacIntyre observed, 'the view . . . that the peasantry can be an independent revolutionary class is entirely foreign to Marx' (1964d: 102). Accordingly, MacIntyre never expressed any hopes for socialism in China, Vietnam or Cuba. In contrast, Guevara, like Mao, regarded the peasantry as a potentially revolutionary class. MacIntyre's orthodoxy here is all the more striking given the influence upon him of the Communist, Hellenist, Hibernianist and, later, Maoist George Thomson, and given his own life-long admiration for peasants' moral agency. Related to this is his objection to Guevara's claim that a socialist revolution can be made by a guerrilla army rather than by a proletarian party. For MacIntyre, workers who are aware of their true class interest in overthrowing capitalism should organize in a democratic centralist party capable of acting as a unitary agent of revolution, as the Bolshevik Party acted in October 1917. Only in this way could a revolution be effected *by* the working class rather than *for* them.

It was in accordance with his orthodox belief in the necessity of party organization that, at the end of 1959, MacIntyre was both a founding editor of *New Left Review* and a member of the Socialist Labour League, newly formed from the more traditional Trotskyist left. In such ways he attempted, in both his own practice and his own theory, to straddle the division within Marxism between Leninist orthodoxy and New Left revisionism. He appreciated the way in which Thompson and others 'had rebelled against the bureaucracy of the Stalinist party machines and the mechanical determinism of Stalinist ideology . . . in the name of a conception of human nature which was authentically Marxist' (1959: 98). On the other hand, he thought that serious revolutionaries, unlike New Left dilettantes, could not stray far from orthodox Marxist theory, from the working class or from Leninist organization.

MacIntyre told fellow members of the Socialist Labour League that 'Marxist theory can provide a guide to what can be done and what must be done. That is why we need a Marxist Party, because only through the

Marxist party can . . . unity of intellectuals and workers really be constructed' (in MacIntyre et al. 1959: 331). Such professional intellectuals and 'politically conscious' individuals as himself, a philosophy lecturer, cannot aim at creating 'the free society . . . except by way of moving with the working class into conscious political action', and this can only be done within 'a vanguard party'. 'The knowledge which liberates' by enabling 'us to change our social relations . . . which Marxism puts at our disposal, is not . . . something which the individual can get out of books . . . ; it is rather a continually growing consciousness, which can only be the work of a group bound together by a common political and educational discipline' (1960c: 23–4). Apart from some such group, a professional intellectual will become 'an educational technician who can safely be charged with training the social administrators of the established order' (1960b: 235).

What MacIntyre was then trying to put into practice was his nascent idea of the unity of theory and practice, a unity that he, like many others at the time – such as the members of Socialisme ou Barbarie in France (on his attraction to which, see Blackledge and Davidson 2007) and of the Praxis Group in Yugoslavia – was reading back into the early, quasi-Hegelian Marx. MacIntyre was exceptional in trying to develop such practice within a traditional, Leninist institution. With Lenin, he 'saw the unity of intellectuals and workers in a Marxist Party as a precondition of a proper unity of theory and practice' (1960a: 10). Such unity, he hoped, could transform actual social relations in overcoming 'the most basic division of labour', that separating mental from physical work and manager from managed. 'In our political work this distinction begins to disappear. As workers become increasingly guided by theory, as intellectuals become increasingly close to the workers' struggle, so the two groups become one' (ibid.: 12).

MacIntyre was well aware that he had been preceded in this hope and endeavour by Lukács, and he was also well aware of Lukács' fate. Not so grim as that of the Old Bolsheviks, Lukács nonetheless renounced his own conception of Marxism as workers' self-activity and reformed himself into a faithful follower of Stalinism. Subjection to party discipline became 'deification of the Party' (1968a: 101), to the leaders of which Lukács therefore willingly submitted his intellect and actions (2006b: 138).

Britain was not like Hungary, and MacIntyre hoped that Trotskyism was not like Stalinism. Despite perceiving that Trotskyists 'share all the dogmatism of the Stalinists without any of their achievements' (1958c: 79), he hoped that this time 'intellectual freedom and party discipline [could] be combined' (1960c: 24). They could not. Instead, he, along with others, was rapidly expelled by the League's own petty Stalin. This second time, however, he did not immediately give up on organized Marxist activity. Instead, he joined another group, the International Socialists, which located itself within 'the Trotskyist tradition' but was more open to the rethinking of Marxism being undertaken by New Left intellectuals. Whilst a member, MacIntyre protested that Marx 'stood at the opposite pole from the kind of élitism which thought that a small, disciplined party of leaders could make the revolution on behalf of the working-class' (1964d: 106), admitting that even Lenin and Trotsky 'on occasion acted as voluntarists' (1963a: 17).

For Lenin and Trotsky to act as voluntarists was to act in disregard of that mechanistic theory of historical materialism that led Kautsky and Mensheviks to oppose their Bolshevik Revolution. MacIntyre often explicitly criticized the latter, but never the former, for the positions they adopted regarding the crucial events of 1917. The unspoken point was that Lenin (unlike Guevara) had been effective in making a Marxist revolution. That the revolution ultimately failed has often been explained as a consequence of Stalin's intentional betrayal, and that such explanation turns upon Stalin's voluntarism, rather than upon the level of development of Russia's forces of production, is at least consistent with the initial privileging of voluntarism. MacIntyre was too conscientious a Marxist social scientist to adopt such an excuse. The idea of state capitalism, which did much to define the particular theoretical position of the International Socialists, enabled him to go some way towards an alternative explanation, but not far. An adequate explanation would presumably have to refer both to intentional agency and its social structural constraints, and the tension between these two is what MacIntyre was trying to negotiate within the context of Marxist theory. It is a tension between, on the one hand, what he perceived as the practical and ethical reasoning at the heart of Marx's Marxism and, on the other, the worryingly mechanistic and disastrously managerial science which 'Marxist-Leninist' tradition had made out of Marx's philosophical sociology.

Marxist consequentialism

When he still hoped to make a moral theory out of Marxism, MacIntyre denied that 'Marx's own judgements were directed only to the future consequences of present actions' (1968a: 130). He quoted Marx that as revolutionary workers associate they recognize ' "the need for society, and what seems a means has become an end" ' (1998b: 47; cf. Marx 1975a: 313). Revolutionary *praxis* is self-activity, here and now. The making of socialism must be the self-making of human beings. It is not a mere process, but an activity.

Nonetheless, there is a real architectonic in traditional Marxist theory that is not simply social but temporal; it is not located in the metaphor of base and superstructure but in the historical process that culminates in communism. According to Marxism's traditional orthodoxy, communism is that for the sake of which the process of history occurs, and history is a narrative of class struggles which communism will conclude. Communism is, then, at the apex of Marxism's architectonic theory and, according to that theory, the real apex of historical progress. It is the final end, the completion, the *telos*, of that temporal process. It is the theoretical goal of actual practice, the aim of cadres of whose actions future generations are to be the beneficiaries. But, being as yet non-existent, it cannot be known as more than the condition under which human potential will at last be released and actualized. Marxists are not utopians; they do not contemplate an unactualized end but only deliberate about means. Therefore, Marxist theory cannot form such a systematic totality as may Hegel's. Capitalist practice raises the level of development of the forces of production; Marxist practice raises consciousness to the level at which the forces of production may be revolutionized. For Stalinists, it is sufficient to say that communism justifies any present means to its rapid attainment. If the law of primitive socialist accumulation dictates that the exploitation of peasants and workers must be increased (through exhortation or coercion), then so be it. In this regard, Trotsky, and even Guevara, share much with Stalin. Meeting human needs is the traditional aim of Marxism, but this aim belongs to a future state of communism and not to the present process of its construction. If the actions of the faithful and theoretically informed Marxist revolutionary are guided by any sense of moral duty, it is not a philosophically Kantian one but rather one informed by what we may call a thoroughgoing 'consequentialism', according to which 'the right action is the one productive of the best consequences' (Anscombe 1958: 12, 9).

Trotsky elaborated his moral position in *Their Morals and Ours*, comparing it to the 'utilitarian' and ' "Jesuit" principle "the end justifies the means" ' (1973: 19). John Dewey famously found much to commend in Trotsky's consequentialism and in his postulated end of ' "increasing the power of man over nature and . . . [abolishing] the power of man over man" ' (Dewey 1988a: 350; cf. Trotsky 1973: 48). On Trotsky's account 'dialectical materialism', lacking any 'dualism between means and end' because 'the immediate end becomes the means for a further end' (Trotsky 1973: 49), indeed resembles Dewey's own pragmatist ethics by postulating a 'continuum of ends-means' (Dewey 1988b: 226, 229). Dewey, for whom nothing could be atemporal or self-sufficient, had already attributed to Aristotle a conception of 'the last end-in-view' of practical judgement as 'simply the adequate or complete means to the doing of something' (Dewey 1979: 38), reducing Aristotle's teleology to that to which he in fact opposed it: an infinite regress of ends and means (in a way criticized by Anscombe; see chapter 1). But dialectical materialism is neither pragmatism nor a pragmatically mistaken and non-metaphysical Aristotelianism. Nor, MacIntyre frequently protested, is its combination of 'the materialist doctrine' with Hegel's totalizing pretensions veritably Marxist. MacIntyre objected that dialectical materialism originated with Engels, not Marx, and that although it was propounded by Plekhanov and, in *Materialism and Empirio-Criticism*, by Lenin, it was abandoned by Lenin after reading Hegel. It nevertheless became the purportedly scientific justification for the closure of Marxist theory against falsification, a closure asserted by Stalinists in order to justify their management of intellectuals and workers.

MacIntyre accepts that Trotsky's morality is utilitarian and criticizes his reduction of his 'moral dissent from Stalinism into a disagreement about what in fact the proximate and remote consequences of certain types of action are' (1968a: 128). Trotsky may have learnt no more from Bentham than did Guevara from Kant, but MacIntyre has consistently argued that the bourgeois moralities theorized by Bentham and Kant were effectively assimilated and applied by Marxist revolutionaries and revisionists who lacked any moral theory of their own. He calls Kautsky a utilitarian and describes the Marxism to which Lukács was forcibly subjected as 'determinist, mechanistic' and therefore 'utilitarian'. 'The mechanistic separation of means and ends is suitable enough for human manipulation, not for human liberation' (1960b: 235). The young Lukács, like the young Marx and Lukács' young Hegel, understood this.

MacIntyre eventually concluded that Marxism had never broken sufficiently from the reasoning of its bourgeois opponents. It had failed to ground its theory in actual practice, as Marx had aspired to do in the *Theses on Feuerbach*. Invoking Lukács' *History and Class Consciousness*, MacIntyre argued that Marxist philosophy had inherited too much from 'liberal categories of thought' (1968a: 136). He restated Lukács' claim that Marxism's theoretical separation of base and superstructure 'derives from the [actual] separation of the economic from the political in bourgeois societies' (1970a: 60; cf. 1968a: 136–7). At first, he blamed the mistaken extension of 'this basis-superstructural model' beyond capitalism upon 'the Engels-Plekhanov version of historical materialism' (1968a: 136–7), but, when he repeated Lukács' claim a couple years later, he asserted that Engels was 'an authentic interpreter of Marx' and denied that we can 'judge and understand Marxist theory as it has really existed . . . in the light of some ideal version of Marxism' (1970: 35, 61).

Beyond the Marxist tradition

Why did MacIntyre finally reject what organized Marxism had become? What attracted him to Marxism was always that which he consistently attempted to theorize: the bases it claimed in the practice of ordinary working people. When he spoke of the unity of theory and practice, what he was articulating was never only that of some revolutionary organization; it was always grounded in the actual and potential consciousness of workers as moral and political actors. He has always had a fine sense of the arrogance and hypocrisy of those in power, and of their desire to close their judgements and actions against criticism from those they consider as their inferiors. Marxism he long saw as the solvent of such elitism, which is why he so fiercely resisted its moral corruption into any new form of elitism.

MacIntyre, I have argued, attempted to overcome the separation of Marxism as social science from Marxism as 'revolutionary practice'. He aspired to a social science capable of assessing the possibilities for developing socialist consciousness and revolutionary activity. This is incompatible with the postulation of iron laws that render us the victims of social processes rather than the authors of social change. Marxism was to be the *praxis* that would allow us to overcome the old dualisms of matter and mind, fact and value, determinism and free will. Indeed, Marxism, as the combination of self-activity and social science, was to overcome the ancient separation of theoretical from practical reason, and of both from production. The revolutionary point of overcoming these oppositions is to overcome, in theory and in practice, 'the hierarchical division between managers and managed' (1998a: 231). If we so understand MacIntyre's basic conception of knowledge and practice, we should acknowledge that he has never abandoned Marx's idea of revolutionary practice. What he has abandoned, he has often said, is only 'the Marxism of the Second, Third and Fourth Internationals', including the Leninist understanding of revolution as an event to be effected by a small community of cadres, using the working class as their instrument. What he continues to understand as truly revolutionary practice is workers' own shared self-activity, in resistance and opposition to any alien power.

MacIntyre's eventual abandonment of political organization was occasioned by the emergence of the second New Left, a left which he condemned as 'petty-bourgeois bohemia close[ly] allied to the *Lumpenproletariat*' and engaged in 'parent-financed revolt' (1970a: 91). His resignation as an editor of *International Socialism* was announced in the summer of 1968. He later characterized 'much student radicalism of the sixties' as a 'Left Nietzscheanism' that attempted to make revolution through 'some gigantic and heroic act of the will' in a way redolent of those 'archaic aristocratic' heroes imagined by Homer and celebrated by Nietzsche (1985a: 114).

Marx himself, MacIntyre notes, failed 'to provide a social psychology' and said little about 'the growth in political consciousness of the working-class'. This allowed 'some vulgar Marxists to suppose that the growth of working-class consciousness would be some kind of automatic reflex of the same economic processes that produced the downfall of capitalism'; but when, in 1929, that downfall seemed imminent 'the working-class turned out to be quiescent and helpless' (1970a: 42–3). When Marcuse advised student radicals to look elsewhere for some agent of revolution, MacIntyre accused him of returning to the elitist ideas condemned by Marx in his third thesis on Feuerbach (ibid.: 64). MacIntyre's notorious conclusion was that 'to be faithful to Marxism we have to cease to be Marxists; and whoever now remains a Marxist has thereby discarded Marxism' (ibid.: 61; cf. 1985a: 262).

The depth of MacIntyre's disillusionment may be gauged from his comparison of 'the epistemological claims of the revolutionary' with those of 'the orthodox [non-Marxist] social scientist' and, worse still, of 'the industrial manager'. All are concerned with identifying 'the necessary and sufficient conditions' of social order in order to make predictions and affect social outcomes. All adhere to what he calls 'the ideology of expertise', which 'embodies a claim to privilege with respect to power'. Sharing such 'epistemological self-righteousness', the revolutionary 'cannot avoid in himself the very elitism which he attacks in others'. (1973: 340–2). If we wish to understand where this critique was coming from, then we may refer to the economic catastrophism at the heart of the theory of the Socialist Labour League and to the corrupt dictatorship at the heart of its practice. Below, I shall elaborate where the critique was to take MacIntyre.

MacIntyre always insisted on trying to keep the tradition of Marxism distinct from capitalism and its ideologies, in opposition to which that tradition had its point and purpose. He insisted on this because he understood Marxism as originally motivated by an ethical first principle of self-activity that he considered an invaluable insight into human needs, and because he fully accepted the Marxist critique of capitalism's systematic alienation of human activity from and subjection to its own social product, as the negation of that principle. Marxism's ethical and revolutionary aim he understood as the actualization 'self-activity as a total form of life'. It was in defence of this aim that he denounced those ex-Communists who criticized Stalinism in the name of other, liberal values. It is also why he, like the Old Bolsheviks and Lukács before him, and even when free from the discipline of any democratic centralist party, and despite his own reservations about many of its particular doctrines, maintained the integrity of Marxist orthodoxy as a distinct conceptual scheme. And yet, even when a dedicated Marxist, he never possessed anything like the purity that he attributes to the tradition. I shall make extensive claims below for the continuing influence of his Marxism upon his subsequent Aristotelianism, but I have noted that his Marxism was already combined with Aristotelian, and Wittgensteinian, influences.

'Aristotelianism'

Another social science

'A moral philosophy . . . characteristically presupposes a sociology', an understanding of how its 'concepts are embodied or at least can be in the real social world' (1985a: 23). In this proposition, *After Virtue* continues *A Short History of Ethics*'s commendation of Hegel and Marx's sociological insight that 'a communal framework [is] presupposed by morality' (1967a: 267). In proposing that moral philosophy has social bases, MacIntyre might be thought to be taking issue most of all with Kant, whose moral philosophy is often regarded as the culmination of what he famously calls 'the Enlightenment project' of justifying the rules of morality nonteleologically. Kant he indeed considers to have been fundamentally mistaken in drawing an elemental distinction between facts and values, but mistaken only about facts and about values and not about his own presuppositions. MacIntyre's appreciation of Kant's conflicting theses is too great for him to accuse Kant of untheorized presuppositions. 'Even Kant', MacIntyre observes, 'implies' a sociological premise 'in his writings on law, history and politics' (how important this premise had already been to MacIntyre we will see below, pp. 189–91). And he himself even implies that it is Kant who best articulates that 'distinction between manipulative and non-manipulative social relations' which he has himself long drawn. For Kant, whilst a moral relationship is 'one in which each person treats the other primarily as a means to his or her [i.e. the other's own] ends', it is immoral 'to treat someone else as a means' in attempting to make 'her an instrument of my purposes by adducing whatever influences or considerations will in fact be effective on this or that occasion'. The latter relationship, if it is to be one in which 'I' am likely to be successful, will be one in which I, as manipulator, draw upon 'the generalizations of the sociology and psychology of persuasion' (1985a: 23–4; cf. 1998d: xiii). Or I may simply lie. MacIntyre later admits that he 'draws upon Kantian resources' in his 'respect for rationality', in his 'rejection of consequentialism' and, therefore, in his condemnation of the 'illegitimate power' of the liar over those whom she deceives (2006c: 140, 137). In this, he takes sides against Trotsky on 'the political value, indeed the indispensability, of truthfulness' (1971f: 24). We may note that he sides also against Dewey on the concept of truth, which he argues is irreducible to warranted assertability. Where he differs from Kant is in objecting to the distinction between 'unenlightened them and enlightened us' (2006d: 172), a distinction used to warrant assertions that those with a scientific understanding of empirical anthropology are entitled to manage those who lack such superior knowledge.

The distinction between manipulative and non-manipulative social relations is, MacIntyre argues, denied by the moral philosophy of emotivism, and it is emotivism that best exemplifies the prevailing attitude towards morality in contemporary society. Emotivism, it turns out, is the analytic, Anglophone analogue of the more vigorous moral philosophy of Nietzsche. For Nietzscheans, moral propositions serve as rhetorical devices that mask a person's manipulation of others. The sociology presupposed by Nietzscheanism is one that reduces all social relations to relations of manipulation. Even lying is legitimate for Nietzsche's aristocratic superman; not, as for the Trotskyist, for consequentialist reasons, but as an expression of his superior will to power.

MacIntyre is utterly opposed to both the sociology and the ethics of Nietzsche. Nonetheless, he recognizes that the way in which Nietzsche moved from the one to the other enabled him to form a single philosophy of great rhetorical and, therefore, social force. In this crucial sense, Nietzsche's philosophy clearly surpasses Kant's tortured attempts to meld his disparate lines of reasoning into a single, architectonic system justifying his ascetic ideal. Nietzsche draws no absolute distinction between empirical activity and ideal activity, as does Kant, nor between present activity and future activity, as does Marx. Instead, Nietzsche draws a picture of empirical and present activity and tells us that this represents the brutal and ineradicable reality of our mutual relations. Those amongst us who have the strength of will to acknowledge and affirm this reality, freeing ourselves from any illusion of a universal truth, or of a heavenly salvation or future communism, must act in accordance with this reality and assert our power over those who lack such strength. If we do, we will form part of the new, Nietzschean aristocracy.

MacIntyre does not argue that Nietzsche is simply mistaken. On the contrary, he acknowledges that Nietzsche's portrayal is an accurate representation of how our real social relations are institutionalized under capitalism. The way in which the more brutal aspects of these relations are explained as necessary by Nietzscheans serves to legitimate the actions that constitute these relations and to delegitimate subversive actions as motivated by immature hopes. We could say that Nietzschean theory and much of contemporary social practice mirror and support one another, but this would be to express matters too passively. As MacIntyre put it, 'a successful ideology tends to make true that which it asserts to be true' (1968b: 27). This proposition owes something to Marx's second thesis on Feuerbach, which states that 'Man must prove the truth . . . of his thinking in practice', but it might owe still more to Anscombe's account of the 'great question' of what Aristotle meant 'by "practical truth"' and, more precisely, to her own answer to this question that things are 'brought about – i.e. made true – by action'. This answer could appear to express a pure pragmatism, or the kind of social science evident in Thomson's statement that primitive 'magic embodies the valuable truth that the external world can in fact be changed by man's subjective attitude towards it' (Thomson 1973: 11). But that Anscombe meant more than this is evident from her careful addition that an unjust action by someone in power 'will have produced practical falsehood' (Anscombe 1965: 157).

The conclusion to which MacIntyre was moving, and to which he had already long been moving as a Marxist, was that Nietzschean theory and capitalist practice had to be opposed in the name not of some theoretical or future ideal, but of some actual and present kind of practice. What he was therefore searching for was still a sociology, a social science, in which to ground a moral philosophy opposed to that falsehood which is expressed by Nietzscheans and institutionalized in capitalism. In this opposition to the capitalist present, and in his recognition of a need to justify conflict not between individuals but of collectivities against capitalism, MacIntyre remained a revolutionary. 'Marx was fundamentally right in seeing conflict . . . at the heart of modern social structure' (1985a: 253).

Social science as managerial ideology

Where MacIntyre departed from Marxist social science was in rejecting its traditional mechanistic and value-free pretensions, not its partisanship.

He has always been keen to contest the claims of the figure normally portrayed as Marxism's foremost sociological opponent, Max Weber ('one Liebknecht [is worth] a hundred Webers'; 1976a: 155). Nonetheless, by the time he wrote *After Virtue* he accepted that many Marxists shared something with those ideologues of management he called Weberians (1998e: 64–6; 1985a 26–7).

> As Marxists organize and move towards power they always do and have become Weberians in substance, even if they remain Marxists in rhetoric; for in our culture we know of no organized movement towards power which is not bureaucratic and managerial in mode and we know of no justifications for authority which are not Weberian in form. And if this is true of Marxism when it is on the road to power, how much more so is it the case when it arrives. All power tends to co-opt and absolute power co-opts absolutely. (1985a: 109; cf. 261)

What MacIntyre denotes by 'Weberian' here is the instrumental and 'bureaucratic rationality . . . of matching means to ends economically and efficiently'. It is successful deliberation, but it is also much more. First, it is the consequentialist institutionalization of certain ends to the exclusion both of other ends and of any rival rationality prohibiting immoral means. Secondly, it is the institutionalized imposition of the conclusions of that deliberation upon those excluded from such deliberation, and therefore their exclusion from responsibility for their own actions and from the ethically educative effects of engaging in cooperative deliberation and responsibility. What he denotes by a Weberian form of justification for authority is a consequentialist justification in terms of the '*effectiveness*' of 'bureaucratic authority', a justification which reveals 'that bureaucratic authority is nothing other than successful power' (1985a: 25–6).

Before we leap to any conclusion that MacIntyre has abandoned a Marxist for a Weberian conception of the state, we should recall that Weber's famous definition of the state took its premise that the state is a coercive *instrument* from Trotsky (Weber 2004: 33), to which Weber added that a state successfully claims a legitimate monopoly in the use of such coercion. We should then note that (as elaborated below, pp. 169–71) MacIntyre has never endorsed any account of the state as a neutral instrument. This said, he had already acknowledged the 'interesting form of argument' advanced by such elite theorists as Robert Michels in answer to the question 'why must politicians and managers rule?' (1966: 186). Michels identified 'the tendency towards aristocracy, or rather towards oligarchy . . . in every kind of human organization which strives for the attainment of definite ends' (Michels 1962: 50). Years before the Bolshevik Revolution, in studying Germany's Social Democratic Party, Michels had concluded that, although socialist parties might aspire to be democratic, all they can practice organizationally is centralism. 'The oligarchical and bureaucratic tendency of party organization is a matter of technical and practical necessity', and such 'organization . . . is the only means of attaining the ends of socialism' (ibid.: 72). After the Revolution, Weber warned Germans against taking the Bolshevik path for the same reason, knowing well that the 'means' used cannot but affect the form of the consequent 'ends'.

MacIntyre acknowledges that Marxists do indeed organize in the way that Michels describes. Marxism is theoretically orientated to the future goal of communism, in relation to which everything now present is too easily regarded as no more than a prior means. The obvious instrument with which to pursue communism is the state, whether it be Kautsky's parliamentary state or Lenin's new kind of state, and the instrument with which to pursue state power is the party. These are the technical means that Marxists have assumed will be effective in actualizing their theoretical end. That Marxist analyses of bureaucracy 'have been notably weak . . . not only affected Marxist analysis of the Soviet bloc; it has also weakened understanding of the bureaucratic neo-capitalism of the West' (1968a: 139).

In turning from Marx and Trotsky to Weber and Michels for an understanding of bureaucratic power, MacIntyre no more capitulates to their arguments than he does to those of Nietzsche. Like Hennis, MacIntyre stresses Weber's Nietzscheanism (even if he makes little of the Nietzschean and explicitly anti-revolutionary way in which Weber attributed to the individual responsibility for determining what values will inform her action; Weber 2004). Both Nietzsche and Weber are theorists of power, and both pose power as ineliminable and effective. Both therefore serve to legitimate the power of the powerful. Nietzsche talks only of the power of the individual superman, but Weber demonstrates how power is socially institutionalized. MacIntyre rejects the elitism of their theories, but he also rejects more empirical accounts of bureaucratic power. Bureaucratic authority is successful power and its effectivity cannot be isolated from the effectivity of belief in that power. Such belief is prevalent amongst bureaucrats, and amongst those subject to bureaucrats' power, and also amongst those social scientists who purport to analyze and measure that power in a value-free way. 'Social science methodology [is] the ideology of bureaucratic authority', he argues (1998e). What is banally theorized by students of organization and management is the real banality of power, and what informs their study is a conceptual scheme that they share with those they study.

There is a tension within *After Virtue*'s account of the power of 'bureaucratic managers'. On the one hand, MacIntyre alleges that managers are really 'impotent', their apparent exercise of power 'a masquerade' (1985a: 75). On the other, he highlights the manipulative power that managers really do exercise over those they manage. But the tension is itself more apparent than real. MacIntyre's position is that managers do have power over others, even if that power is largely explicable by the imputation of authority to them by those others, but that they do *not* possess that power to produce extraneous outcomes to which they pretend and which is (or was) often imputed to them by the supposedly detached and neutral observations of social scientists. We might therefore refine MacIntyre's suggested 'possibility' that managers 'do not even succeed in controlling their own corporations' by specifying that (at least in the absence of strong unions) they do normally succeed in controlling their workers but not in controlling their markets. This is, in part, why he talks here of 'manipulation' rather than of power. His polemical point here is made against such 'radical critics' as Marcuse and C. Wright Mills who believe that a managerial elite 'control[s] the United States' (1985a: 75). Social reality is less tractable than they supposed, and MacIntyre is amongst those social scientists who long and consistently predicted the collapse of the Soviet Union and its ultra-bureaucratic institutions. In realizing that neither the 'ends of socialism' nor even many more modest goals can be achieved by 'oligarchical and bureaucratic' means, MacIntyre's social science proved superior to that of most of those he called Weberians. All too often, manipulation is subtly or brutally successful; bureaucratic planning seldom is.

Towards a new philosophy of action

After Virtue's philosophical critique of the mechanistic character of generalizations in social science and of their lack of predictive power may now appear unremarkable. The New Right's Hayekian critique of 'constructivist rationalism' in defence of 'spontaneous order' went some way towards deflating social scientific positivism, whilst the second New Left's decline into a complementary 'postmodernist' and consumerist apology for capitalism went further still. Even *After Virtue*'s casting of philosophical critique into a historical form might also now seem unremarkable. It shares much with postmodernists' Heideggerian and genealogical critique of the will to scientific knowledge and technical power, which in turn shares something with Hayek's late extension of his own historical critique (Hayek 1988; a position similarly influenced by Brentano, but via Carl Menger and

Austrian School economics). Where MacIntyre's critique may appear less radical than these others is in tracing the epistemological project it attacks only so far back as the early Enlightenment and not all the way to Aristotle. In this, it resembles more the German critique of positivism made in the name of a specifically Aristotelian practical philosophy. However, it differs from all of these others politically. All of these other critiques are conservative, sometimes in their rhetoric, always in their practical implications. All serve to justify the New Right project of 'freeing the economy', and especially the newly 'flexible' labour market, from those rigidities promoted by positivist and utilitarian planners. All legitimate the claim that what is required, given the fact of bureaucratic and managerial structures, is strong and decisive leadership. All serve to legitimate what Margaret Thatcher upheld (against British miners) as 'a manager's right to manage'. What this 'right' consists in is the power of any line manager over her subordinates. This is necessary, said Thatcher, because 'there is no alternative'. Before addressing MacIntyre's sociological and political alternative we must, though, identify what underpins it: his different philosophy of the causation of action.

The only idea of causation admitted by most Enlightenment philosophers was that of mechanical or efficient causation, with its value-free mode of explanation. As MacIntyre says, this replaced the medieval Aristotelian location of

> efficient causes in a world to be comprehended ultimately in terms of final causes. Every species has a natural end, and to explain the movements of and changes in an individual is to explain how that individual moves towards the end appropriate to members of that particular species. The ends to which men as members of such a species move are conceived by them as goods, and their movement towards or away from various goods are to be explained with reference to the virtues and vices which they have learned or failed to learn and the forms of practical reasoning which they employ. Aristotle's *Ethics* and *Politics* . . . are as much treatises concerned with how human action is to be explained and understood as with what acts are to be done. Indeed within the Aristotelian framework the one task cannot be discharged without discharging the other. The modern contrast between the sphere of morality on the one hand and the sphere of the human sciences on the other is quite alien to Aristotelianism. (1985a: 81–2)

This is a fine exposition of how the conceptual, explanatory and evaluative scheme of Aristotelianism differs from that of the protagonists of the Enlightenment, and yet when he wrote this exposition MacIntyre was still almost as reticent to embrace that scheme as were our post-war German practical philosophers. He again acknowledges that 'after Kant the question of the relationship between such notions as those of intention, purpose, reason for action . . . and the concepts which specify the notion of mechanical explanation . . . becomes part of the permanent repertoire of philosophy', whilst those first 'notions' belonging to the philosophy of action have become detached from the concepts of 'good or virtue' which 'have been handed over to the separate subdiscipline of ethics' (ibid.: 82).

The first 'relationship' – between concepts of intentionality and of efficient causation – had, as we have seen, long exercised him, and rather fruitlessly so. His failure to combine Marxist social science with the revolutionary ethical insight of Marx's *Theses on Feuerbach* he attributed to the extent to which even Marxism, 'the most influential adversary theory of modern culture' (ibid.: 61), had itself failed to break sufficiently from the ethos of that culture. He concluded that 'nothing less than a rejection of a large part of that ethos will provide us with a rationally and morally defensible standpoint from which to judge and to act' (ibid.: x). Clearly, his position is antithetical to Ritter's 'doctrine of "ethos"'.

After Virtue attempted to move on from this failure. In it, citing once again the third of Marx's *Theses*, MacIntyre rejects 'the Enlightenment's mechanistic account of human action' (ibid.: 84), now including not only its Weberian but also its Marxist variants. In looking for an alternative (and implicitly acknowledging Winch's critique of his earlier efforts; ibid.: ix; cf. 1998d: xvi), he concentrates upon the second relationship – between that part of contemporary philosophy studying action and that part called ethics. In this, he follows Anscombe more than Marx. He well realizes that, if what a moral philosophy presupposes is a sociology, then such a sociology must include a philosophical psychology capable of explaining action. Practical reasoning, in its syllogistic form, concerns concrete wants and consequent actions, and concrete wants contrast with abstract 'oughts'. The Greeks made an ethics out of such reasoning, first in the 'prephilosophical' form described by Homer and then in the practical philosophies of Plato and, especially, Aristotle (1967a: 5–99), in all of which what one should do is conditional on one's social role (1971g). For Anscombe, 'the ethical syllogism as such is not an ethical topic . . . because human goodness suggests virtues . . . and one does not think of choosing means to ends as . . . courage, temperance, honesty, and so on' (Anscombe 1963: 78), but MacIntyre found guidance elsewhere in appreciating how '*arete* ensures that a man has the right goal, while *phronesis* cares for the means of attaining that goal' (*NE* 1144a7–9; quoted in Adkins 1960: 334). Anscombe was less ready than MacIntyre to accept Aristotle's proposition that every action aims at a good, acknowledging only that the practical syllogism could *contribute* to 'a philosophical system of ethics' which, in any case, she was not 'trying to construct' (1963: 78). After elaborating its sociological presuppositions, MacIntyre was to try to elaborate an Aristotelian ethics and politics that gave a central place to the practical syllogism.

Histories

Reflecting upon the failure of his earlier project, MacIntyre concluded 'that if Marxism fails, it fails as history and not just as philosophy, and any approach that seeks . . . to claim its inheritance must also succeed as history and not just as philosophy' (1976a: 156). He attempted such an approach in *After Virtue*. Its approach to history is neither mechanistically explanatory nor, in the sense of a Hegelian metaphysic, teleological. Rather, it is one which, recognizing that 'participants' understanding of social and economic activity is integral to and partially constitutive of such activities', seeks to present 'rationally defensible explanatory narratives' (1984a: 254). It is an approach that deals in particularities and not the universal. It is therefore an approach which, MacIntyre implies, is consistent with the kind of generalizations that Aristotle admitted into the study of 'human affairs', which apply only ' "for the most part" ', rather than with the kind of generalizations made by 'the modern social scientist' (1985a: 159). Nonetheless, it is an understanding of history that Aristotle lacked. It is, MacIntyre then proposed, an alternative foundation for Aristotle's practical philosophy to that of his own 'metaphysical biology'.

Against many recent commentators on Aristotle's practical philosophy (and not just Dewey or German practical philosophers), MacIntyre readily affirms that its 'teleology presupposes his metaphysical biology' (ibid.: 162). *This* theoretical basis, MacIntyre repeatedly asserts in *After Virtue*, must be rejected. He replaces it with a basis in social history and historical sociology. This is a modern supposition; one indebted to Kant, Hegel and Marx, and to Hume and Smith and, as he more readily acknowledges, to Ferguson, Collingwood, Gadamer and Karl Polanyi. It is a history expressed in terms of 'tradition' but not, he protests, one indebted to Burke. Burke's idea of tradition is conservative but, MacIntyre insists, his own is not. Why not?

MacIntyre justified his use of the concept of tradition as a counterbalance to his concept of conflict. His concern with conflict originates with his Marxism but, dissociated from historical materialism and its determinist account of ideology, he was aware that all his talk of conflict might appear to commit him to a Nietzschean or 'Heraclitean view of social life', and it was in order to prevent such misapprehension that he 'introduced' his concept of tradition (1998e: 67; first published in 1979). This concept, he proposed, is itself inseparable from a concept of revolution. Burke 'understands tradition as essentially conservative and essentially unitary' and 'counterpose[s] tradition [to] reason and tradition [to] revolution'. Against this, MacIntyre, following Kuhn's argument about the structure of scientific revolutions, proposed that traditions 'are the bearers of reason, and traditions at certain points actually require and need revolutions for their continuance'. Against Burke's presumption that traditions are 'essentially unitary', he argued, first, that 'conflict arises . . . between traditions and . . . tests the resources of each contending tradition' and, secondly, that it is a 'mark of a degenerate tradition that it has contrived a set of epistemological defences that enable it to avoid being put in question' (2006e: 16, 12; first published in 1977). This second argument he had already advanced against Stalinism. What we should now add is that the first argument may be advanced against Gadamer, even though he is the source of much that MacIntyre learned 'about intellectual and moral tradition' (1998c: 265). Gadamer practised a way of dealing with the history of ideas that avoided some of the errors in the idealism of a Collingwood, as well as those in the determinism of an Engels. Where Gadamer differs from MacIntyre and agrees with Burke is in conceiving tradition only in the singular. But, then, at the time he wrote *After Virtue* MacIntyre had himself not yet adequately worked out his idea of the rationality of rivalry between traditions.

After Virtue identified a 'classical tradition' or 'tradition of the virtues', which it went on to call 'Aristotelian'. MacIntyre intended the book's history of moral theories to demonstrate that Nietzsche's genealogy of morals fails as history. He had long recognized that Nietzsche offered 'a scheme of *the* virtues' which Nietzsche presented as specifically 'aristocratic virtues, as class virtues', in opposition to Kantian and Enlightenment schemes of universal moral rules (1969: 81). Later, he admitted that his voluntarist, relativist and partially genealogical argument in *A Short History of Ethics* (*partially* genealogical only, because its first half traces a progression culminating in Aristotle) 'should perhaps have ended by giving Nietzsche the final word' (1998c: 261).

His second attempt at a history of Western moral theories argued that the final word should be given not to Nietzsche but to Aristotle. Nonetheless, as in his first – and also in his third, *Whose Justice? Which Rationality?* – *After Virtue* followed Nietzsche in giving the *first* word to

Homer. Against Nietzsche, MacIntyre here aimed to demonstrate that the Homeric world of warring aristocrats should be understood not in terms of simple self-assertion but of social roles. Against the Enlightenment's exaltation of theory (and therefore *with* Nietzsche), he aimed to demonstrate that the real origins of Aristotle's central ethical concepts of *agathon* (good) and *arete* (virtue or excellence) were not in his metaphysical biology but in Greek history and culture. Therefore, Aristotle's own theoretical 'presuppositions' should be replaced with ones that are sociological and reflexively historical.

MacIntyre has long argued that philosophy is inseparable from its history. Even so, historical success is not tantamount to success as philosophical argument. It is *here* that he breaks decisively from Hegel's historicism. In *After Virtue* he acknowledges the historical success of Nietzsche's critique of the Enlightenment, but also looks forward to the critique of Nietzscheanism he presents in *Three Rival Versions of Moral Enquiry*. Nietzscheanism's historical success was contingent upon its sole rival being an Enlightenment theory that refused to explicate its own sociological presuppositions within its therefore abstractly moral theory (that this charge of abstraction does not hold against Mandeville or Hume is later acknowledged by MacIntyre in his account of Humean tradition, and we may add that Hegelianism's implosion in Germany was followed by its spread elsewhere), and MacIntyre structures the argument of *After Virtue* upon the premise that the Nietzschean critique has not been tested against the kind of concretely grounded theory that the Enlightenment itself defeated but that he revives and revises. As Nietzscheans recognize, historical development is more a matter of contingency than of Hegelian logic. For example, the defeat of Aquinas's Aristotelian and Augustinian project was, MacIntyre later argued, a matter of historically contingent misunderstanding (1988a: 206–12; 1990b: 151–69). In *After Virtue* he argues that Aristotelian practical philosophy was historically defeated because its teleology presupposed that of Aristotle's discredited metaphysical biology. The earliest protagonists of Enlightenment were correct, he here suggests, to reject Aristotle's metaphysical biology in favour of a mechanistic and non-teleological *natural* science. Their mistake was to throw the baby of teleological ethics out with the murky bathwater of teleological metaphysics, instead of bathing it in the fresh water of a purely social science.

Ends and means

In *After Virtue*, MacIntyre criticizes both mechanistic social science and non-teleological moral theory. The two targets are combined in his criticism of the way in which 'anti-Aristotelian science sets strict boundaries to the powers of reason' so that 'in the realm of practice . . . it can speak only of means. About ends it must be silent' (1985a: 54). 'Bureaucratic rationality is the rationality of matching means to ends' that are 'predetermined' and therefore beyond the reach of reason (ibid.: 25). Bureaucracy he has always considered to exemplify a 'functional view of work' and a 'means-end concept of activity' (1964c: 6), opposed to his own concept of self-activity. Capitalism he had already criticized for being 'essentially rationalistic in its approach to means, even if absolutely irrational in regard to ends' (1963b: 5), or for being concerned only with the means of production and not with its end. Such a form of practical rationality is altogether less rational than one that encompasses ends as well as means. To this thought, *After Virtue* adds that the logical structure of such superior practical rationality is 'teleological' and, therefore, identifiable with the practical philosophy of Aristotelianism.

Despite saying that 'Aristotle does not in his writings explicitly distinguish between two different types of means-end relationship' (1985a: 148), MacIntyre draws an interpretive 'distinction between internal and external means to an end'. Virtues are 'internal' in the sense that 'the exercise of the virtues is itself a crucial component of the good life for man' so that it, as the 'end', 'cannot be characterized independently of a characterization of the [virtues as] means'. Although the distinction 'is not drawn by Aristotle himself', MacIntyre insists that 'it is an essential distinction to be drawn if we are to understand what Aristotle intended' (ibid.: 184). Evidently, then, it is not meant to correspond to Aristotle's juxtaposition of 'internal *goods*' to those 'external goods' which, as necessary conditions of the good life, could be described as means, and nor does it relate to Aristotle's reference to the 'external actions' exemplified by master craftsmen (see above, p. 31). Attempting to rescue a 'teleological' ethics from that theoretical philosophy which he regards as the discredited 'presupposition' of Aristotle's own practical philosophy, MacIntyre disregards Aristotle's metaphysical distinction of *energeia* from *kinesis* (rather as he earlier disregarded the concept of *entelecheia* in his account of a *telos* as the temporal terminus of 'an activity'; 1967a: 81). That this distinction could be thought to approximate to that which MacIntyre articulates in terms of 'internal' and 'external means' indicates both that he may be closer to Aristotle's metaphysics in *After Virtue* than he admits and that he would do well, as a self-proclaimed Aristotelian, to employ something more like Aristotle's own metaphysical idiom.

The distinction between internal and external means was originally (see e.g. Hardie 1968: 254–7; Cooper 1975: 22) drawn by L. H. G. Greenwood in his commentary on Book Six of the *Nicomachean Ethics* (Greenwood 1909: 46–8, 53–5), at a time when the practical philosophy inspired by Mill's utilitarianism was being challenged in Britain by that inspired by Green's idealism. Later, the distinction was adopted and elaborated by both Anscombe and von Wright (Anscombe 1965: 150; Wright 1963: 162–8) and, then, by numerous other commentators. Most notable amongst these is Ackrill, with his inclusivist interpretation of *eudaimonia* upon which (although conducted in Oxford's 'armchair style' of ordinary language philosophy; 1985a: ix) MacIntyre draws (1985a: 158, 175; 1988a: 142–3). Ackrill argues that the 'intellectualist' interpretation (see chapter 1) of *Ethics* Book One is mistaken, and he suggests that when Aristotle appears to describe a hierarchy of means to ends culminating in the final good of *theoria*, what he enumerates are 'not just means' to but 'constituents of or ingredients in' *eudaimonia* (Ackrill 1997b: 184; cf. Austin 1961: 42). In this he echoes Greenwood, whose initial terminology of 'internal means' is replaced by that of 'ingredient part[s]', 'actual ingredients' and 'component parts of . . . happiness' (Greenwood 1909: 79, 80, 84), and anticipates others (e.g. Wiggins 2002: 219–21; Cooper 1975: 81–2; Nussbaum 1978: 170. For critiques, see McDowell 1998a and 1998b; Broadie 1988; and Kraut 1989: 210–37).

We might well agree that, if some such distinction is to be drawn, it is better expressed as one between, first, 'essential constituents' (see below) of the good life and, secondly, 'means to an end' as conventionally understood (and, also, as terms in which we may interpret Aristotle's accounts of the relation of external to internal goods, of the architectonic content of political deliberation, of the movements of animals, and of the relation of producer to product). As MacIntyre often puts it, Aristotle is concerned with both 'the good and the best' (cf. *NE* 1094a22). When (as we shall see) he repeatedly describes 'the function of the virtues', what he implies is less that moral virtues are productive and exhaustible means to a separate end than that they are parts of some more inclusive good. If we accept his interpretation of Aristotle's ethical teleology as predicated on the teleology of his metaphysical biology, then Aristotle's account of *the* human good and *telos* should presumably not be understood in terms of any temporal process and end to be causally effected by some 'means' or other, but, rather, as an account of a characteristically human *entelecheia*, or state of completion, and *energeia*, or self-activity. *Eudaimonia* should, accordingly, not be understood as a condition of 'happiness' consequent upon all of the goals of practical reasoning, but as the very condition of the 'flourishing' human being in virtuously reasoning and acting (however 'doubtful' may be Aristotle's concept of flourishing; Anscombe 1958: 18).

To assert this here is, though, to anticipate a conclusion that has yet to be justified.

Internal means and functional concepts

MacIntyre's critiques of both capitalism and traditional Marxism may be construed in terms of their refusal of any idea of 'internal means' or 'essential constituents'. Capitalism treats workers as 'human resources' in and expendable means to the production of saleable 'goods' and profits. Traditional Marxism postulates communism as a future goal independent of any present means to its attainment. The aim of neither is conceived as being *constituted* by the activity of those who actualize it. Both conceive of end and means in the manner of mechanistic social science.

MacIntyre's sociological use of 'internal' and 'external' in *After Virtue* is continuous with his earlier use of the terms in relating beliefs to actions and in differentiating reasons from causes. So understood, his use of the term 'teleology' may itself be understood as consistent with its intentionalist usage by others in the philosophy of action and of social science from the 1960s onward. Accordingly, what appeared immediately innovative about *After Virtue* was the way in which it introduced *this* concept of teleology, as purposiveness, to moral theory without making any concessions to the very different meaning that the term 'teleology' already had there (cf. Cooper 1975: 87–8) in denoting that utilitarian consequentialism condemned by Anscombe.

But how far does reasoning in terms of 'means' and 'ends', and of a teleology itself understood in these terms, really get us beyond the logic of utilitarianism? After all, it was John Stuart Mill who called teleology 'the doctrine of ends' (Mill 1987: 140), thereby warranting later textbook contrasts of teleology with deontology and provoking MacIntyre to argue simultaneously against the one's consequentialism and the other's abstractness. MacIntyre acknowledged that his own attempt at 'devising some new teleology' is preceded by that of utilitarianism (1985a: 62) and, later, that Mill shares the idea of what he calls an internal means: for Mill, 'virtue is originally valued only as a means [to happiness], but then, as a result of experience of the life of virtue, it comes to be valued also as an end', so that 'virtue is desired for *its* own sake precisely because it is . . . a part of [the end that is] happiness' (2006c: 117). It was only after *After Virtue*'s first edition that MacIntyre made sufficiently clear that for him, too, virtues are to be valued as more than just means to other ends. When pressed, he echoed Ackrill in saying 'that we value the virtues both for their own sake and for the sake of *eudaimonia*' (cf. *NE* 1097b2–4), adding that to value them for the sake of *eudaimonia* is to value them precisely as 'essential constituents'. The greater complexity now shifts to valuing virtues 'for their own sake'. This we should do 'because unless we value the virtues in and for themselves, we cannot be virtuous . . . and so will be deprived *both* of those goods that virtues themselves are *and* of . . . additional goods, such as the goods of good community' (1983a: 461–2). To this he added, in the postscript to the second edition, his opposition to any 'means-end distinction according to which all human activities are either conducted as means to already given or decided ends or are simply worthwhile in themselves' (1985a: 273). We may here note that activities conducted as means to already given or decided ends would be regarded by Aristotle as productive processes, whilst activities worthwhile in themselves are what he called *praxeis*. MacIntyre might call himself an Aristotelian, but he clearly opposes something elemental in Aristotle's conceptual scheme.

We might also ask how far *After Virtue*'s understanding of teleology in terms of means and ends gets us beyond that of Hegel, who remained the elephant in the room for some years after MacIntyre had ceased to invoke his authority. For this period, what MacIntyre understood to be valid in the idea of teleology remained something thoroughly temporal and historical. This said, it is evident from his occasional allusions to a cosmically teleological order how little he took from Kant and Hegel's distinction between 'external' and 'internal' teleologies; had he taken more, he would have got closer to a pre-Thomistic Aristotelianism.

MacIntyre may be on firmer Aristotelian ground in his argument for understanding ' "man" as a functional concept'. In the past, he had dismissed any such concept (e.g. 1964c: 12). Now, with a nod to contemporary deontic logic (that of Prior, not von Wright), he approximates to Aristotle's *ergon* argument in drawing an analogy of the 'essential nature and [the] essential purpose or function' of a human being with those of an artefact – a 'watch' – and of a worker – 'a sea-captain' or 'a farmer'. An individual, when acting in the capacity or performing the function of a farmer, ought to do whatever a farmer ought to do; in other words, she ought to do whatever it would be right for a farmer to do qua farmer under given circumstances. As the concept of a farmer is a 'functional concept' inseparable from a concept of the specific purpose of a farmer and from the concept of a good farmer who actualizes that purpose, such a proposition has normatively prescriptive content. He notes that such functional concepts controvert the familiar Humean denial to factual premises of evaluative conclusions. Linked to such a functional concept as that of a sea-captain or farmer, 'ought' ceases to be an abstract universal and becomes an imperative specific to a social role (1985a: 56–9; cf. 1967a: 89–90, 263–5).

The significance of the concept of a social role we have already noted regarding MacIntyre's sociological account of the development of Greek ethics, but he now (cf. e.g. 1967b: 72) opposes this concept's equation with that of a social function. This is because he opposes sociological functionalism's positivist way of explaining action 'in terms of social structure' rather than 'of the agent's reasons' (1986a: 95; this is a similar distinction to that drawn in chapter 1 regarding Charles's 'functional model' and 'agency model' of explanation). A social role – whether played by Odysseus or Hesiod, James Cook or Jethro Tull – furnishes its occupant with reasons for acting (for Aristotle, in the form of goods to be actualized). Or rather, on MacIntyre's historical account, social roles provided individual actors with sufficient reason to act in the time described by Homer and Hesiod, and long after, but were ceasing to do so in Europe by the time of Tull and Cook – not only in Europe but also in Polynesia, as evinced by the similarity of Europe's 'oughts', abstracted from any particular role, to Polynesia's taboos. It was under the combined influence of Anscombe (1958), Steiner (1956), Collingwood (1939: 63) and Adkins (1960: 2–3, 253, 329) that MacIntyre had argued that the idea that we ought to 'do what is right for its own sake' is what most decisively divides modern from Greek ethics (1967a: 85), which lacked the 'ought' of an impersonally individualist universalism. For the Greeks, what it was to be a good man was identified with particular roles, and therefore excellence was identified with the exercising of particular qualities and skills. *Arete* denoted 'the production of the correct result, in a given situation, irrespective of the manner in which the result was produced or the intentions of the agent' (Adkins 1960: 332). *Aretai* were, on this account, productive means to ends. Where Kant drew an absolute distinction between skill and pure practical reason, and where von Wright drew an attenuated distinction between the *'technical goodness'* of 'abilities and skills' and those 'features', 'traits of character' or virtues 'which possess a utilitarian value for safeguarding the good of man' (Wright 1963: 137; Wright 1989: 791), the distinction drawn by MacIntyre is still more muted. As Pinkard observes, in conceptualizing 'practical reasoning as a kind of skill' MacIntyre still shares something with Hegel (2003: 192).

What MacIntyre wanted to rehabilitate from the Greeks in *After Virtue* was the idea that '"man"' is itself a 'functional concept' (1985a: 58–9), so that some specific good may be attributed to humans qua humans. However, as he had already argued that the goodness of actions was 'pre-philosophically' specific only to particular social roles, and as he dismissed

Aristotle's theoretical philosophy of natural species and their good of activity, it was as yet unclear how any such human good might be specified.

The logic and history of practical reasoning

Where the philosophical argument of *After Virtue* first goes beyond anything in *A Short History*'s genealogy of moral theories and forms of life is in advancing a teleological argument for morality. Traditionally, this argument took the form of a 'threefold scheme':

1 A conception of the human good as that of 'man-as-he-could-be-if-he-realized-his-essential-nature' or 'human-nature-as-it-could-be-if-it-realized-its-*telos*'.
2 A conception of 'untutored human nature' or 'man-as-he-happens-to-be'.
3 'The precepts of rational ethics', by which MacIntyre intends straightforward moral rules as well as those 'precepts which enjoin the various virtues' (1985a: 52–3).

The third 'element' in the scheme (3) identified and prescribed the means by which an individual moved from the condition of (2) untutored human nature to (1) the desired end of human potentiality fulfilled. It is this end (1) that now requires revision because of what MacIntyre regards as the untenability of Aristotle's metaphysical biology.

The tripartite structure of what MacIntyre presents as Aristotelianism's formal argument for morality is similar to the logical structure of a syllogism (and of Hegel's dialectic). The argument's first element may be understood as its major premise, its second element as its minor premise, and its third as its conclusion. Because it is a theoretical argument about practice, this conclusion is not an action (as in MacIntyre's account of a *practical* syllogism), but the proposition of a set of rules to be followed and virtues to be cultivated. Unfortunately, MacIntyre proposes, the argument's major premise is erroneous. Therefore, the argument can only be saved if a replacement is found. Aristotelianism now requires a new major premise.

MacIntyre wants to maintain that a justification of moral precepts can still be inferred from the juxtaposition of one's actual condition to some concept of rational desire. He had long hoped to rescue morality from its Kantian opposition to desire, which is why he had been fascinated with the Greeks' morality of happiness. More generally, he had hoped to overcome the Kantian separation of values from facts. If it could be reconstructed in some tenable form, a threefold scheme of practical reasoning would achieve these aims. *After Virtue's* central metaethical argument is not that Aristotelianism's traditional threefold scheme provides an apodictic justification for morality. Rather, it is that any successful justification for morality must take the general form of such a scheme, within which morals are the necessary means to one's rationally desirable end (1985a: 52–5).

After Virtue's metaethical argument may be distinguished from what could be called its central historical argument, so long as the two arguments are understood as complementary. The book's historical argument is that, before the Enlightenment, morality was justified in terms of Aristotle's threefold scheme, but that the Enlightenment gave actors reasons to try to justify their actions without recourse to any teleological conception of the human good. All that therefore remained were the scheme's second and third elements, and what was eliminated was the first element's motivation for morality. Without it, morality was supposed either to supply its own motivation (as with Kant's 'good will') or to be motivated by some pre-rational aspect of human nature (as with Smith's 'impartial spectator'). Any such twofold scheme is, MacIntyre argues, bound to fail as a justification. Therefore, the unintended consequence of the Enlightenment project was social demoralization. This effect was then amplified by Nietzscheanism's explanation of moral claims as attempts to impose one's will upon others, and by its explanation of the Enlightenment's moral failure as a failure of morality as such.

The core concept of virtue

As a Marxist, MacIntyre was well aware of the critique of morality as a form of ideological manipulation. His own early attempt to formulate a non-manipulative morality shared something with Nietzsche. He looked back to the Greeks' ethic of 'doing well and faring well' (cf. Adkins 1960: 252–6), which he understood as successfully fulfilling one's social role and achieving one's corresponding goals. Whilst Nietzsche advocated one's resistance to manipulation by replacing moral discourse with a private language justifying the manipulation of others, MacIntyre's hope was to formulate a morality of self-activity and cooperation that eschewed manipulation altogether.

After Virtue's 'moral philosophy', its teleological virtue ethics, 'presupposes a sociology', an understanding of how its 'concepts are embodied or at least can be in the real social world'. This sociology MacIntyre elaborates as what he calls 'the core concept of virtue'. This comprises another three-fold scheme, but this time a non-syllogistic one. Its constitutive concepts are those of:

1 'A practice'.
2 'The narrative order of a single human life'.
3 'A tradition'.

These three concepts are the 'three stages in the logical development of the concept' of virtue, as he attempts to revive and sociologize it. 'Each later stage presupposes the earlier, but not vice versa' (1985a: 186–7). Taken together, these concepts are intended to substitute for Aristotle's meta-physical *telos* of 'man-as-he-could-be-if-he-realized-his-essential-nature'. They are the sources of those ends in relation to which moral virtues may be understood as internal or constitutive means. He proposes that, rightly understood, these sources have nothing to do with manipulation and every-thing to do with personal activity and interpersonal cooperation in pursuit of ends that initially lie beyond the self, and that it is by adopting and *inter-nalizing* some such aims, and therefore practising the virtues, that individ-uals can learn to move from their initial, 'untutored' condition to the actualization of their *telos*.

When MacIntyre adds that 'progress in the development of the concept is closely related to . . . the history of the tradition of which it forms the core', we might well still detect a Hegelian resonance (1985a: 187; cf. 2006f: 84–5). However, MacIntyre does not postulate any simple substitute for Aristotle's metaphysical *telos* because he lacks any adequate standpoint from which to do so. He has become a more dialectical thinker than Hegel, in that he retains a Hegelian conception of history as conflict and contes-tation but without Hegel's belief in the temporal necessity of reconcilia-tion. We are temporal beings incapable of any atemporal view from nowhere, or even from any temporary vantage point above the fray of com-peting traditions. Rather, traditions, lives narratively understood and prac-tices all have a 'teleological' structure in the sense that they are orientated to some developing concept of a particular 'internal' goal and good. MacIntyre's post-Wittgensteinian (see below) account of practices is of activities that 'generate new ends and new conceptions of ends' and are therefore alien to any 'version of the means-end distinction according to which all human activities are either conducted as means to already given or decided ends or are simply worthwhile in themselves' (1985a: 273). They are neither Aristotle's *poieseis* nor *praxeis*.

Even though his chosen antagonist is 'the last metaphysician', Nietzsche, we might think that, as MacIntyre now regards Hegel and Marx's teleological way of dealing with time as too metaphysical and insufficiently historical, he may betray some hint of the Heideggerian influence so important for Gadamer and his philosophical compatriots. Whether, and if so how, MacIntyre is more successful than any German in modernizing the teleological presupposition of practical philosophy will depend upon the 'logical development' of his core concept of virtue. What is already clear is that virtue's conceptual basis – social practices – transgresses a conceptual boundary regarded as basic by German neo-Aristotelians.

A non-metaphysical Aristotelianism

MacIntyre draws attention in *After Virtue* to what he (like Gadamer) considers a 'tension between Aristotle's view of man as essentially political and his view of man as essentially metaphysical', between the 'local and particular' and the 'cosmic and universal' (1985a: 158, 148). However, he does not take the easy path of simply dismissing *theoria*, not least because he has long recognized that it is in 'the nature of all intellectual inquiry' that its end is internal to the activity (1964c: 19). Theoretical activities are therefore paradigmatic practices.

Earlier, MacIntyre had excoriated Marcuse's speculative 'metaphysics' and 'biology' (1970a: 87). Marx, who he had praised for bringing 'down to earth the hitherto metaphysical themes of alienation', he had nonetheless criticized for 'insisting on the possibility of a more than empiricist understanding of social facts' (1968a: 140). More recently, and more favourably, he has taken this so far as to say that Marxism retains 'the same metaphysical and moral scope of Christianity and it is the only secular postenlightenment doctrine to have such a scope' (2006g: 146). In between, in *After Virtue*, despite criticizing the fallacies of empiricism (1985a: 79–81), despite asserting the need to break from the ethos of modernity in order to contest its hierarchical social order, and despite accepting the importance of Aristotle's *theoria* for his ethics and politics, MacIntyre still refuses to countenance Aristotle's metaphysical biology. Why?

Part of the reason is philosophical, a legacy of MacIntyre's earlier Humean and Wittgensteinian understandings of morality as customary and a language game, according to which 'one cannot justify . . . morals as a whole in non-moral' terms (1957b: 202). But part of the reason is political, and this in a Marxist rather than an Aristotelian sense. In *A Short History of Ethics* MacIntyre attributed much of Aristotle's theorizing to his 'class-bound conservatism' in defence of 'upper-class Greek life'. Despite describing Aristotle's ethics as concerned with creating 'a form of life' in which 'doing well and faring well' go together, an idea which he considered revolutionary if extended to all, he well realized that it would be 'mistaken' to make 'Aristotle sound like a revolutionary'. Instead, he regarded the theoretical substance and metaphysical substances of Aristotle's universalist theory as little more than an 'apology for this extraordinarily parochial form of human existence' and for its own 'kind of hierarchical social order' (1967a: 68, 67, 60, 83; cf. Nussbaum 1988a: 184, 177). As I argued in chapter 1, there is much justice in such an indictment. And when MacIntyre now says sanguinely of Aristotle's 'ill-founded exclusion of women, slaves, and ordinary productive working people from the possibility of the virtues of rule and self-rule' that 'later Aristotelian tradition' has shown 'how Aristotle's central theses and arguments are in no way harmed by [the exclusion's] complete excision' (1998d: xviii), I would add that this cannot be said of all of the central theses of that metaphysics in which Aristotle's ethics was 'ill-founded'. In this respect, the tradition still needs to rework its central arguments. I shall argue below that MacIntyre indicates how such revision should best proceed.

Social Ethics

Practices and institutions

It was in reflecting upon his own political and professional practice that MacIntyre developed his 'socially teleological' (1985a: 197) concept of a practice: 'insofar as universities are genuinely places of independent inquiry, the activities carried on there are activities which are worthwhile in themselves rather than as means to anything else'. And it was in contradistinction to another concept that he proposed that of a practice: 'the history and structure of a practice is never to be identified with the history and structure of the institutions which are the bearers of that practice' (1970b: 562).

MacIntyre formulated this general lesson about ethical practices and organizational institutions in the context of reflection upon the way in which his own intellectual practice was caught in the conflict between student radicals and university managers in the late 1960s. Given this genesis, it might be thought that the same kind of critique can be made of his sociology that he had made of Aristotle's metaphysical biology and philosophy of *praxis*: that it is an ornate conceptual scheme masking parochial interests. To think in this way would, though, be to ignore not only the uses to which he has subsequently put this distinction but also its prior formation in his own thought.

MacIntyre had criticized both 'bourgeois democrats and Stalinists' for failing to appreciate that it is 'logically impossible' for the state to 'control' art or science. 'You cannot make [artists or scientists] do art as you bid them or science as you bid them; for art and science move by their own laws or development.' To 'rescue and maintain genuinely free enquiry is in a class society itself a partisan activity' (1960c: 23–4). His partisan maintenance of his practice of free enquiry against both managers and Marcuseans was therefore informed by his revolutionary idea of self-activity, an idea in which he argued we all have a common interest. Assaults by the children of the privileged upon an imagined system of psychological control were an ostensibly revolutionary politics that he never took at face value. 'The children of those who define social reality in technocratic, bureaucratic, and academic terms aspire to a definition of human reality which will escape all institutional constraints' (1971h: 11). Such an imagined reality MacIntyre condemned as readily as had Hegel. Where he, like Marx, differs from Hegel is in denying that our actual institutional constraints are the only rational ones. His reconnecting of 'practical intelligence and the moral virtues' is intended to contest the 'exaltation of bureaucratic expertise' institutionalized by contemporary capitalism (1985a: 155).

MacIntyre's juxtaposition of practices to institutions separates manipulative from non-manipulative activities in a way that raises the possibility of non-manipulative practices being sustained and advanced even if their managing institutions are reformed or replaced. Institutions, with their formal rules and structures, are, he has admitted, necessary temporal 'bearers' of practices. Nonetheless, it is less the case that production (still less *excellent* production) depends upon managerial effectiveness than that managerial institutions are ancillary to productive and other practices. As a practice is distinct from its institutional bearer, it can survive the overthrow of that bearer and the creation of some alternative. Society's more elemental constituents are practices, not institutions.

The distinction between practices and institutions – unlike Hegel's distinction between state and civil society, or even Marx's derivative one between superstructure and base (ibid.: 61) – is intended to controvert rather than apprehend bourgeois and 'liberal categories of thought'. However, we might well think that it also controverts Aristotle's categories of technical and practical rationality. Aristotle contrasted practice not to institutions but to production and to theory. Indeed, he identified political

practice with its institutional bearers, the *archai* that comprise its constitutional principles and offices. To these considerable extents, MacIntyre's
concept of practices is unAristotelian.

Goods internal to practices

As MacIntyre says, the social logic presupposed by his moral theory contrasts with the metaphysical presuppositions of Aristotle's ethics. For
Aristotle, 'internal goods' can only denote goods that are internal to the
substantial being of some particular individual or, derivatively, to some
specific kind of being. Similarly, *energeiai* and *praxeis* are necessarily predicated of individual subjects or their species. In contrast, MacIntyre speaks
of 'practices' that are not predicated of individual beings but describe a kind
of relation between humans as social actors. Practices are functions of such
social relations rather than of individual beings.

   Such a concept might be thought to share less with Aristotle's idea of
action than with his idea of craft, in that each craft aims at a particular kind
of good that is irreducible to the wills or intentions of individual artisans
apart from their work as artisans. However, *After Virtue*'s concept of practices is clearly influenced less by Aristotle's account of craft production than
by Wittgenstein's anti-Platonic and conventionalist account of rule-
following and anti-Augustinian and conventionalist account of language
games. In *After Virtue*'s famous definition of 'a "practice"', it is:

> any coherent and complex form of socially established cooperative
> human activity through which goods internal to that form of activity are
> realized in the course of trying to achieve those standards of excellence
> which are appropriate to, and partially definitive of, that form of activity,
> with the result that human powers to achieve excellence, and human con-
> ceptions of the ends and goods involved, are systematically extended.
> (Ibid.: 187)

Among the examples of practices he cites 'are the enquiries of physics,
chemistry and biology, and . . . the work of the historian', but practices are
certainly not confined to the academy. He also lists as practices 'arts, sciences, games, politics in the Aristotelian sense, the making and sustaining
of family life' (ibid.: 187–8). We might regard it as significant, though, that
he chooses the example of a game, chess, to illustrate what he intends by
'internal good'. Long before, he had followed Wittgenstein in proposing
that 'what is true of chess is also true of morality', but what he then claimed
is true of chess was only that without 'an established and shared right way

of doing things . . . the notion of authority' is vacuous (1967b: 53). What he now adds is that what gives a shared way of doing things moral author- ity is its possession of an internal good; that the goodness of a practice derives from having standards of excellence that allow progress in both the history of the practice and in the intellectual and moral excellence of those individuals who adopt and pursue the excellence of the practice, enabling them to move from their prior, untutored condition to the actualization of their *telos*. Here MacIntyre does, at least nominally, repeat Aristotle's juxta- position of internal to 'external' goods. A child may be enticed to learn to play chess by the lure of candy, which is a good external to the game. By contrast, 'the achievement of a certain highly particular kind of analytic skill, strategic imagination and competitive intensity' and, more generally, of excellence in whatever 'the game of chess demands' are goods internal to chess as a practice. What is most valuable in chess, MacIntyre suggests, is not the production of wins, nor of such external 'goods as prestige, status and money' (1985a: 74), nor candy, and nor can it be the process of effecting any of these. Rather, what is valuable is the activity itself; or, to be more precise, what is valuable is progress in the practice, both collective and indi- vidual. The good internal to chess has been advanced by Wilhelm Steinitz, and further by Mikhail Botvinnik, and further still by Gary Kasparov, each of whom has achieved this by developing their own game.

The choice of a game to exemplify a practice with internal goods has been taken by many readers of *After Virtue* to indicate that MacIntyre's par- adigm of a practice is of something essentially unproductive, in the same way that Aristotle conceived *praxis* as essentially unproductive. Although a central argument of MacIntyre is indeed that practices are good in them- selves, and although this is a central reason why he already identifies his position as Aristotelian, a central argument that I wish to advance is that (even in *After Virtue*) MacIntyre draws no distinction between notionally unproductive activities and other practices. In this, his Aristotelianism differs radically from that of post-Heideggerians and (not just on their account) from that of Aristotle. Many of what MacIntyre calls practices are productive of what Aristotle himself would call 'external goods', products that serve the good of others.

The son of a doctor, much of MacIntyre's reflection upon the rational- ity of practice was conducted, in the years immediately prior to the publi- cation of *After Virtue*, upon the rationality of the medical profession. For Aristotle, that other doctor's son, medicine was merely a skilled activity that is valuable when productive of health in the patient but is of no good to the medic other than as a source of income and esteem. MacIntyre disagrees. For him doctoring is a practice with its own standards of excellence, and the meeting of those standards is as great a good for the actor as is the meeting of standards of excellence in a game, in politics or, even, in theorizing. Even if the patient dies, if the doctor did the best that could be done in treating the patient then she has done an excellent job as a doctor. Even productive activity can be good in itself and therefore of value to and in the actor, quite apart from the good of the product. Of course, the standards of excellence internal to medicine are standards set in actualizing the goals of the practice, but so too are the standards internal to a sport, a theoretical discipline, or politics. Just as with these other activities, so too with medicine and other productive crafts, to meet and sustain those standards is to act and practice excellently.

To say that practices have goods internal to them is to deny that their value is reducible to, or dependent upon, their location in any architectonic, hierarchical and politically teleological order, or to any more particular relation to superordinate activities, aims or beneficiaries. However, MacIntyre does agree with Aristotle that some activities are undertaken for the sake of others, differentiating between a practice and the exercise of a mere skill. 'Bricklaying is not a practice; architecture is' (ibid.: 187; he later confirms that building, too, is a practice). A practice is more than a particular skill and 'is never just a set of technical skills . . . even if the exercise of those skills can on occasion be valued or enjoyed for their own sake'. That said, 'every practice does require the exercise of technical skills'. Therefore, to engage in any practice one must go through the discipline of learning the requisite skills. Unlike Aristotle, MacIntyre does not contrast practice to production. What he does say is that, within a practice, 'technical skills serve' the 'goods and ends' of the practice (ibid.: 193). Bricklaying may therefore be regarded as one of the technical skills required by a social practice of building. 'The word "skills"' is used 'to lump together heterogeneous abilities and capacities' (1998f: 868), and those that are most valuable are those used in actualizing goods internal to practices.

Capitalist production requires technical skills, but MacIntyre does not describe capitalism as a system of practices. 'Put to the service of impersonal capital', work 'on a production line, for example', embodies 'means-end relationships' which 'are necessarily external to the goods which those who work seek; such work . . . has consequently been expelled from the realm of practices with goods internal to themselves.' Work is here, for workers, merely their means to 'biological survival'. To those for whom they work, it is the means employed in 'institutionalized acquisitiveness'. '*Pleonexia*, a vice in the Aristotelian scheme, is now the driving force of modern productive work' (1985a: 227). It is, MacIntyre has more recently noted, the 'character trait necessary for success in capital accumulation'. But 'the more effective the employment of capital, the more labor becomes no more than an instrument of capital's purposes, and an instrument whose treatment is a function of the needs of long-term profit maximization and capital formation', needs which 'impose upon capitalists and upon those who manage their enterprises a need to extract from the work of their employees a surplus which is at the future disposal of capital and not of labor' (2006g: 148–9). MacIntyre therefore still endorses Marx's critique of the means-end relation of labour to capital. Indeed, he has become more appreciative of 'the labor theory of value' (ibid.: 152), noting that both Aristotle and Aquinas 'held a version' of the theory (1988a: 199). But what now follows for MacIntyre from Marx's critique of capitalism's exploitation and alienation of labour is that such labour cannot be understood as engaged in practices with internal goods. And this, from what MacIntyre calls his Aristotelian standpoint, is what is most fundamentally wrong with capitalism. The way in which he had always sought to link 'evaluation and explanation' he now declares to be 'characteristically Aristotelian' (1985a: 199).

Although 'internal good' denotes a property of practices, MacIntyre's use of the expression indicates a deliberate ambiguity. What internal goods are internal to primarily is social practices, but they are also internal, in a secondary sense consistent with his 'core concept of virtue', to the narrative unity of a human life and, thirdly, to a wider tradition. Rather as with Hegel's project of dealienation through reconciliation of the individual to the social constraints upon her, MacIntyre suggests that the self's rationality and morality is constituted through and guided by participation in social practices. The goods internal to the practice of chess are goods internalized by chess-players, and in this way his sociological sense of 'internal goods' corresponds to Aristotle's usage.

MacIntyre's account of practices complements his social scientific and moral critique of alienation by elaborating upon its opposite. Where he had spoken of individuals' self-activity and of the intelligibility of their actions to others, he now talks of shared practices, of practical rationality and of actors' participation in such particular practices and their particular rationalities. As it is characteristic of a practice that pursuit of its internal good enables a person to give narrative order to her life, practices might be thought of paradigmatically as vocations. But this would be to go to the other extreme from regarding mere pastimes as paradigmatic. MacIntyre observes that individuals typically participate in a number of different practices. Jobs are centrally important practices to both individuals and societies, but they are far from exhaustive of practices. A person might well consider their participation in the practice of family life as more important and, very likely, a greater source of good than is their employment under capitalism. Even if someone is utterly alienated from their own paid production, they may not be alienated as a spouse or parent, or when participating in some sports team, or when participating in some other social practice. Alienation is real, but seldom as total as postulated by Marcuse. Insofar as individuals are *not* alienated – insofar, that is, as they participate in practices the goods of which they can themselves adopt, internalize and pursue in cooperation with others – they have resources to resist their further alienation.

Virtues as means and ends

In *After Virtue* MacIntyre defines a virtue as '*an acquired human quality the possession and exercise of which tends to enable us to achieve those goods which are internal to practices and the lack of which effectively prevents us from achieving any such goods*' (1985a: 191). Although he adds, in conformity to his 'core concept', that virtues also enable us to sustain both our search 'for the good life for man' and our shared tradition (ibid.: 219, 223), it is their importance for practices to which he accords priority. Virtues are 'those qualities of mind and character which would contribute to the realization' of 'some good recognized as their shared good by all those engaging in' such 'a common project' as, for example, 'the founding and carrying forward of a school, a hospital or an art gallery' (ibid.: 151). They are, it would seem, valuable instrumentally, as means to ends or goods internal to practices.

This ethical prioritization of practices was criticized by many, and in his defence of the book's argument MacIntyre found himself referring his critics to the secondary and tertiary elements of his core concept (e.g. 1984b: 37–8; 1985a: 275) in responding to their allegation that he could not discriminate 'evil practices' (cf. 1985a: 199–203). This is the problem of relativism. Having discarded metaphysical biology, human nature cannot serve as a measure. Nor can he yet deal with the problem as Aristotle did, by reference to an architectonic order which culminates in a final good and provides a criterion by which to judge the goodness of all subordinate aims and activities. Such an order he had good reasons to shun (as noted in chapter 1), first because Anscombe argues that Aristotle's case for a final end giving point to all subordinate ends rests upon a fallacious assumption that all ends *must* culminate in such a single end, and secondly because Aristotle's case for such an order legitimates exploitation and oppression.

If the standard of goodness is internal to a plurality of practices, then it is relative to each of those practices. Reference to the second 'stage' in his core concept, the narrative unity of a human life, seemed to allow no more than the 'provisional conclusion' about the human *telos* that 'the good life for man is the life spent in seeking for the good life for man' (ibid.: 219). But it cannot be even a provisional answer to relativism to say that individual man is the measure. MacIntyre therefore attempted to answer by reference to the third stage, 'tradition'. He could be happy that his theory provided no 'view from nowhere' of moral claims, but not that cultural convention should take the place of such objectivity. His aspirations remained revolutionary, and therefore what would do for a Gadamer or Burke could not do for him. Nonetheless, as we shall see, it was by increasingly locating his own concept of virtue within the metaphysical scheme of traditional Aristotelianism, by working back from the final ends of Thomistic Aristotelian enquiry to its first principles, that he was to find a non-relative measure for moral claims in that very metaphysical biology upon the rejection of which his original identification with Aristotelianism was predicated. With this increasingly certain but no less reflexive partisanship, his account of tradition was elaborated into a metatheory challenging the Enlightenment's epistemological pretensions. Its place as the sociological core concept's third element was taken by 'the goods of community' (1994a: 284).

MacIntyre's move in the direction of a robust account of the nature of human being and action is already evident in *Whose Justice? Which Rationality?*. He here subordinates talk of 'internal goods' to a new terminology of 'goods of excellence'. This expression clearly implies that these excellences, *aretai* or virtues are properties primarily not of practices as social phenomena but of their participants as individual human beings. MacIntyre's deliberate ambiguity in the older expression remains in the new but the focus has shifted significantly, from the sociology of practices, with goods internal to them, towards the logic of individuals' practical rationality as participants in such practices.

The later book again alludes to Greenwood's exegetical distinction between external and internal or 'constitutive' means to an end (1988a: 132), albeit in a way that is more equivocal and limited than that of the earlier book (and explicitly acknowledges the influence of John Cooper; see ibid.: 135; cf. Cooper 1975: 1–2, 7–8, 19–22, 81–2). As before, MacIntyre makes this contrast without reference to Aristotle's own distinctions between *energeia* and *kinesis* or *praxis* and *poiesis*. Despite its attenuated presentation, this omission is all the more striking in *Whose Justice?* given this book's exposition of his metatheory of the rationality of traditions' rival conceptual schemes, and his greater commitment to Aristotle's philosophy in rivalry to others. This book also repeats the proposition, first made in clarification of the earlier's argument, that the virtues are 'valued *both* for their own sake *and* for the sake of the *telos* (1988a: 111). They are valued both as ends and means or, he wishes to maintain, as 'constitutive means'. As yet, we might think, the idea of teleology has not adequately escaped such unAristotelian ideas as Dewey's pragmatist 'continuum of ends-means'.

Schools of excellence

What *Whose Justice? Which Rationality?* and numerous essays since *After Virtue* most importantly add to its core concept is explanation of the ways in which practices serve as schools of the virtues. Therefore, if their relation is to be expressed in terms of means and ends, we should consider practices to be means to the end of virtue and not vice versa. Practices are the shared activities within which individuals may find goods apart from and greater than those valued by their untutored desires and passions, and within which they may therefore learn how to advance beyond their 'untutored human nature' by disciplining those desires and passions and cultivating virtuous habits of intellect and character. It is no longer virtues that are means – even 'internal means' – to goods internal to practices but practices that are means to the achievement, the actualization, of the good life of human activity and excellence. Practices 'are constitutive means to the end of our flourishing' (1999b: 102). It might well be thought that this conceptual reversal makes good sense, at last, of the terminology of 'internal means'. If something is valued as a means to an end, then presumably its place might be taken without loss by something that serves equally well as a means to that end. This is one reason why it makes little sense to describe virtues as means to some other end, and still less if one adheres to the Thomistic and Aristotelian idea of the unity of the virtues. However, this is precisely MacIntyre's position with regard to the plurality of practices that may serve individuals as schools of the virtues. An individual may learn the same virtues through participation in any one of many different practices. We might indeed therefore say that practices are internal or constitutive means to the goods of excellence of their participants. Habituation into virtues is a temporal process, whereas, as Aristotle argued, the exercising of the virtues is something that is good in a way that is atemporal. We come to flourish by cultivating the virtues, but what human flourishing comprises is the moral virtues' active exercise.

If particular practices school actors in virtues that they may learn equally well in other practices, those particular practices also school actors in skills, standards and rules internal and specific to them. MacIntyre proposes that within practices the learning of skills proceeds hand in hand with the learning of virtues, not least because an education in self-discipline and practical judgement is likely to supervene upon an education in skill. It is 'through education into the skills and virtues . . . and through an understanding of the relationship of those skills and virtues to the achievement of the goods internal to [a] practice' that we 'acquire a capacity for becoming reflective about norms and goals' within 'a teleological scheme'. I do so by learning how to distinguish, first, between what my untutored 'appetites and passions' would have me do and what I would do if 'I were to do what would make me excellent in the pursuit of the goods internal to . . . the practices in which I am engaged' and, secondly, 'between what it would be to achieve what is good and best unqualifiedly and what is good and best . . .. for me, at my stage in the education of my capacities, to do' (1998g: 140; the same argument is made at 1998h: 121; 1988a: 30–1; and 1990b: 61–2). To learn such lessons is to progress as a practical reasoner. It is to progress in terms of technical skills and of the self-control and prudential reasoning that one learns through the discipline of learning such skills. It is progress gained through cultivation of the architectonic virtue of ordering and exercising one's own capabilities to a single good, through turning original aspiration into actual achievement, through learning how to cooperate with others in the pursuit of shared achievement, through learning to acknowledge the veritable excellence and authority of those from whom one learns and, therefore, through learning the virtue of justly treating others as they deserve on account of their own relative excellence and achievement. This, MacIntyre proposes, gives us an idea of authority as something other than successful power.

A good internal to a practice is 'the concept of the best, of the perfected, [that] provides each of these forms of activity with the good towards which those who participate in it move' (1988a: 31). In pursuing such a good, individuals better both themselves and the practice. Where Charles attempts to draw an 'ontological' distinction between the amoral and 'external results' of productions and the ethical and 'internal results' of actions, MacIntyre argues that it is precisely through subordinating their prior desires to the pursuit and production of goods that are external to the self but internal to social practices that individuals typically learn to become moral beings. Charles's ontological distinction repeats that of Aristotle but also resembles the Cartesian distinction of mind from matter, a distinction overcome in MacIntyre's Wittgensteinian understanding of 'the connectedness of the inner life and the outer'. More importantly, MacIntyre's account of the internalization of practical rule-following takes us a long way towards satisfying Charles's demand for 'a proper understanding of *consequentialism*' of the kind characteristic not of modern moral philosophy but of a teleological ethics.

Where MacIntyre agrees with Charles is that only its master craftsmen are likely to advance the standards of technical excellence internal to a practice. If a professional builder plays chess, he engages in the same kind of practical reasoning as does a professional chess grandmaster, but it is the grandmaster who is more likely to play a part in advancing its standards of excellence by, say, inventing a new variation of some particular opening. Conversely, it is master builders who establish and advance standards of excellence in building, and a chess grandmaster who dabbles by building an extension to his house will benefit by learning from the techniques and maxims developed by professional builders. As practitioners advance towards the concept 'of the perfected', whether that be of a house or a game of chess, that concept is itself further advanced, if the practice is in good order, so that practitioners always have a goal ahead of them. In attempting to achieve a good internal to a practice, a practitioner has 'initially to learn as an apprentice learns' from the standards already established (1985a: 258). These standards are those established by the master craftsman, the *phronimos* of a practice's particular kind of rationality. Although her innovation is more a matter of learnt skill and judgement than of individual genius, 'the greatest achievements in each area at each stage always exhibit a freedom to violate the present established maxims' (1988a: 31). It is in this unmanagerial way that scientific, industrial, artistic and other practices and practical rationalities progress.

Theory and production

Rather as MacIntyre relates the learning of technical skills to the habituation of virtues, so too he links intellectual with moral virtues. Whilst he agrees with Aristotle that moral virtue is learnt through practice and habituation whereas intellectual excellence is acquired through instruction, and although he criticizes those Renaissance Aristotelians who disregarded this distinction (1999a; 2006a), he has never revoked his claim that, as *phronesis* is both an intellectual virtue and a virtue of character, 'these two kinds of moral education are intimately related' (1985a: 154). What he calls his 'teleological' conception of practical rationality involves an account of practices and of individuals as practitioners, and this account of individuals as practitioners locates intellectual virtues, moral virtues, moral rules and technical skills in our lives as practical reasoners. It is through such an understanding of the relationship of 'skills and virtues to the achievement of the goods internal to [a] practice . . . that we first find application in everyday life for . . . a teleological scheme'. Practitioners 'become evidently, even if unwittingly, Aristotelians' (1998g: 140). Even though they may seldom, if ever, explicate their practice in terms of a philosophical theory, a teleological scheme is evident in practitioners' ordinary language as ' "good at", "good for", the virtue words, the expressions which appraise performance of duty, and "good for its own sake" are at once socially and semantically ordered' (1998i: 274). MacIntyre happily acknowledges that ordinary workers are often more aware than academics of goods of excellence, and that 'Aristotelian theory articulates the presuppositions of a range of practices a good deal wider than Aristotle himself was able to recognize' (1994a: 301). Whilst Anscombe describes Aristotle as the 'ordinary man's philosopher' (Anscombe 1991: 1), MacIntyre depicts Aristotelianism as the ordinary actor's philosophical theory and tradition.

As we have seen, MacIntyre's broadening of the concept of practices compared with Aristotle's own concept of *praxeis* includes as practices those academic activities that Aristotle counted as *theoretikon epistemon*, theoretical sciences. For MacIntyre, 'achieved understanding is the *theoretical* goal of the *practical* activity of enquiry' (1998j: 183). In *Three Rival Versions of Moral Enquiry*, he proposes that both Plato and Aristotle regarded philosophy as 'a craft, a *techne*'. For Aristotle, he notes, quoting the *Nicomachean Ethics*, ' "every good . . . is the *ergon* of a *techne*" (*NE* VII: 1152b19), and what a particular *techne* produces in those who practice it is some particular capacity (1153a23), a capacity to be achieved, as are the other end-products of any *techne*, only with true reasoning (VI: 11[4]0a20–1), which itself requires both intellectual and moral virtues'. He also cites the opening passages of both the *Ethics* and the *Metaphysics* to establish that, for Aristotle, 'the master-craftsman', the *architekton*, 'is the model of the person with *sophia*' (1990b: 61), and goes on to describe philosophy as 'the master-craft of master-crafts' (ibid.: 68; cf. pp. 127ff.). All of this is familiar ground to Heidegger and to those of Heidegger's followers who regard themselves as neo-Aristotelian practical philosophers. However, they draw the very different conclusion that *sophia*, because a *techne*, cannot be counted as practice.

In *After Virtue* MacIntyre criticized the 'blindness of Aristotle' which rendered 'invisible' 'the peculiar excellences of the exercise of craft skill and manual labor' (1985a: 159), even whilst himself insisting on a redrawn distinction between practices and skills. He later filled in the details of practice's widened scope, clarifying that, for example, both 'architects and construction workers engaged in developing good housing' are included within its ambit (1998g: 140). As the third element in his tripartite 'core concept of virtue' is now conceptualized in terms of 'the goods of community', we should not be surprised when he says that those practices which are 'productive crafts' are valuable both because 'the craftsperson is perfected through and in her or his activity' and because of their 'good product' (1994a: 284). Even in *After Virtue* he had said that the 'first' internal good of practices is that of 'the excellence of the products' (1985a: 189). Conversely, he rejects any purely utilitarian evaluation of those 'productive practices' which, he admits, suffered a 'lack of attention' in that book (1994a: 284). Practices are not to be valued only for their consequences, their external results, their products. They are also to be valued for their own sake. That is, social activities are to be valued when they are genuinely sites of cooperative activity in accordance with shared standards of excellence, in which individuals may learn and exercise virtues and not just skills, and in which they do so in actualizing goods specific to the practice. When this is the case, practices are to be valued both for their own sake *and* for the sake of their products.

Unlike Stalinists and many other of Hegel's heirs, MacIntyre does not pretend that moral and material development are bound to coincide in some 'absolute ideal' of actuality and rationality. It is perhaps here that we can see most transparently the moral point of the distinction between 'internal' and 'external' goods that he presents in 'sociological' terms. Our internal well-being is conditional upon our material welfare, but the former is in no way to be reduced to the latter and, whenever there is a conflict between the two, it is the latter, which is of merely instrumental value, that we should subordinate to the former, which is our *telos*.

Institutions versus practices

It is in *After Virtue* that MacIntyre most clearly juxtaposes – and opposes – institutions to practices:

> Practices must not be confused with institutions. Chess, physics and medicine are practices; chess clubs, laboratories, universities and hospitals are institutions. Institutions are characteristically and necessarily concerned

with . . . external goods. They are involved in acquiring money and other material goods; they are structured in terms of power and status, and they distribute money, power and status as rewards. Nor could they do otherwise if they are to sustain not only themselves, but also the practices of which they are the bearers. For no practices can survive for any length of time unsustained by institutions. Indeed so intimate is the relationship of practices to institutions – and consequently of the goods external to the goods internal to the practices in question – that institutions and practices characteristically form a single causal order in which the ideals and the creativity of the practice are always vulnerable to the acquisitiveness of the institution, in which the cooperative care for the common goods of the practice is always vulnerable to the competitiveness of the institution. In this context the essential function of the virtues is clear. Without them, without justice, courage and truthfulness, practices could not resist the corrupting power of institutions. (1985a: 194)

No such distinction is to be found in Aristotle. The distinction upon which this distinction in turn depends – that between goods internal and external to practices – is (as we have already seen regarding 'internal goods') indebted to Aristotle but importantly different from Aristotle's own, between goods that are internal and external to the psyche and character of a human being. The difference is, again, that between MacIntyre's 'socially teleological account' of the virtues and Aristotle's 'biologically teleological account' (ibid.: 197). Nonetheless, those goods which MacIntyre calls external – money, power and status – are amongst those that Aristotle, also, counts as external. (And, of course, this is unsurprising when we recall that MacIntyre's original motivation in elaborating his account of practices was to form the first 'stage' in his sociological 'core concept of virtue'.)

External goods are 'never to be had *only* by engaging in some particular kind of practice (ibid.: 188). If a grandmaster were to give up chess for building because he calculated that he could earn more money as a cowboy contractor than as an excellent chess-player, then he would be acting in pursuit of goods external to any practice. He would, thereby, be pursuing the goals of his untutored desires and foregoing his best opportunity of cultivating the virtues.

The most important difference between internal and external goods for MacIntyre is also one shared with Aristotle. It is that internal goods are rightly understood as good in themselves, whereas external goods ought always to be valued only instrumentally, as what MacIntyre calls 'external means' to the end of actualizing internal goods. Here, once again, MacIntyre draws upon Aristotle's critique of *pleonexia*, extending that critique from material acquisitiveness to include also greed for power and status. External goods differ from those internal to practices in 'that when achieved they are always some individual's property. Moreover, characteristically they are such that the more someone has of them, the less there is for other people' (ibid.: 190).

MacIntyre has said that external goods are necessary to institutions and that institutions are necessary to practices. Although the tension between goods internal and external to practices is therefore ineradicable, MacIntyre argues that, just as an individual should order her activity so that external goods subserve internal goods, so too should participants in a practice ensure that its organizing institution's instrumental goods of power and money are deployed in subserving the practice's goods of personal and practical excellence. The danger posed by institutions is that they will 'corrupt' practices by reducing them to the position of means to the end of accumulating power and wealth. Such is the position of practices under capitalism, within which they are subordinated to the bureaucratic institutions of state and corporation. So subordinated, individuals are denied opportunities to pursue goods of excellence, subjected to institutionalized demoralization and encouraged to believe that social interaction can comprise nothing other than a competitive struggle over zero-sum, external goods.

It is in his awareness that institutions, with their formal rules and structures, are necessary to practices (rather than in anything like Charles's championing of an account of the cognitive status of productive practices inferred from Aristotle against one inferred from Wittgenstein), that MacIntyre's 'Aristotelian' account of practices advances most decisively beyond Wittgenstein. Of course, what MacIntyre means by 'a practice' is not what Wittgenstein calls '*eine Praxis*', according to which any instance of ' "obeying a rule" is a practice' (Wittgenstein 1958: 81, 81e [§202]). We have seen that MacIntyre's definition is far more specific, and that, on his account, organizational 'institutions and practices characteristically form a single causal order' (on causal orders, see 1976a: 150–4). Such an account can withstand the anti-Wittgensteinian criticism (e.g. Turner 1994) to which others may be vulnerable, that they cannot explain how 'practices' are sustained through individuals' behaviour (which McDowell would likely call 'the illusion of a problem'; McDowell 1999: 193). We might suspect that the idea of a causal order betrays something of a functionalist model of explanation, but such a fear should be allayed by MacIntyre's consistent stress upon intentionality and upon conflict.

MacIntyre's idea of practices may owe most to Wittgenstein but it also shares much with Weber. Our institutionalized confinement within

Weber's famous 'iron cage' is formed precisely out of our commonly prioritized 'care for external goods [*äusseren Güter*]', a proposition which (especially if understood in terms of more specifically 'material goods'; Weber 2002: 123) is redolent of those that the love of money is the root of all evil and that the state's aim is to facilitate the accumulation of capital. As Hennis says, positivist sociologists fail to match Weber's concern with character, conduct and moral choice. In this, it is MacIntyre (especially in *A Short History*, and notwithstanding his own disavowals), and not them, who is the better Weberian. We may add that Weber, in acknowledging the historical specificity and contingency of institutionally formalized rationality, and of its manipulative and behavioural effects, shares more with MacIntyre's than with Nietzsche's conception of the nature of human character and activity.

We might again compare MacIntyre's position to that of Ritter, for whom ' "praxis" has reality . . . in its integration into the . . . institutional order'. MacIntyre's account of practice also integrates actions into a social order and, much more clearly than in *A Short History*, he now agrees that there is a single institutional order expressing a more or less coherent ethos, even if its ethics is justified only by a historical *bricolage* of moral theories. He *disagrees* in arguing that this ethos should be contested by a rival ethos of practices even though, except where it is unified in what he later calls practice-based communities, this rival ethos lacks the coherence of that institutional order unified by the state. To say that practices and institutions form a single causal order no more implies that there is no conflict between the two than does an account of proletariat and bourgeoisie together constituting capitalism.

Ritter, like Gadamer and Nederman, considers the distinguishing feature of Aristotelian ethics to concern the predetermination of individuals' norms by a unitary cultural and institutional ethos. This MacIntyre denies in his 'threefold' teleological moral theory and his core concept of virtue. For MacIntyre, Aristotelian practical philosophy is concerned with the rational determination of ends as well as means, and ends are rationally, cooperatively and progressively determined within social practices. Within practices, individuals determine what is good, deliberate about how to actualize that good, act, by repeatedly acting habituate themselves to act to secure what they have determined to be good, and thereafter characteristically act immediately to secure that good, and do so in resistance to institutional manipulation. It is in this opposition of practices to institutions that what MacIntyre has already said of 'Weberianism', of emotivism, of manipulation and of management gains its greatest point.

Compartmentalization and management

The institutions to which MacIntyre is most opposed are, then, those that correspond to the ideal-typical form of impersonally bureaucratic or managerial organizations. These involve the social structural 'compartmentalization' of different value spheres and moral discourses. This critique of compartmentalization continues MacIntyre's earlier, Lukácsian argument about the separation of the economic from the political. Liberalism's 'view of the world as divided and compartmentalized' reflects society's 'division and compartmentalization' (1968a: 132). He then juxtaposed a life 'split up into rival and competing spheres, each with its own set of norms', to Marx and Lukács' 'notion of a form of human life in which man would' achieve 'clarity about means and ends' (1971i: 66). He still now considers such a complete and unalienated life to be incompatible with 'capitalism', which 'provides systematic incentives to develop a type of character that has a propensity to injustice' (2006g: 149). To operate within such a compartmentalized structure an actor must compartmentalize her own life, and she is therefore likely to believe it appropriate to behave as one kind of person in the office and another at home. A compartmentalized society teaches that flexibility is a virtue and integrity a vice. A compartmentalized life is one incapable of completion.

After Virtue's critique of mechanistic social science informs MacIntyre's critique of 'the peculiarly managerial fiction embodied in the claim to possess systematic effectiveness in controlling certain aspects of social reality', whilst its critique of emotivism informs his argument that 'the manager represents in his *character* the obliteration of the distinction between manipulative and nonmanipulative social relations' (1985a: 74, 30). Although the 'role' of 'the manager' is that of the 'dominant figure of the contemporary scene', MacIntyre argues that what managers' 'claims to effectiveness and hence to authority' (and to 'power and money') constitute is a 'culturally powerful' 'moral fiction' legitimating their 'manipulation of human beings into compliant patterns of behavior' (ibid.: 27–8, 74, 86). Their exercise of such effectiveness should not, he is adamant, be considered a social practice. It belongs instead to 'the characteristic institutional forms of twentieth-century social life' (ibid.: 87). Their concern is not with goods of excellence internal to any particular practice, but 'with technique, with effectiveness in transforming raw materials into final products, unskilled labor into skilled labor, investment into profits' (ibid.: 30).

Ever since *After Virtue*'s critique of 'the manager', so-called business ethicists have attempted to defend the rich and powerful against its critique of corporate capitalism. Many of the books for businessmen and manuals for managers produced by this well-funded academic discipline are written in an idiom of ends, means and excellence, consistent with the institutionalized rhetoric of 'mission statements', 'human resources' and 'quality assurance'. Some authors describe this idiom as teleological and Aristotelian, and some (surveyed in Beadle and Moore 2006) have even cited MacIntyre in claiming management itself to be a 'practice' with its own 'internal goods'. Accordingly, a health care manager, for example, is committed not to good health care but to good management. We would be surprised if someone managing a hospital ward were not a medical professional, but, so the argument goes, we should expect the hospital itself to be managed instead by a professional manager, expert in the efficient use of resources. One does not have to be a Heideggerian to recognize here a substitution of instrumental reasoning for authentic *praxis* nor a Marxist to recognize the operation of ideology, but perhaps one has to be more than either a Heideggerian or a Marxist to recognize what is of greatest value in the Hippocratic tradition that is here threatened. But, to see this, one also has to see further than Aristotle, who recognized what it is to be a good doctor but did not allow that becoming a good doctor might make one a good human being – might, but need not. For example, Heidegger was himself both 'a very great philosopher and a very bad man' (2004a).

It is in criticizing compartmentalization that MacIntyre has clarified the 'crucial distinction between a virtue and a skill'. Within a compartmentalized society, each role has ends 'set to which the formation of habits are means. The virtues, as understood in the past, enabled us to identify the ends towards which good individuals are to direct themselves, and virtues, unlike skills, direct us only to good ends'. This is a distinction expressed in what MacIntyre regards as thoroughly Aristotelian terms. He goes on to say that it is in compartmentalized societies 'that virtues come to be understood only as . . . effective means to the achievement of [institutionally] predetermined ends, that is, as socially relevant and effective skills' (2006h: 117). Contemporary society shares too much with the kind of society celebrated by Homer and Nietzsche. In these new dark ages, where excellence is again equated with effectiveness but where power is newly bureaucratized, it is managers who consider themselves aristocrats.

Beyond Hegel?

MacIntyre echoed what Anscombe said about 'practical falsehood' when he described managers' real ideological and institutionalized power as a 'moral fiction', and *After Virtue* shared with Anscombe the idea of a single intelligible and non-fictitious type of practical reasoning. In the year after the appearance of the book's first edition, MacIntyre took what might appear to be the decisive step towards his famous metatheory of rival traditions of practical rationality. He contended 'that Anscombe, like Aristotle, has correctly characterised one centrally important kind of practical reasoning, but that what she treats as an erroneous philosophical account of practical reasoning – in essence Hume's account – is in fact a true account of another distinct type of practical reasoning'. We may indeed see here an anticipation of *Whose Justice?*'s juxtaposition of Humean to Aristotelian traditions. However, the contrast is as yet entirely continuous with *After Virtue*'s 'threefold' account of the logic of teleological justifications of morality, in that 'Hume's account' merely describes the practical reasoning of 'untutored' and unsocialized human nature. MacIntyre's contention is that 'Humean practical reasoning is what we all as very small children start out with' in that 'all appeal is to some "I want"', so that 'progress in practical rationality consists precisely in the transition from Humean to Aristotelian practical reasoning, from entirely personal contexts to contexts of practice'. (1982a: 301–2)

MacIntyre had always been impressed by Hume's empirical and psychological explanation of morality, but his use of Hume here is indebted to Hegel. Hume's practical reasoner is the agent of Hegel's 'abstract right'. Hegel's idea of ethical progress may be as readily understood as that of the maturation of an individual as of humankind. The progress is from the infant's abstract right of 'I want' to the adolescent's naive assertion of unconditional principle to the adult's acknowledgement of necessary institutional constraints, and from the comfort of the family to the alienation of civil society to the responsibilities of citizenship. In keeping with such a Hegelian narrative, MacIntyre still here understands teleology in terms of temporal progress. His understanding of the agent's progress from 'untutored human nature' via education in 'the precepts of rational ethics' to the actualized freedom and rationality of self-activity may be understood in Hegelian terms. The 'tutoring' of the individual by her relations with others, by moral rules, by practices and institutions is similar to the that educative process of socialization or enculturation which Hegel called *Bildung*.

Again, we might easily interpret MacIntyre's 'core concept of virtue' in Hegelian terms. If 'the narrative order of a single human life' corresponds to Hegel's moment of individuality, and if 'a tradition' corresponds to the moment of universality, then the intermediate place and mediating moment of particularity is taken by 'a practice'.

If we understand MacIntyre's treatment of Hume's account of practical reasoning in these ways, then we may interpret MacIntyre's understanding of the superiority of Aristotelianism as similar to Hegel's understanding of the superiority of his own position to that of Hume or Hobbes. And yet there are differences. Hegel tells a story of the history of philosophy that culminates in the maturity of his own system, in a way that parallels the sublation of Hellenism by modernity and of childhood by adulthood. In contrast, MacIntyre tells a story that culminates in the fragmentation, not the progress, of moral philosophy. Whereas in Hegel's history providence trumps conflict and universality sublates particularity, in *After Virtue* conflict is ineradicable and particularity unsurmountable. These, though, are not the most important of MacIntyre's differences from Hegel in *After Virtue*.

MacIntyre's most important difference from Hegel was his refusal of Hegel's postulation of a determinable rationality existing apart from the reasoning of individuals, of a final end standing above and directing the conscious ends of ordinary actors. He rejected Hegel's temporal and spatial extension of what we have called the functional model of teleology, an extension that presents the universe as a rationally organized totality. In this, he rejected what Hegel regarded as the great achievement of 'speculative', theoretical philosophy. Where Hegel claimed to perceive through the appearance of particularity and conflict a rational actuality of universality and harmony, MacIntyre reasserted the elemental reality of conflict and the secondary reality of its ideological denial. Therefore, whereas Hegel regarded the highest purpose of *Bildung* to be the recognition by individuals of that universal rationality, MacIntyre argued that moral education should prepare individuals for social and intellectual conflict.

MacIntyre became 'irremediably anti-Hegelian in rejecting the notion of an absolute standpoint' when elaborating his account of rivalry between traditions (1994a: 295). We may interpret both the metaphysics which he repudiated up until *After Virtue* and the Hegel that he has repudiated since in terms of the kind of epistemologically unchastened architectonic system once promoted by 'Old' or 'Right Hegelians', and which such post-Kantians as Pippin, Pinkard, Brandom and McDowell are now attempting to supersede, but we will below find grounds to question MacIntyre's continuing antipathy to Hegel.

Rival rationalities, rival traditions

In *After Virtue* MacIntyre raised the Marxist question of '*whose* will', the question of 'what particular and specific interests' are served by the ideologies he criticized there, but he added that 'to answer that question is not my task here' (1985a: 110, 24). The question is intended to unmask claims to moral authority, expecting to reveal not mere expressions of arbitrary emotion but real and cognizable structures of power. Accordingly, by the time of *Whose Justice?* MacIntyre's idea of rival 'practical rationalities' was accompanied by an account of rival 'forms of social structure' (1998h), one structured by goods internal to practices, the other by goods external to practices. External goods, in parallel to the book's redesignation of internal goods as goods of excellence, he renames 'goods of effectiveness'. He says of such goods what Aristotle says of skills: that they are potential means to either good or bad ends. Rather as Aristotle says that the exercising of skills tends to preclude the exercising of excellence, so MacIntyre says that pursuing goods of effectiveness tends to substitute for pursuit of goods of excellence.

MacIntyre's conceptual distinction between practices and institutions cuts across those drawn by Aristotle. That Aristotle's distinctions between *praxis* and *poiesis*, *phronesis* and *techne*, were rehabilitated by our post-Heideggerian practical philosophers we have seen. We could now add that this rehabilitation was anticipated in that distinction of 'substantive rationality' from merely formal, technical or 'instrumental rationality' which was postulated by Weber and later extrapolated by Marcuse and other members of the Frankfurt School (most of whom were, and are, happier to acknowledge the influence of Weber than of Heidegger), and that MacIntyre surely felt some of their influence (as well as that of Weber more directly). Like them, he had identified instrumental rationality predominantly with the bureaucratic state and managerial institutions of corporate capitalism. On his account, managerial reasoning is calculation about means to institutionalized ends. These ends are not shared by those employed in their pursuit. To manipulate someone is to get them to act for the sake of the manipulator's aims rather than their own. This is not to exclude the possibility that the subject of manipulation may also benefit in some way – payment – from what they do (as Kant said of 'mercenary art'), but it is to exclude the possibility that they will benefit in the same way as the manipulator, and it is to allow that they may benefit in the same way (and perhaps to a greater degree) from pursuit of the different aim of some other manager. What differentiates the directive action of a master craftsman from such manipulation is that the director and the directed share in the same kind of reasoning, act for the sake of the same aim and benefit in the same way from the actualization of that aim. Therefore, MacIntyre does not identify the technical skills internal to practices with the kind of techniques used in compelling others to act as one wills or in pursuit of such institutionalized ends as that of transforming 'investment into profits'. The latter kind of skill (of telling a lie convincingly, for example) is regarded as such because its exercise effects manipulation. The first kind of skill is to be counted such because its exercise produces goods internal to practices. Here we may note that MacIntyre would agree with Charles's interpretation of Aristotle's account of a master craftsman as engaged in the same kind of activity as an apprentice, and not of a manager.

A focus upon managerial institutions may neglect the extent to which capitalism can be understood in terms of individual demand and, correspondingly, the extent to which instrumental rationality can be understood still more in the terms of Hume than of Weber. MacIntyre understands Aristotelianism as a tradition of reasoning about ends as well as means, whereas he regards its rival as concerned with reasoning only about means to ends that are assumed to be beyond reason's reach. In *Whose Justice?* he acknowledges Hume as seminal to that rival tradition. Certainly Hume – like his friend, Smith, and like their follower, Hayek – well understood the instrumentality of civil society's structure for the satisfaction of what MacIntyre calls untutored desires. On Hume's account, an individual's ends are dictated by her pre-rational passions so that practical rationality is concerned only with the calculation of the most effective means to those given ends. On what MacIntyre characterizes as Aristotelianism's account, in contrast, an individual who learns the virtues rationally intends the ends of her action. This characterization of Aristotelianism is discordant with any imputation to Aristotle of an efficiently 'causal' alongside a 'teleological' explanation of intentionality (e.g. Charles 1984), and here we recognize the importance of MacIntyre's specification that what is distinctive to Aristotelianism as a tradition of both theoretical explanation and practical rationality is its first principle of the reasonableness of final ends (e.g. 1998j).

We may say, however oversimply, that MacIntyre's account of rival traditions of practical rationality presents goods of effectiveness and goods of excellence as the conflicting priorities of two such traditions. The one tradition allegedly privileges the kind of activity exemplified by the kind of competitive, manipulative and managerial relations fostered within institutions, whilst the other privileges that kind of cooperative and emulatory activity which MacIntyre says characterizes practices. The first encourages people to think of their relations with others in terms of power, influence and effectiveness. The second encourages people to focus instead upon the excellence of themselves, their colleagues and their products. Such traditions are not simply traditions of philosophical enquiry. They are, on MacIntyre's account, also broader traditions of social activity and of reflection upon that activity. As such, traditions are similar in conception to what he would earlier have called ideologies, denoting by this not simply false consciousness but a particular kind of shared consciousness that both informs a particular kind of activity and is informed by a particular kind of interest in activity. We might therefore consider Marx 'the ancestral begetter' (1985a: 110) of MacIntyre's idea of tradition. The tradition that dominates is usually that which warrants the institutionalized subordination of excellence to effectiveness, and of manipulated workers to managerial power.

It is in this way that MacIntyre combines the concepts of tradition and conflict into a single account of social reality. This account builds upon the way in which he negotiated the tension between *After Virtue*'s imputations to managers both of manipulative power and of actual impotence. He there turned, once again, to Marx's third thesis on Feuerbach. What Marx understood was that someone who wishes to manage others' behaviour in accordance with social scientific laws has to understand her own manipulative action 'as exempt from the laws which govern the behavior of the manipulated' (ibid.: 84). Now acknowledging rivalry between traditions of practical rationality, MacIntyre accepts that the tradition concerned with managerial effectiveness facilitates what he there called 'the application of a real technology' of manipulation (ibid.: 85). However, that technology is not warranted by any claims admitting of the same standards of falsifiability as natural science, and therefore such effective exercise entails neither that its own explanation of what is going on is uncontentious nor that its claim that there is no alternative must be accepted.

Each tradition is informed by a particular kind of social activity. What is at issue between them politically is which type of activity should dominate the other. However, one tradition's hegemony is now so great that its claim that there is no alternative is seldom questioned, let alone challenged. What is in contention between these traditions of practical rationality philosophically is the explanation and evaluation of individuals' social activity. The politically dominant tradition regards choice of ultimate ends as subjective, contingent and beyond the scope of reason, its conception of rationality applying only to the choice and use of means. For it, the most securely rational activity is that undertaken in accordance with bureaucratic procedures. The other tradition, on MacIntyre's account, maintains that ultimate ends are amenable to reason, as is the failure of actors to so reason. This Aristotelian tradition therefore renders some activity intelligible in terms of its own theorization of right reasoning and acting, some *in*activity intelligible in terms of the failure of actors' wills, and yet other activity intelligible in terms of what he continues to call 'mistaken' kinds of rationality that are 'made true' only by being 'embodied in institutionalized social life'. To this he adds that Aristotelians may apprehend more than their rivals by understanding the traditional reasoning of those rivals as a 'second first language' (1988a: 370–88), an elaboration of the tactic of immanent critique into a strategy that will, he hopes, demonstrate that Aristotelianism is the best theory of practical rationality so far.

What we might add is that, to operate within capitalism, actors pursuing goods internal to practices are obliged to understand the propriety of its contractual and procedural norms as if a second first language. If the goods of excellence are to inform their vernacular, then actors need to exercise the virtue of practical wisdom in judging when to speak in this and when in the language of official power.

Politics

Starting out all over again

A decade before the publication of *After Virtue*, MacIntyre was writing an abortive history of Marxist philosophy. Even when *After Virtue* itself eventually appeared, he described it as a product of his long-standing preoccupation 'with the question of the basis for the moral rejection of Stalinism'. His answer to that question, contrary to that of almost all other critics of Stalinism, was that Marxism's 'harm-engendering moral impoverishment' is due largely to 'what it has inherited from liberal individualism' (1985a: x).

For MacIntyre, Marxists' greatest success was 'in constructing an immanent critique [o]f liberal individualism'. Their 'concept of emancipation has had a purely negative content' and they 'have proved quite incapable of creating or even apparently of envisaging worthwhile human community' (1985b: 246–7). What is betrayed by reformists' account of socialism as 'state-sponsored planning plus automation' (1963b: 5), by Lenin's reduction of communism to 'Soviet power plus electrification', and by Trotsky's admission of utilitarianism, is a practical concern with goods of effectiveness to the exclusion of goods of excellence. What this practical concern in turn betrays is a failure of revolutionary theory.

This appraisal of Marxism informs MacIntyre's assessment of C. B. Macpherson. Despite saying that 'everything that he is against I am against too' and commending his argument 'that the modern notion of property . . .

is part of the individualist and capitalist conceptual scheme', MacIntyre attributes to Macpherson a non-' "possessive" ' but 'cooperative and creative individualism' that itself fails adequately to break from that scheme. Unfortunately, when MacIntyre argues that 'pre-capitalist concepts of community must be [crucial] for socialists' or that 'individualism is and always was the doctrine of successful thieves from the community', all that most liberals can hear is the word 'community' and not the argument (1976b: 178–9, 181). His critique of rights talk is not just of an abstractly normative individualism but of the expropriation and accumulation of labour's products as capitalist private property, and he seeks to build upon Marxism not just as an immanent critique of liberalism but 'as a body of theory designed to inform, direct and provide self-understanding in the practice of working-class and intellectual struggle against capitalism' (2006g: 157).

What was wrong with Stalinism is that it substituted the coercive and regulatory power of the state for the self-activity of workers. What is wrong with orthodox Marxism is that it sustains no objection to such a substitution. In criticizing Hegel for describing the state as standing above rather than being based upon civil society's system of material needs and private property relations, Marxism suggested that the state is no more than the instrument for the oppression of one economically defined class by another. Accordingly, when private ownership of the means of production is abolished, the state is supposed to become redundant and wither away. Control is treated as a simple function of ownership, and the absence of private ownership is therefore assumed to entail common control. Hegel's treatment of bureaucrats as a universal class standing above and apart from the particular property relations and materialist motivations of civil society, and therefore lacking any class interest of its own, was inherited by Stalinism.

MacIntyre *does* challenge the idea of bureaucratic and managerial neutrality. His conceptual opposition of institutions to practices and of goods of effectiveness to goods of excellence makes it clear that the state should never be substituted for workers' self-activity. Power corrupts and absolute power corrupts absolutely. With Aristotle, and with Weber, he speaks of our constraint by 'external' and not only by 'material' goods. And, with Weber, and with the Christian tradition, he proposes that we are constrained by the presence of external goods and not just by their absence. Such goods are properly treated as means and not as ends, but this is only possible when we have conceptualized an end that is better than the mere accumulation of means.

Marx never elaborated a philosophical justification for conceiving of self-activity as a good and, therefore, as a political goal, even if he originally criticized capitalism for its negation of such a good. Without a coherent idea of self-activity as the human good, and without a critique of power extending beyond the power of money, the expropriation of private capital can only result in the accumulation of state capital and therefore of bureaucratic power over ordinary actors. Any such revolution, however popular, cannot but be self-defeating.

Marx's mistake was, then, to reject philosophy 'at a stage at which his own philosophical enquiries were still incomplete and were still informed by mistakes inherited from his philosophical predecessors' (1998a: 224). Instead of completing his philosophical enquiry into the nature of self-activity, Marx turned his attention to that British political economy which treated workers' activity in terms of a brute 'labour' that is manipulated at will by capitalists and alienated from its human essence. After the eventual collapse of Stalinism, MacIntyre argued against those who claimed the triumph of the West to be a vindication of capitalism. 'Marxism was not defeated, and we were not defeated, by the protagonists of the standpoint of civil society.' Rather, 'Marxism was self-defeated and we too, Marxists and ex-Marxists and post-Marxists of various kinds, were the agents of our own defeats, in key part through our inability to learn in time some of the lessons of the theses on Feuerbach. The point is, however, first to understand this and then to start out all over again' (1998a: 234).

State power

The least bad kind of state, according to MacIntyre, is one that is small, tolerant and leaves local communities relatively free to organize their own affairs. It is therefore unsurprising that he, like many dissenters of the past, feels most at home in the United States. America is, though, only marginally less bureaucratic and paternalist than other capitalist states. Following Michels as well as Marx, MacIntyre observes that such states 'are oligarchies disguised as liberal democracies' (1998k: 237). He regards 'the contemporary state and the contemporary national economy as a huge, single, complex, heterogeneous, immensely powerful something or other' (2006i: 211). The state is itself a 'hierarchy of bureaucratic managers' (1985a: 85) integrated into the structure of capitalist civil society, its 'civil service' serving the accumulation of capital.

MacIntyre's critique of the state is sometimes characterized as instrumentalist. Insofar as this implies that he regards the state 'as the guarantor of individuals' [right to pursue] self-chosen goals' (rather than the guarantor of their capability to pursue such goals), such a characterization is not inaccurate, but it is incomplete. When such an incomplete reading is undertaken by a republican or communitarian who conceives of the state as a 'political community' of citizens, it can inspire an abstractly normative appeal to MacIntyre to put 'more emphasis upon [the state] as the site of their shared purposes' (Beiner 2002: 473). What this misses is that MacIntyre, like Marx, regards the idea of citizenship as an ideological mask, worn by an institution that is structurally incapable of admitting its subjects to the kind of shared reasoning that would be necessary for the formation of a veritably 'shared purpose' and 'political community'. The characterization is more seriously misleading insofar as it implies that MacIntyre, like liberals and others, understands the state as an instrument freely available for deployment in pursuit of any end that may be proposed. This has never been his view, and he has even criticized Marx and Engels for occasionally evincing 'belief that the state is . . . neutral as between rival classes and economic interests' (1963b: 6). As he has consistently maintained, the state is 'united in an indissoluble partnership with the national and international market'. It is therefore 'never merely a neutral arbiter of conflicts, but . . . acts in the interests of particular and highly contestable conceptions of liberty and property'. Besides having their own interests in status and power over their subordinates within and outside the state, its managers share a 'common need' with those of private corporations 'for capital formation, for economic growth and for an adequately trained but disposable labour force, whose members are also compliant consumers and law-abiding citizens' (2006i: 209–11). Such institutionalized interests preclude the state from ever becoming an instrument with which to pursue what MacIntyre regards as a veritably Aristotelian conception of the common good.

What is dangerous in the misconception of the state as either a communal or neutral instrument is its disregard of the state's real power to 'co-opt', to incorporate practice-based institutions into its overarching apparatus of social management and project of capital accumulation. MacIntyre's understanding of and opposition to the state's power to co-opt may be traced back, beyond his critique of Leninism, to his Leninist critique of reformism and corporatism. He followed Lenin in warning 'the working-class movement' against 'abandonment of revolutionary aims' and 'adjustment to trade union goals' (1961a: 21), even if he went beyond Lenin in applauding syndicalists' revolutionary aims of 'ownership by the workers in each particular industry' being '*taken* by the workers, not given to them' (1960d: 5). For all his hopes of the shop stewards' movement at the time of his expulsion from the Socialist Labour League, he well realized that things had changed since Lenin's time and that capitalism had 'learnt some degree of rationalization and of control' (1961a: 21). Against reformists, 'all the old Leninist arguments still apply anyway; but the changed character of state power itself is probably more important'. He realized that 'the extension of state activity into economic and social life', which was promoted by reformists, was causing 'a dissipation of the old unitary state into a multi-farious network of institutions' (ibid.: 23). The state and economy were already turning into a single, heterogeneous, immensely powerful appara-tus of management, and MacIntyre was already analyzing this social trans-formation. Even then, he observed that it is managers, not shareholders, who are the primary 'controllers of capital' and that directors' decisions 'are only part of a total process of decision-making in which the substance of power is widely shared' (1963b: 5). He quickly appreciated that the National Economic Development Council (founded in 1962 as Britain's forum for bargaining between capital's managers, trade union leaders and government ministers) was 'a model for the new bureaucratised corporate capitalism' under the conditions of a strong but bureaucratized labour movement. The state and corporate managers of this new capitalism thereby co-opted trade unions into 'actually helping to administer' capital-ism 'in a way that old style capitalists never could' (ibid.: 6–7). As he has verified since the defeat of social democracy, Marxist predictions have 'turned out to be true' 'that, if trade unions made it their only goal to work for betterment within the confines imposed by capitalism and parliamen-tary democracy, the outcome would be a movement towards first the domestication and then the destruction of effective trade union power' (2006g: 153). A politics that trusts to collective 'bargaining power' under capitalism is always likely to be determined instead by wealthy 'economic elites' (2004b: 216).

Functionalist ideology and conflictual practice

In opposing co-optation, MacIntyre has consistently rejected any attempt to pass off pursuit of money, power and status as virtuous promotion of the common good. He has commended Marx's critique of the idea of 'different classes in society as differentiated by function, each performing its cooper-ative part in producing a common outcome'. Despite criticizing Marx for retaining bourgeois categories in defining class in terms of legally private and alienable ownership of the means of production (and thereby allowing socialism to be defined as state ownership), he has never wavered in endors-ing Marx's critique of any such functionalist 'theoretical schematism' (1968a: 134–5).

When MacIntyre asks the university to 'justify itself by specifying what its peculiar and essential function is, that function which, were it not to exist, no other institution could discharge' (1990b: 222), he clearly suggests that practices may contribute to the common good of some wider community. Nonetheless, he rejects any positivist functionalism that attempts to explain human actions in terms of social functions ('one Jaurès is worth a hundred Durkheims'; 1976a: 155). This is perhaps why, ever since he first identified himself as an Aristotelian, he has distanced himself from John of Salisbury, who (as we saw in chapter 2) Nederman places at the centre of the medieval revival of Aristotelian practical philosophy. And, as we have seen, it was John's idiosyncratic way of providing a metaphysical and biological under- pinning for the social order of his day to which may be traced both our idea of organization and an influentially functionalist rationalization and legiti- mation of political actuality. This is not a tradition that MacIntyre traces.

On MacIntyre's account of the medieval Aristotelian tradition, one figure alone is utterly outstanding: Aquinas. MacIntyre's Aquinas is (like John) a defender of tyrannicide (1999a: 78), who also wished to subvert 'the incipiently bureaucratic extension of centralized authority and power' of 'the emerging nation-state' by posing, 'at the level of theoretical enquiry', an alternative 'set of legal, political, and moral possibilities for structuring communal life' (2006j: 50, 42). This claim depends upon a contextual reading of Aquinas which might be thought to make the best possible case for regarding him as a social critic (and for the University of Paris as an insti- tution sometimes serving the practice of theoretical enquiry as opposed to that of royal power), but MacIntyre's more elemental point is the familiar one that Aquinas' appeal to nature as a source of 'law' provides a univer- salist standard by which to judge the particular laws issued by temporal rulers. Aquinas provided philosophical premises for criticizing political actors and institutions. In his writings on politics, he was therefore able to avoid conflating rationality with actuality or providence with politics, even if, as I suggested in chapter 2, we sometimes find such a conflation in his writings. I also suggested there that if, as MacIntyre suggests, we should understand Aquinas as setting out premises for an alternative to the pre- vailing political order, then that alternative might be described as a com- munal functionalism.

Whereas Nederman accuses Aquinas of 'distaste for the mechanical arts', MacIntyre claims that Aquinas regarded 'education in the mechanical arts' as morally good 'insofar as it serves the proper ends of those individ- uals who receive it' (1998l: 105). MacIntyre refers to the philosophical importance of the institutionalized 'structure' of a craft in 'a craft guild'

(1990b: 61) but is too faithful to Aquinas to pretend that it prefigured that holistic social Catholicism which invoked his authority in organizing workers and other groups marginalized by capital, the manifestos of which were Ketteler's *Die Arbeiterfrage und das Christentum* and Leo XIII's *Rerum Novarum* (cf. 2006g: 148). MacIntyre's Aquinas is no such reformist, despite MacIntyre's own admiration for those Catholics who, like mendicants and Marxists before them, engaged with the real concerns of workers. Rather, Aquinas' social criticism is sharpened by MacIntyre into a revolutionary position. He is an antagonist of any 'fundamentally conservative . . . functionalist generalization' about social harmony and a protagonist of arguments that virtues 'are dysfunctional to and disruptive of certain types of social and cultural order', that 'the virtuous person may be committed to overthrowing rather than sustaining the established forms of social life', that 'the practice of the virtues is at revolutionary odds with those forms', and that even the Aristotelian 'virtue of *sōphrosunē* [temperateness], like other virtues, can be a virtue of revolutionaries' (1988b: 11, 2, 7).

MacIntyre acknowledges that 'possession of the virtues' is now likely to 'hinder us in achieving external goods' (1985a: 196), that doing well is likely to prevent us from faring well. If one is truthful one tells the truth, even though one may lose money or power or respect by so doing. One does not calculate what one has to gain or lose by so acting; one acts because one knows that it is the right thing to do if one is to avoid evil and achieve the good. Cultivation of such virtue is necessary to resist co-optation, and so too is cultivation of a fine sense for discriminating between the virtues and their rhetorical simulacra in others and, also, in ourselves. But this can only be a necessary condition of successful resistance, not a sufficient one. Were this sufficient to resist co-optation, it would have been neither St Benedict nor Trotsky who he extolled as moral exemplar but Robespierre (1985a: 256–63; cf. 1985a: 238; 1995: 227). Trotsky, we should note, MacIntyre has always regarded as such an exemplar, despite Trotsky's theoretical consequentialism and its misguided justification for lying, because of his lack of dogmatism, his resolution in pursuit of a good cause, and his willingness to relinquish power and withdraw into opposition with a small community of comrades. In comparison, Lukács, despite his superior theory, acquiesced in the practical suppression of himself and his theory. MacIntyre's message to revolutionaries, and to workers, and to moral philosophers, is that correct theory is never enough; if theory is to be vindicated, it must always be combined with correct practice.

Where once he had accepted, and even radicalized, Marxism's traditional account of the revolutionary agency of 'the dispossessed' proletariat,

MacIntyre now understands present socialist consciousness to be based in unalienated forms of life and practice that already possess some internal good of excellence. He once famously argued that 'the basic antagonism in our society [is] *at the point of production*', and that it is at this point that 'people are [most] formed in their social activities' and 'begin to act and think for themselves' and to 'react' against capitalism (1959: 99). In an important sense, he seems still to believe this. But his political point then was that revolutionary struggle should be based on the shop floor of capitalist industry, where workers are in direct and continuous conflict with managers over the control of their own labour power. Now, by contrast, he argues that it is where the social activity of production is free from capitalist management that producers can best think and act for themselves. Where this is the case, they are often motivated to defend their shared practices against the depredations of state and capital. In illustration, he turns to what his old comrade Thompson said 'of the communal life of the hand-loom weavers of Lancashire and Yorkshire', contrasting this with what Marx did *not* say 'of the militancy of weavers in the insurrection of the Silesian weavers of the Eulengebirge in 1844' (1998a: 231–2; cf. Marx 1975b: 202, 204; others have argued that this insurrection '"unleashed" in Marx' what became 'his definitive break with all the implications of Young-Hegelianism': Löwy 2003: 84). For MacIntyre, Marx 'seems not to have understood the form of life from which that militancy arose, and so later failed to understand that while proletarianization makes it necessary for workers to resist, it also tends to deprive workers of those forms of practice through which they can discover conceptions of a good and of virtues adequate to the moral needs of resistance' (1998a: 232).

State ideology

As MacIntyre has always argued, 'theories are themselves part of the social life which they attempt to describe' (1961a: 21). This idea informs alike what he says as a Marxist of ideology and as an Aristotelian of tradition. The liberal individualism of Hobbes and Kant, which he has always opposed, is 'actually embodied not just in the thought, but also in the activities characteristic of civil society'. This is why he persists in arguing that 'to regard individuals as distinct and apart from their social relationships is . . . not only a theoretical mistake. It is a mistake embodied in institutionalized social life . . . which cannot be corrected merely by better theoretical analysis' (1998a: 228–9).

Such a theoretical mistake is embodied in the modern state, which 'has to present itself' as 'an institutionalized set of devices whereby individuals may more or less effectively pursue their own goals, that is, it is essentially a *means* whose efficiency is to be evaluated by individuals in cost-benefit terms'. MacIntyre here says that the state 'is' such a set of devices (2006k: 163). Conversely, he later describes the state as 'presenting itself . . . as a bureaucratic supplier of goods and services' (1994a: 303). It *presents* itself as a 'supplier' but this does not entail that it *is* a means that may be used, either by individuals or electorates, in pursuing their own freely chosen goals. As has often been said, if voting could change the system it would be abolished, but for this there is no need because whoever you vote for the government gets in.

No one ideological mask is sufficient to legitimate state power. 'The state' is always a particular state, a nation-state, in rivalry and potential conflict with others, and states always require justification not only in terms both of rights and – however contradictorily – utility, but also of patriotic identification. 'In the one capacity it requires us to fill in the appropriate forms in triplicate. In the other it periodically demands that we die for it' (1998a: 227). Justification in terms of utilitarian effectiveness may take either a Stalinist collectivist or a liberal individualist form. Justification in terms of patriotism may take a communitarian or republican or more straightforwardly nationalist or even racist or *völkisch* form, and 'the philosophers of the *Volk* are Herder and Heidegger, not Aristotle' (1998k: 241). MacIntyre therefore endorses liberals' criticisms of communitarians as heartily as he does communitarians' criticisms of liberals. Even the American state is 'living out . . . a central conceptual confusion' of liberal universalism with communitarian patriotism (1995: 228). Because the state requires both of these two contradictory justifications for its legitimation, that legitimation, although usually effective, is always incoherent.

MacIntyre does not overrate the significance of this observation, as he follows Marx in recognizing 'how very little the exposure of incoherence generally achieves' (1998a: 227). What is important is the fact of legitimation, and that a successful ideology makes true what it asserts to be true. Contemporary liberals are more successful in solving the state's problem of political obligation than were Locke or Kant. They succeed in part because of their 'Weberian' acceptance of what they present as the fact of an 'irreducible plurality of values' (1985a: 109), allowing them to defend the state's incoherent admixture of contractarian, utilitarian and patriotic justifications; in part, also, because of their renewed ability (after the so-called death of Marxism) to represent 'the standpoint of civil society'

(1998a: 223) as one of individuals freely pursuing such a plurality of values, rather than as one dominated by capitalist acquisitiveness; and in part because of their rhetorical assertion that the contemporary state is both neutral and a democracy, and that the state's laws and policies should therefore be understood as the outcome of trade-offs between the plurality of its citizens' values and interests. What is made true by this ideological success – as well as by 'power and money' (2006d: 181–2) – is not participative citizens collectively ruling themselves but subjects attributing 'democracy' to the state, accepting that they are morally obliged to obey its commands and, even, to participate in its electoral rituals. Indeed, so successful has been contemporary liberalism that the idea of the good is now widely regarded as private and merely subjective whilst that of right has been detached from it and identified with the law enforced by the state, justice being equated with adherence to the state's procedures. Our only shared morality is that of acquiescent obedience to power, and what the powerful tell us to fear is any appeal to first principles or final ends. A more insidiously demoralizing ideology of passivity and manipulation is hard to imagine.

An Aristotelian politics

When he exposed the theoretical mistake involved in state ideology in papers in the 1980s, MacIntyre usually carried on to contrast the modern state with the Athenian *polis*. He has not drawn such a simple contrast since. 'The contrast has become one between types of social relationship which can be found in many different social orders, rather than one between the Greek *polis* and all other social orders' (2006h: 111). He has often implied that this change should be attributed to his reading of Aquinas and certainly it is strikingly made in *Whose Justice? Which Rationality?*, where he announced allegiance to a specifically *Thomistic* Aristotelianism. Having previously presented Greek intellectual history as a relatively simple progression from that of the 'heroic society' described by Homer to that of the *polis* as described by Aristotle, he now poses a 'division of the post-Homeric inheritance' between protagonists of goods of effectiveness – including Thucydides, the sophists and Isocrates – and such rival protagonists of goods of effectiveness as Socrates, Plato and Aristotle.

In *After Virtue* MacIntyre aligns what Aristotle calls politics with what he himself calls sociology (1985a: 148, 116). As we have seen, he lists amongst the practices that are basic to his sociology 'politics in the Aristotelian sense'. He has also told us that Aristotle's *Ethics* and *Politics* are as much concerned with how human action is to be understood and explained as with what is to be done. He has since proposed that Aristotle's 'error' in excluding women, slaves and artisans may be due in part to a false inference from empirical 'characteristics of the dominated' of a kind that is 'typical of ideologies of irrational domination'. The error is that of failing 'to understand how domination of a certain kind is in fact the cause of those characteristics'. This, it may be fairly added, is an explanation characteristic of modern sociology, with its understanding of the effectiveness of socialization, of nurture rather than biological nature. What MacIntyre might add to this is observation of a second error of Aristotle's: a failure to draw inferences from the truth of what he says of the importance of education and the harm of its absence, and, more generally, of the importance of 'external goods' – in Aristotle's own sense of the term – and of the harm of their absence. If 'the best kind of *polis*' is to provide a desirable model for an alternative to the modern state, then it can be provided neither by Aristotle's Athens nor even by Aristotle's uncorrected argument for a politics of goods of excellence. Rather, the best kind of *polis* 'would require a restructuring of' the occupational roles of women and artisans 'of a kind inconceivable to Aristotle' (1988a: 105). It transpires, then, that Aristotle's politics has to be corrected by MacIntyre's sociology.

Politics in the Aristotelian sense is, says MacIntyre, a practice. It involves 'the making and sustaining of forms of human community – and therefore of institutions' (1985a: 194), combining what Aristotle distinguishes as the productive process of making a political constitution and the practical activity of sustaining political order. What this does not tell us is what kind of institutions are to be made and sustained. Any nominally Aristotelian politics must be one that aims at the common good of the members of a particular political community, as Aristotle stipulates at the beginning of the *Politics*, but any number of different political ideologies, from across the modern political spectrum, would claim to aim at such a common good. Nor, given the foundational status of the *Politics* for modern politics, can this inconvenience be easily excused. Both 'the common good' and 'Aristotle' are names widely available for invocation. MacIntyre does carefully differentiate a common good understood in terms of goods of excellence from one understood in terms of goods of effectiveness (1998k: 239–43), but he is all too aware that offering one more abstractly normative and prescriptive theory is likely to achieve even less than does unmasking the incoherence of rivals. 'Debate and conflict as to the best forms of practice have to be debate and conflict between rival institutions and not merely between rival theories' (1990c: 360).

What distinguishes a veritably Aristotelian politics is, MacIntyre recognizes, stipulated less crucially at the start of the *Politics* than of the *Ethics*. This recognition, occasionally evident in *After Virtue*, is most unambiguously expressed in *Whose Justice? Which Rationality?*. He here loyally reports that politics was, for Aristotle and fellow Athenian protagonists of goods of excellence, 'a higher-order, integrative form of activity, whose *telos* was the achievement of a structured communal life within which the goods of the other forms of activity were ordered, so that the peculiar *telos* of the *polis* was not this or that good, but *the good and the best* as such' (1988a: 44). An institutionalized politics that really promotes the excellence internal to the members of a community is, then, one which orders all social practices architectonically for the sake of that final good. Having corrected Aristotle, MacIntyre adds that in 'the best kind of polis' this hierarchy must be 'one of teaching and of learning, not of irrational domination' (1988a: 106). To talk of a hierarchy of teaching and learning is to speak of an order within which those who learn participate in the same kind of reasoning and acquire the same kind of knowledge as those who teach. Therefore, political reasoning and knowledge are not the peculiar preserve of some distinct class of political rulers (and, incidentally, teaching is not the peculiar preserve of some distinct practice). MacIntyre's Aristotelian politics is a practice, but it cannot be a vocation in the sense that it is limited to a professional elite, institutionally compartmentalized from the rest of society.

The political good must be one common to all members of the community. In the case of a territorial political community, MacIntyre differs from Aristotle in holding that its members must be understood to include all of the inhabitants of that territory. This stipulation made, MacIntyre agrees with Aristotle's account of the best kind of *polis* that it is 'the form of social order whose shared mode of life already expresses the collective answer or answers of its citizens to the question "What is the best mode of life for human beings?"'. Such a rational social order comprises a hierarchical 'ordering of means to their ends, in which the ultimate end is specified in a formulation which provides the first principle or principles from which are deduced statements of those subordinate ends which are means to the ultimate end'. Various practices are 'integrated into an overall rank-order by the political activity' of citizens (1988a: 132–3).

We can see here how it is Aristotle's politics that corrects what MacIntyre now considers an error in the sociology he propounded in *After Virtue*. There he postulated an ineradicable likelihood of tragic conflict between incompatible and often incommensurable goods, so that there is an ineradicable danger that doing well will prevent one's faring well. Now, having divided the post-Homeric inheritance between rival traditions, he replaces the message of Sophocles with that of Aquinas. He retains a dialectical pluralism in writing of citizens' 'answer or answers' and of 'the first principle or principles', but his hope is for the teleological ordering of this plurality within a *polis* that '*already* expresses the collective answer or answers' to the question of what is good and best.

This Aristotelian and Thomistic revision of MacIntyre's sociology entails that goods and standards of excellence internal to practices may be internal, also, to a veritably political community. Such an institutional extension of the practical rationality of moral and intellectual excellence throughout society is possible only if two conditions are met: first, that practices are rationally and cooperatively ordered; secondly, that all individuals actively participate as citizens. Citizenship in this sense is not simply the abstractly and legally equal status that its name is now taken to denote. Rather, it is an activity of learning and of teaching, and of discussing, judging, executing decisions and – if, when and as necessary – of defending one's community. It is also an activity that is not compartmentalized from participation in other practices. Rather, one participates in political community by participating in reasoning about the good served by one's particular practice within the structure of goods internal to the entire political community.

Since correcting Aristotle on the inclusivity of political community, MacIntyre has corrected his own endorsement in *Whose Justice?* and *Three Rival Versions* of Aristotle's hierarchism. He now stresses our mutual dependence, so that relations between practices are not of the asymmetrical kind whereby one aims at the benefit of another without reciprocity. Principles of just distribution and 'just generosity' (see below pp. 184, 199) contravene the hierarchical order of Aristotle's 'for the sake of' relations, although MacIntyre persists in proposing the teleological nature of political order. The rationale, and not just the intention, of his politics is now that of a thoroughly inclusive common good.

Passive resistance and active projects

The question remains as to how such a politics can be practised here and now. How does MacIntyre propose that debate about the best forms of practice can cease being merely between rival theories and become 'debate and conflict between rival institutions'? What is to be done? Three answers will be offered.

First, one should refuse that minimal amount of participation which the state allows its subjects in the name of citizenship. This strategy of withdrawal was evident when MacIntyre declared that 'the only vote worth casting' in a presidential election 'is a vote that no one will be able to cast, a vote against a system that presents one with a choice between Bush's conservatism and Kerry's liberalism. . . . The way to vote against the system is not to vote.' Whereas liberals sometimes propose an obligation to vote, MacIntyre, taking seriously the fact of legitimation, proposes 'a duty to withdraw' (2004c).

This refusal of co-optation or 'collaboration' (1998c: 265) reflects MacIntyre's famous commendation of St Benedict's strategy of communal withdrawal; even though he can 'not see any prospects of overthrowing the dominant social order', he proposes that 'it ought to be rejected' and that 'perhaps it can be outlived' (1984a: 252). It also reflects his advocacy of a 'politics of local community' (1998k: 246–50). He denies 'that there is anything good about local community as such' (1999b: 142), but also identifies what can be good about it. A local network of social relations affords little room for duplicity. If one is an excellent person, one will be known as such. If, conversely, one manipulates others, then one will have a reputation for manipulativeness and will not be entrusted with power. Nor would such a person be trusted in economic exchange. At the local level, buying and selling can be a matter not only of freedom or utility but also of friendship and justice. Beyond locality, any norms of a just price or just wage are likely to lose their purchase. MacIntyre is not opposed to real markets, only to those metaphorical markets in which buying and selling is compartmentalized from other social relations. Against these markets, local markets should be protected. Politically, locality is important because it can afford participation in rational deliberation and decision-making to all. However, his recently repeated celebration of such goods of local community has been sympathetically criticized for, *inter alia*, replacing Marcuse's 'glorifying [of] sub-cultural elites' with a 'veneration of peripheral social orders', failing 'to contest the managerial view of the large-scale', and generally failing to make any satisfactory politics out of his account of practices (Breen 2002: 198; 2005: 497).

A partial response to such charges is furnished by MacIntyre's second answer, proposing that a politics of locality can itself create debate and conflict with managerialist institutions. 'Founding a community to achieve a common project', such as 'the founding and carrying forward of a school, a hospital or an art gallery', requires the cultivation and exercise of virtues by members of that community if the project is to succeed. It also requires the development of rules or 'laws' (1985a: 151). Such projects satisfy his criteria of 'politics in the Aristotelian sense': 'the making and sustaining of forms of human community – and therefore of institutions'. Such communities require cooperation between different practices. Practices he compares with 'more inclusive and relatively self-sufficient forms of systematic activity which serve distinctive human goods, so that the *telos/finis* of each is to be characterized in terms of' that good. For example, the practice of 'tree-felling' may 'be part of and embedded in an architectural project of building a house or a manufacturing project of making fine papers or an ecological project of strengthening a forest as a habitat for certain species' (1998j: 182). In each of these cases, the lumberjack's practice will be subserving some other and further good external to his practice. Strengthening a forest need not be a good external to the practice of a lumberjack, but MacIntyre is careful to specify a case in which it is. Or, at least, we might suppose that if the ecological project were one funded by government and contracted to the lowest bidder, then those employed to fell the trees would have their tasks dictated by managers and play no part in decision-making about the project. Under such conditions, we might say that the workers are simply exploited for and alienated from their labour. Under these conditions, we might suppose that they will be demoralized by their work and have no special interest in the success of the project or, therefore, in doing a good job. If this is so, the work will be of no benefit to them apart from their wages. They might still hone their skill in tree-felling but would perhaps be no better able to rationalize their doing so than to say that it would enable them to work more effectively and therefore, hopefully, earn more money in less time. If so, the cultivation of skill is as likely to be accompanied by the cultivation of vices as of virtues. Like their bureaucratic managers, their reasoning about their work would be primarily in terms of income and efficiency; even if less than those managers in terms of power, status, buck-passing and directing others' labour. All of this would likely be the case under present, compartmentalized conditions but, MacIntyre suggests, matters would likely be different if practices were ordered towards a project's goal so that all practitioners had a hand in deciding upon its execution. Under *these* conditions, all could regard the project's actualization as their common goal. He invites us:

> [to] consider, for example, the project of founding a new neighbourhood school. . . . Architects, construction workers, teachers and parents all have a part to play, so that the goods of architecture and of building, of education and of family life, all serve the common good of the children. Such projects characteristically founder when either those engaged in each practice have become so specialized that they are unable to cooperate except on their own terms or when administrators substitute

themselves for practitioners, imposing some bureaucratically acceptable form on the enterprise. But such projects do not always founder. (2003: 47)

To participate in such a cooperative project is, MacIntyre maintains, to engage in 'a distinctively philosophically enterprise . . . insofar as the conception of human flourishing that it expresses is articulated, so that it can become a subject for enquiry and debate by those whose practice has committed them to it'. Those who so participate should thereby be able to advance their own understanding of human flourishing and of how to rank-order different goods in their own life. This they can learn through practice, through mutual support and also and importantly through mutual criticism, but only if they 'find some institutionalized way of coming together that is generally not provided for in our culture' (ibid.: 48). The more we are able to integrate and order the different goods that we pursue in our lives, the greater will be our personal integrity. However, we can only so integrate our different goals if we can integrate the different practices in which we participate, and we can only do this with the cooperation of fellow participants. If, for example, someone participates as both a parent and a builder or architect or teacher in the founding and sustaining of a school, then they will have gone far towards overcoming the compartmentalization that is normally imposed upon us by our culture. One will, on MacIntyre's account, be subverting those cultural norms with a contrary, practical and philosophically Aristotelian activity and normativity, rather as, he has told us, Aquinas sought to subvert the norms and institutions of his time.

The making and sustaining of such a communal institution as a neighbourhood school would not at all comprise a politics in the Aristotelian sense if the making were contracted by government to some capitalist corporation, to be dictated by managers and imposed on workers and neighbourhood alike. Nor would sustaining the school comprise such a politics if it involved imposing a curriculum and a managerial structure on both teachers and parents. Although what is determinative here is not the funding, MacIntyre well recognizes that money is necessary to any such project. Being consistent in his criticism of the unjust maldistribution of wealth in our society, he is certainly not advocating self-help only for those who can afford it in the capitalist market. Here we may note that, before becoming a lecturer in private American universities, he was a tutor in a project greater than that of any neighbourhood school: the Workers' Educational Association. Education – whether theoretical, technical or moral – he has always regarded as necessary for adults, and not just for children.

MacIntyre has always believed that 'above all the task of education is to teach the value of activity done for its own sake' (1964c: 21), and that providing *all* children with such an education would be 'dangerous' to the dominant order. 'A society in which fishing crews and farmers and auto mechanics and construction workers were able to think about their lives critically and constructively' on the basis of such formal education 'would be a society on the verge of revolution'. However, he recognizes that to achieve an excellent education for all, 'we would first need a revolution to bring about the massive shift in the allocation of resources', a revolution against that partnership of state and capital which benefits from schools' production of compliant consumers. If, therefore, 'the prospect of revolution is Utopian, then [his educational] proposals are Utopian' (2002b: 15). He has added that such ideas are 'no more utopian than the politics of those who wish to influence the state' (2004a).

Local politics and practice-based communities

For such a project as a neighbourhood school to be pursued, resources may have to be obtained from the state. Therefore, MacIntyre's second answer to our question of what is to be done qualifies the first. What is crucial is that such means not corrupt the end, and he warns against any compromise of the rationally cooperative self-activity of practitioners with state or corporate power. 'Between the one politics and the other there can only be continuing conflict' (1998k: 252).

The making and sustaining of a school would constitute a politics in MacIntyre's Aristotelian sense if resources of money, power and status were subordinated to the goal of education, if the practices of parents, of teachers of various disciplines, of builders, janitors and others were also ordered to that final end, and if all of those involved in the project were involved also in reasoning about that *telos* and its actualization. In this case, MacIntyre claims, it would not only be the common good of the children that would be served, but also that of all of those engaged in the project, as they, too, would benefit from it as an education in the moral and intellectual virtues, and especially in that virtue of practical wisdom which must be constantly exercised in treating with alien powers. However, they would only so benefit if they excluded those who would corrupt or usurp decision-making about the project from their own cooperative deliberations. For example, in the case of a health project, 'physicians, nurses, therapists of various kinds, actual and potential patients and those who have responsibility for children or the aged' should all be involved in practical reasoning about the project; 'representatives of insurance companies or . . . bureaucratic managers' should be excluded (1999b: 144).

After all of this has been said, it remains the case that neither a hospital nor a school nor even Aquinas' University of Paris can be regarded as a fully political community in any Aristotelian sense. A fully political community would include some system of representation of all practices in deliberation and decision-making, would be self-sufficient and would determine its own coercive and property relations. If it were an Aristotelian political community, its participants would understand that 'justice is a precondition of practical rationality' (1988a: 129). If they uphold 'both justice as understood by St Paul' and by Marx (2006g: 154), then they may try to institutionalize 'a revised version of Marx's formula for justice in a communist society, "From each according to her or his ability, to each, so far as is possible, according to her or his needs" ' (1999b: 130).

A project is something far less than such a community, even though it too orders practices for some more encompassing good. That said, participation in any such project would provide a practical, if partial, education in how a political community might be institutionalized through cooperative ordering of the self-activity of its various members. If practices are schools of the virtues, projects provide the best schooling in how to order practices architectonically within one's community.

MacIntyre cites as examples unspecified 'alternative institutions' created by 'Thomists', which were 'isolated from the contemporary social order in an attempt to integrate intellectual, moral and social formation'. Although such institutions suffered 'real and seriously damaging' inadequacies, 'the moral' of such 'projects' is 'to re-embark on the task of creating alternative institutions, in which Aristotelian and Thomistic concepts are embodied in institutionalized forms of practical reasoning aimed at the achievement of a multiplicity of goods' (2006h: 122). That he believes it possible to subordinate goods of effectiveness to goods of excellence within an institutional structure that extends far beyond the local scale is evident from his allegiance over the past two decades to the Roman Catholic Church, under Aquinas' inspiration. In 'the Pauline doctrines of the church and of the mission of the church to the world' he finds the definition of a life 'informed *both* by the hope of the Second Coming *and* by a commitment to this-worldly activity in and through which human beings rediscover the true nature of their natural ends and of those natural virtues required to achieve those ends' (1998d: ix–x). More specifically, the Catholic Church has always been the single most important institutional bearer of the Thomistic Aristotelian tradition. Despite his criticisms of Protestantism, and despite his theological differences from other religions, he would presumably extend to many of their institutions the same dignity of subserving shared religious practices (for a more ambitious account of churches, as 'political communities', see Bielskis 2005: 145–62). We should note here, however, that religious affiliation can never suffice as the basis for any wider community. What unites any comprehensive community can only be a shared allegiance to a common good and not 'any notion of civic unity as arising . . . from some shared ethnic or religious or other cultural inheritance' (2006a: 39).

Less antagonizing has been MacIntyre's account of the family as a 'practice-embodying institution' (1994a: 290). The family's structure, he proposes, allows 'the kind of mutual trust that will enable our shared decision-making to be implemented in activities through which the common goods that give point and purpose to [it] can be achieved' (2003: 68). As such, it is the main institution within which most people experience mutually beneficial relations of giving and receiving and of critical scrutiny of actions and reasons. The principal criterion for judging those reasons and actions should be the common good of all of its members. But he knows that this is not always the case, and that the family is condemned by many as an inherently patriarchal and therefore oppressive institution. Even such 'practice-embodying institutions' are 'always corruptible and often corrupted' (1994a: 290); presumably, in the case of the family, most often by men's pursuit of coercive, sexual and earning power apart from the goods of excellence internal to family life. Conversely, the family may be the site of what others have called an ethic of care, and MacIntyre has endorsed such a characteristically female ethic in opposition to the idea of a masculine virility that has so coloured the traditional idea of virtue (1999b). Such an ethic exemplifies resistance to compartmentalization.

The importance of the family as an institution within which goods are ordered has decreased with the compartmentalization of the economy from the household. No longer is the household the basic economic unit that it was in the times of Aristotle and of Aquinas, and MacIntyre now warns of 'the imminent disappearance of the family or household farm and with it of a way of life the history of which has been integral to the history of the virtues from ancient times onwards' (1998k). Neither projects nor families are so self-sufficient that they can easily order goods in ways that resist the very different priorities of state and capital. More self-sufficient have been 'some relatively small-scale and local communities' based upon the 'communal practices' of 'some kinds of modern cooperative farming and fishing enterprises', although such communities are threatened with 'being reduced to the status of instruments of this or that type of capital formation'. When he declares that 'what is most urgently needed is a politics of self-defence for all those local societies that aspire to achieve some relatively self-sufficient and independent form of participatory and practice-based community and that therefore need to protect themselves from the corrosive effects of capitalism and the depredations of state power', it is likely that this urgency is due most to threats to social orders that already have a measure of self-sufficiency (2006g: 155–6). Whereas once, some farming and fishing communities were central to capitalism, they are now, indeed, often peripheral. They are threatened with the same fate as those 'Welsh mining communities' that, until recently, enjoyed goods internal to 'a way of life informed by the ethics of work at the coal face, by a passion for the goods of choral singing and of rugby football and by the virtues of trade union struggle against first [mine]-owners and then the state' (1999b: 143). As a social scientist, MacIntyre has always well understood such destructive processes (e.g. 1967b), but it is also as a moral philosopher that he understands their causes. It is undoubtedly important whether handloom weavers, farmers and fishermen own their looms, land and boats, but it is also important for defence of a way of life that that form of life is understood as ordered to goods internal to its particular practices.

Active resistance

We come to MacIntyre's third and final answer to the moral and political question of what is to be done. In our social order, institutions dominate practices. All that most people can do in their work is to try to engage in shared reflection upon the good of their practice and to try to act in pursuit of that common good in defiance of institutional obstruction. As MacIntyre has told us, 'the essential function of the virtues is clear. Without them, without justice, courage and truthfulness, practices could not resist the corrupting power of institutions'. So, people learn the virtues through participating in social practices, but those virtues need to be exercised if practices are to survive the temptations of money and power. It turns out that virtuous activity is valuable both for the virtuous actor and for maintaining others' opportunity of education into the virtues. The virtues exemplified in cooperative resistance to and subversion of institutional power MacIntyre calls 'goods of conflict'. 'To be good . . . is to be engaged in struggle and a perfected life is one perfected in key part in and through conflicts' such as 'those engaged in by members of some rank and file trade union movements, of some tenants' associations, of the disability movement, of a variety of farming, fishing, and trading cooperatives, and by some feminist groups, and on the other by those who are at work within schools, hospitals, a variety of industrial and financial workplaces, laboratories, theaters, and universities in order to make of these, so far as possible, scenes of resistance to the dominant ideology and the dominant social order' (2006l). The conflict between institutions pursuing goods of effectiveness and practices pursuing goods of excellence is not tragic or even dilemmatic; it is one that should be resolved by subordinating the former to the latter. Nor does MacIntyre just advocate 'resistance'; he also advocates, 'where possible, the abolition of institutions that systematically generate injustice' (2006g: 146).

Even though capitalism has issued not in socialism but in a bureaucratic barbarism, MacIntyre refuses to passively accept the domination of those who 'have already been governing us for quite some time' (1985a: 263). Although often accused of pessimism, he has always exemplified the virtue of hope. His is no longer a hope for a future communism, but it remains a hope for a future in which alienation will be overcome institutionally. This hope remains at one with that of Marx, in that such a future is to be brought about through the practical rationality and self-activity of ordinary actors. In this, Aristotle is corrected by 'Marx, Marx himself, that is, rather than those Marxist systems that have been apt to obscure Marx' (1998k: 251). Aristotle could never have accepted resisting the corrupting power of institutions as a justification of the virtues; still less could he have accepted as an aim the overthrow of rulers by workers.

MacIntyre's working class is not now composed of that socially divided but theoretically unified 'labour' regarded as a factor of production by classical political economists and, under their influence, by Marx. It includes many who survive on a wage, but also self-employed producers maintaining some control over their work by struggling against corporate forces and bureaucratic regulations. It is a class divided along those craft lines decried by Leninists. If such workers require 'a politics of self-defence' less urgently than do some local communities, this is both because their unions still afford some institutionalized defence and because their production remains socially necessary. Nonetheless, increasing managerial power and an increasingly flexible labour market are causing deprofessionalization, casualization, deskilling and demoralization of such practitioners. Too many practices are being derationalized and proceduralized. A politics of collective self-defence is needed, and such a politics requires ethical legitimation.

The conflict in which MacIntyre understands himself to be engaged is between rival philosophies of practice. The one, which he associates with Thucydides, Hobbes, Hume, Nietzsche, Weber and very many others, precludes reasoning about ends and is concerned only with the effective management of the many by the few. The other, which he associates above all with Aristotle, Aquinas and Marx, identifies practical rationality with cooperative activity in pursuit of shared and fully intended ends. Politically, the second, but not the first, aims at an architectonic ordering of goods for a commonly understood and agreed end. The conflict between the two he regards as irreconcilable.

In this, MacIntyre again disagrees with Hegel. We have seen that MacIntyre rejects Hegel's 'speculative' (or 'dialectical') sublation of conflict in rationalizing actuality as a universal and organic whole. We may now add that he also rejects the way in which Hegel moves from description to prescription, from functionality to agency, philosophical theory to institutional practice, organism to organization. For Hegel, the modern state reconciles Augustinian conscience with Aristotelian order, individuality with politics. The task of the modern state is to finally actualize the kind of architectonic and ethical order rationalized by Aristotle. For MacIntyre, such a project of governmentalization can only increase the management and demoralization of us all as ordinary actors. In the terms of Aristotle's metaphysical scheme, it reduces activity to process. Having explored (with Charles and Reeve) the possibility of ethical action supervening upon production, and having noted (with Riedel) Hegel's dissolution of Aristotle's distinction between the two, we should now acknowledge (with MacIntyre) the danger of that which Aristotle valued in action being replaced by that which he devalued in production. What MacIntyre would assert against Hegel's politics is that for an architectonic ordering of activities to subserve the good of actors, then that order must be informed by the discursive deliberation of those same actors. With Aristotle, and against Hegel, he would warn that the larger the polity, the greater the danger.

Before *After Virtue*'s publication, MacIntyre identified that conflict which he was soon to characterize in terms of rival traditions as one between rival views of consumption and work. 'On the first view my fundamental interest . . . is in how large a share of the product of work I consume; on the second view I can have *no* fundamental interest in the continuance of an order that represents work, interest and rewards in the way that the first view does.' If the first view is widely held, 'conflicts over interests will be local, manageable' and marginal. Conversely, 'if the second view were ever to be held by even a substantial minority of workers, then conflict between them and the managing and investing classes would be endemic, central and possibly interminable'. (1998e: 55) It is the second view that MacIntyre has since been elaborating. What his account of self-activity within social practices offers is a solution to Marxism's 'problem of justification' (Brudney 1998: 192–226) for revolutionary *praxis*. His justification for such action is not that it will enable others to flourish in the future, but that it enables us to work towards our own flourishing as complete and uncompartmentalized human beings in cooperation with one another. 'Marx's errors . . . were *our* errors and the defeat of Marxism has been *our* defeat' (1998a: 234). If that defeat is to be reversed, then we must reinterpret our activity within the world in order to change it.

Aristotelianism's Reformation

Teleology as narrative

The late twentieth-century revival of Aristotelianism has privileged what Aristotle said of practice over what he said of theory. In this, it differs from the medieval revival (and from that revival's early modern continuation) which privileged Aristotle's logic, natural science and metaphysics over his ethics and politics. In both cases, the privileging is due less to factors internal to Aristotle's corpus than to the intellectual preoccupations of the respective periods. The medieval revival of Aristotle's work had to accommodate it to a theological framework, whether Islamic, Judaic or Christian. These frameworks stipulated much about how one should live but less about how one should enquire into nature. Once Islamic scholars had demonstrated how to accommodate Aristotle to the theistic idea of Creation, the way was open to use him in filling in the detail. By contrast, modern natural science has seemed to preclude consideration of Aristotle's teleological biology. It has been claimed that the technical methods and mechanistic explanations of such science have 'discredited . . . "our shared portrait of ourselves as self-conscious creatures with . . . the power of reason" ' (1998f: 865, quoting Churchland), and it is in defence against colonization by such 'bald naturalism' (McDowell 1996c) that Aristotle's account of human affairs as admitting of a less determinate kind of knowledge has been rehabilitated. This is as true of the appropriation of Aristotle by analytic philosophers as it is of that by Gadamer and his compatriots.

Such appropriations often seek to ally Aristotle to Kant and to Hegel. We have already explored Hegel's importance for MacIntyre's approach to Aristotelianism's teleological ethics in *After Virtue*, noting that MacIntyre repudiated Hegel's functionalist version of teleological explanation according to which society is unified and history progresses in accordance with a rationality that is impersonal and universal. We have not yet explored how deeply MacIntyre has drawn upon Kant, even though we have noted *After Virtue*'s brisk dismissals of Aristotle's metaphysical biology and its invocation of Kant in normative condemnation of manipulation. Since then, MacIntyre has acknowledged that 'the social norms respect for which is a condition of shared rational deliberation [are] identical with . . . the central precepts of what Aquinas called the natural law and Kant the moral law' (2003: 68), and that 'distorted conceptions' of autonomy 'involve a repudiation of the Kantian standpoint just as much of the Thomistic' (1994b: 191). This he says despite his continuing opposition to Kant's moral voluntarism and political contractarianism. Earlier, he considered himself still closer to a Kantian standpoint or so, at least, it appears from a paper published in 1977, the year in which he 'began to write the final draft of *After Virtue*' (1998i: 268; cf. 1977: 43). Kant's *Religion Within the Bounds of Reason Alone* and writings on history are here described as presenting a moral theory with a 'teleological framework' (1977: 38). The *telos* at the apex of this framework is *not* that state of heavenly salvation for which Kant argued in the second Critique. Rather, the *telos* is perceptible in 'a crucial metaphor, that of the life of the individual and also [the life] of the human race as a journey towards a goal'. What is important in this metaphorical *telos* is the purposive journeying, not the goal. 'Human life is a quest', and this, we should note, is the same quest of which he speaks in *After Virtue* (ibid.: 33–4). There he calls the idea that 'a narrative quest' is constitutive of the good life for humankind 'a provisional conclusion' (1985a: 219); here he says that 'any attempt to specify the true end for man by describing some state of affairs, the achievement of which will constitute that end, is bound to fail' (1977: 38).

Unlike Lobkowicz, MacIntyre proposes that the paradigmatic description of such a 'state of affairs' was advanced by Aristotle. He then ridicules Aristotle's non-metaphorical specification of the human *telos* as a 'comic' creation of an 'upper middle class Athenian gentleman devoted to metaphysical enquiry'. Similarly unconvincing, he continues, now in concurrence with Lobkowicz, is the 'earthly Utopia' of 'the communist society that Marx envisaged at the end of history'. It is to any such 'understanding [of] the true end for man as a state of affairs' that he opposes his claim 'that the meaning of a particular life' lies 'in the agent's having traversed a course which is part of a larger moral history in which death and suffering are not merely negative deprivations'. One such 'dramatic narrative' is that recounted in 'the Marxist tradition': not its historical metanarrative of material progress, nor even its political project of 'building socialism', but the partisan narrative of 'the revolutionary proletariat'. This narrative can make sense of 'the struggle of the Paris Commune' within its 'larger history', motivating and explaining the self-sacrificial death of a Communard as a fully intelligible part of proletarian life and a heroic contribution to revolutionary struggle. We might say that a proletarian fighting on the barricades to save his Commune is as morally 'noble' as an aristocrat fighting uphill to relieve his *polis*. The justification of such action is not an ideal of some future state of affairs but the self-understanding of those already engaged in an actual form of life. Some such 'enacted narrative' is, MacIntyre proposes, what can best give human existence a moral meaning (ibid.: 38–40).

MacIntyre used the idea of enacted narrative to frame a practical philosophy that accommodated both moral imperatives and personal virtues. This framework 'restored' teleology but, he proposed, 'in a form very alien to . . . Aristotle's thought' (ibid.: 34). It had a threefold structure, albeit one different from *After Virtue*'s teleological justification of morality. The first stage of this earlier conceptual structure is 'the enacted narrative of the individual's life' which (secondly) 'derives its point from its place in the enacted narrative of the group or the institution', as the Communard derives his point from his membership of the Commune. 'And this, in turn [thirdly], may derive its significance from some more extended narrative', as the Commune derives its significance from its place in the history of the revolutionary proletariat (ibid.: 40). Although different from *After Virtue*'s justification of morality, we might think this threefold scheme similar to the book's 'core concept of virtue'. It differs from the latter in only two major respects. First, it is more subjectivist (and Kantian) and less sociological in its prioritization of the individual to what MacIntyre here calls 'the group or the institution' but in the book specifies as a practice. Secondly, in the book he replaces the vague notion of a 'more extended narrative' with the concept of tradition.

The 'tradition of the virtues' that MacIntyre champions in *After Virtue* is, of course, neither so Kantian in its philosophy nor so particular in its enactment as this episode in its conception might lead one to expect. The tradition's enactment is that of participants in practices, its drama that of the defence of practices against managerial institutions. Had he persisted in elaborating the argument of *After Virtue* as a 'left Kantian' romantic historical narrative written in postmodern terms, the book's significance would now be incomparably less than it really is. Instead, whilst rereading Gadamer (1980: 173), he returned to his own earlier, Aristotelian conception of practical reasoning.

That the young MacIntyre was regarded as an Anglophone expert upon existentialism and Heidegger we have already indicated, but it does not follow that he was familiar with the obscure texts and unpublished lecture courses in which the young Heidegger elaborated that interpretation of Aristotle which was later to prove so influential. It is therefore likely that it was Gadamer's use of this Heideggerian Aristotle that first suggested to MacIntyre the possibility of detaching Aristotle's practical philosophy from the universalism of his theoretical philosophy. Given MacIntyre's animosity to the latter (Gorovitz and MacIntyre 1976: 56–62), this was crucial for his characterization of *After Virtue*'s moral theory as Aristotelian and, therefore, for the subsequent trajectory of his thought. Unlike Gadamer, he has never supposed that Aristotle himself intended his practical philosophy to be independent of his metaphysical and biological theory, but detaching the one from the other – albeit, as we shall see, only temporarily – enabled MacIntyre to propose his own sociological theory of practices and institutions as an alternative basis for a 'teleological' and 'Aristotelian' ethics.

MacIntyre's early use of the idea of narrative was two-pronged, attacking the idea of atemporal objectivity in scientific as well as moral theory. He argued 'that it is quite implausible to give two different accounts of causality, one for nature and one for society', and it was in trying to find a replacement for traditional Marxism's nomological and mechanistic account of causation that he concluded that he must 'examine in depth the idea of historical narrative' (1976a: 139, 158). As he said later, 'any account of practical rationality which fails as a causal account fails altogether' (1988a: 125). Whilst his celebration of the particularism of narrative understanding and 'partisan' (1976a) explanation was gradually replaced by adherence to a profoundly universalist tradition, his theory of morally educative practices already supplied a robust account of what a Humean might reject as 'external reasons' for action (cf. 1983b: 116ff.). Such an account could, he argued, form the basis for an explanatory and normative social science that is defensible in terms that are at once Wittgensteinian and Aristotelian (1986a: 92–100), as well as for his core concept of virtue. In his further elaboration of that account, narrative has now been replaced by teleology and enactment by actualization.

A Thomist practice of theory

What remains to be told of MacIntyre's own story concerns his partial acceptance of that Aristotelian metaphysics and biology which, like post-Heideggerian practical philosophers, he had dismissed up to and including

After Virtue; a dismissal the progressive retraction of which we might date from the second edition's omission of the first's claim that his teleology 'does not require the identification of any teleology in nature' (1981: 183; cf. 1985a: 196). His increasing acceptance of a metaphysical and biological understanding of teleology might seem to lead him towards specifying the human *telos* as some state of affairs, but the narrative of this movement will not reach any definitive identification of a natural human *telos*. This is the case even if he is understood to postulate some *super*natural salvation. Such a postulate is fundamentally at odds (notwithstanding neo-Platonic and medieval interpretation) with Aristotle. Having, since *After Virtue*, reconciled his own 'Aristotelian' practical philosophy to an Aristotelian metaphysic he has expressed Aristotle's intellectualism as the position that 'all rational practical activity has as its ultimate final cause the vision . . . of what God sees' (1988a: 143; cf. 2006m: 210). For Aquinas, the final human end is not seeing what God sees but 'seeing God', which is possible only in another, beatific life. MacIntyre elaborates a historical narrative that identifies Aquinas as the executor of Aristotelianism's fully coherent synthesis with Christianity, whilst allowing that syntheses may have been effected with Judaism or Islam and that any acknowledgement of a supernatural end derives from faith rather than reason. Such a final end cannot be, as it was for Kant, a deduction from practical reason.

If MacIntyre was to establish that Aristotelianism is the best theory so far, he had to demonstrate that it can deal coherently and adequately with social and natural reality. He was therefore impelled to enquire into first principles in a way that he had avoided since abandoning first his Calvinism and then, if not his Marxism, at least what he indicted as Marxists' 'epistemological self-righteousness'. In pursuing this enquiry into first principles, he was soon to argue that human beings are 'culture-transcending rational animals' and that 'claims to truth . . . are claims to have transcended the limitations of *any* merely local stand-point' (1994b: 187; 1998m: 214). The first principle of Aristotelian enquiry is truth; not the truth of such apodictic foundations for theoretical enquiry as those proposed by Descartes and exposed as mistaken by the failure of the Enlightenment project, but truth as achieved understanding, as the goal, the final end, of enquiry, and as the adequacy of intellects to the object of their enquiry (1998j; 2006m). Accordingly, Aristotelianism may be characterized as the tradition most self-consciously aware of itself as a particular tradition aiming at universal truth. Long before he asked 'whose justice?', MacIntyre had learnt from Marx 'that there are no neutral standards to which appeal can be made' (1964d: 103) in the conflict between conceptual schemes, and that intellectual progress is therefore always progress from some particular theoretical point of view. Truth always requires that the propositions of a theoretical scheme logically cohere with one another, but truth also involves the correspondence, the conformity, the adequacy of an intellect to an object. This is a realist account of truth, according to which, he now says, 'the standard by which the truth or falsity of human beliefs and judgments is measured is provided by the things about which human beings form beliefs and make judgments' (2006m: 210). Although he remains too partisan to describe this as a 'neutral' standard, it is a standard against which all traditions must, in their own ways, measure the adequacy of their claims. Progress within a tradition of enquiry must involve progress in that tradition's ability to explain reality, and a tradition always faces the possibility of running into an epistemological crisis in which its protagonists find that their scheme is no longer adequate to explain its objects. A tradition that is in good order must be open to the possibility of its claims being falsified, and MacIntyre frequently calls for claims to be subject to empirical research. But his most emphatic point is that to ask, to quest after truth, is to presuppose the possibility of some true answer.

From this anti-relativist and anti-perspectivist acknowledgement of *the* truth as the final end and therefore first principle of practical questioning and, especially, of theoretical enquiry, MacIntyre strode into the metaphysically structured domain of Thomistic Aristotelianism. Viewed from outside, what had impressed him about this structure was the way in which it was formed from Aquinas's reconciliation and synthesis of two previously rival traditions. Such a process is what Hegel understood as the dialectical form of intellectual progress as such, and Aquinas demonstrated that it is indeed possible to combine rather than simply shift and replace intellectual paradigms. Therefore, even when understood in terms of rival conceptual schemes, intellectual history can be understood and intellectual enquiry practised in terms that are not genealogical but genuinely progressive.

The philosophical 'boundary situation' that MacIntyre presents Aquinas as having initially occupied he owed to Albertus, who taught Thomas to understand Aristotelian terms as those of a second first language (1990b: 114–15; 1988a: 168). Where MacIntyre credits Aquinas with having gone far beyond his teacher is in having melded Aristotelian and Augustinian terms into a unified philosophical language and coherent conceptual scheme. His achievement was to express the claims of Augustinian Christianity in the terms of Aristotle's metaphysics and the propositions of Aristotle's ethics in terms of Augustinian psychology, and in the process to resolve philosophical issues arising from each. Other traditions of enquiry came and went, but Aquinas was responsible for giving Aristotelianism a radically new, modernized lease of life. In the historicist world of philosophical traditions, this achievement immediately warrants Thomistic Aristotelianism's pre-eminence. At the same time, by raising Aquinas's Aristotelianism above the fray of other attempted medieval syntheses, and by adding that the singularity of Aquinas's success was not appreciated by his immediate successors, MacIntyre freed Thomistic Aristotelianism from culpability for the eventual failure of Aristotelianism as a scientific tradition. Aquinas's metaphysics of eternal and natural law made philosophical sense of theological truths about Creation, human community and our final end of salvation in a way that did not impinge upon the truths of natural scientific enquiry, precisely because it postulated truth as the provisional adequacy of an intellect to its objects and as a *telos* to be further actualized and *not* as some dogmatically given state of affairs. That eudaimonic or beatific contemplation of ultimate and unchanging truth which Aristotle postulated as the final end of practice, Aquinas defers to an otherworldly future.

Having entered the domain of Thomistic Aristotelian enquiry, MacIntyre's central concern is no longer to complete that metanarrative, *A Very Long History of Ethics*, which he has often joked that he was long engaged in composing, and of which a *A Short History, After Virtue* and *Whose Justice?* might be understood as successive drafts. 'An Aristotelian ethics presupposes an Aristotelian metaphysics', he now tells Gadamer (2002a: 169). His earlier dismissal of that presupposition he explains by admitting that he simply 'had not understood' it (1998c: 263); he had not yet learnt to speak in Aristotelian terms as a first philosophical language when he originally composed *After Virtue*. Now that he has learnt, he acknowledges that our understanding of our good must be informed by an understanding of our being, nature and animality. To his admission of error in dismissing metaphysics he therefore adds that he was 'in error in supposing an ethics independent of biology to be possible', adding to this that 'no philosopher has taken human animality more seriously' than Aristotle (1999b: x, 5). To reason metaphysically in Aristotle's terms about the good of any being or group of beings is to reason in terms of its specific *telos* and of its specific kind of flourishing, and whether some such individual or group 'is flourishing is a matter of fact and generally a very plain matter of fact' (2003: 33; that he would not now dismiss 'facts' as he once famously did is yet another mark of his Aristotelian realism). It is not a matter of fact that he considers to conflict with the empirical findings or theoretical claims of modern natural science. Indeed, he proposes that 'some kinds of rejection of Darwinism' (to be less coy, pseudo-scientific – and often Calvinist – creationism) 'that have flourished in some quarters very recently' are so discredited that they should not even be tolerated (2006i: 218–19). Biological science is a practice of enquiry with its own history and standards of excellence, and MacIntyre has no trouble acknowledging those standards. As standards of excellence internal to a tradition of enquiry that has proven the most adequate theory so far in explaining biological reality, MacIntyre is happy to defend the provisional truthfulness of claims that meet those standards.

MacIntyre is no theological foundationalist. He identifies the source of his moral and political ideas as a temporal tradition, not God. When he negotiated his reconciliation to theism his condition was the retention of a practical rationality free from divinely coercive commands (1986b). Nonetheless, commitment to a theistic tradition prohibited him from divorcing metaphysics and ethics in the way that Heidegger's neo-Aristotelian followers understand to be elemental for both Aristotle and themselves. For Aristotle, God is utterly separate from the world and *theoria* is therefore separate from *praxis*. Theism differs from Aristotle in postulating God as the source of human being and of morality and, indeed, of nature and of what is good and right by nature. This is what Aquinas theorized in terms of natural law. However, MacIntyre depicts Augustinianism as the heir of Stoicism and Cicero as much as of Christianity and Paul (1988a: 147ff.), so that natural law may be accorded a thoroughly philosophical origin. In striking contrast to this invocation of influence and the logic of tradition, MacIntyre refrains from referring to the philosophical authority of fellow Thomists. His regard for Thomist tradition is far less than his regard for Aquinas. He has always objected to 'degenerate modern versions of scholasticism' (1964b: 525), and continues to observe that there are 'many Thomisms' whilst referring back to their common source. Aquinas, he argues, should not be understood as some neo-Thomist epistemological foundationalist, theorizing nature as an objective source of constraints upon subjective action. Therefore, he has been prepared to look outside of such a circumscribed tradition, even to Lutheranism, for a way of theorizing a universalizable ethical demand (Fink and MacIntyre 1997) and an 'ought' of exceptionless moral principles of the kind that he once thought lost, but would now reintroduce, to modern philosophy.

Any attribution of authority to a theistic tradition is now widely perceived as dangerous (e.g. Nussbaum 1989). To this MacIntyre responds that faith is distinct from philosophical enquiry, just as it is from the enquiries of natural science, and that it should also be distinct even from political reasoning. The real danger is not in attributing authority to shared beliefs but in institutionalizing authority in any way that insulates it from rational enquiry or criticism. Heidegger, after his abandonment of theism, personifies for MacIntyre the political danger of philosophy, whereas Edith Stein represents its victims. That both theism and Marxism have proven oppressive in the past is no reason to reject them and to embrace a liberalism which denies its own theistic origins. Rather, past oppressions provide reason to uphold the virtues of practical self-activity and theoretical contestation against theocratic, Stalinist and liberal dogmas alike.

Biology and virtue

In now accepting some of what Aristotle and Aquinas said of metaphysics and biology, MacIntyre is certainly not dismissing all that he said before of 'sociology' and practices. What he now acknowledges is that what he said of these is compatible with more of traditional Aristotelian theory than he then realized, and that *After Virtue*'s teleological justification of morality and 'core concept of virtue' are enhanced rather than undermined by such acceptance.

When, in *Dependent Rational Animals*, MacIntyre prefaces his analysis of human flourishing with an analysis of dolphins, as another intelligent species, a central point is to establish the importance to dolphins of their social practices, about which, he claims, they too engage in reasoning. But normativity precedes reasoning. He has always been happy to describe humans as 'rational animals' but he now stresses that 'we are animals before we are rational animals and the initial source of human normativity is in our animal nature' (2003: 53).

In *A Short History* he had said that 'the choice of a form of life and the choice of a view of human nature go together' and that therefore we cannot 'look to human nature as a neutral standard, asking which form of social and moral life will give it the most adequate expression' (1967a: 268). This he would now correct by observing that there can be no neutral choice that an actor can make apart from and between rival traditions, and that what is mistaken in relativism is its failure to acknowledge the significance of the fact that all particular traditions of enquiry agree in making claims to a truth that is universal. As a Marxist, he emphasized, besides what he regarded as the historicity of human nature, its more elemental potentiality and basic needs (1998b: 45–9), and he now once again emphasizes both our natural needs and potentialities. The good of self-activity, of *praxis*, is a good for human beings as such.

Three Rival Versions of Moral Enquiry affirms Aquinas's identification of an accountable agent over time to be that of 'a soul-informed body', whilst still describing one's identity 'as a teleologically ordered unity' in the weaker sense that it 'has the continuity and unity of a quest . . . to discover that truth about my life as a whole which is an indispensable part of the good of that life' (1990b: 196–7). MacIntyre has since added to this theologized conception of a quest that the 'physical activity' of 'this soul-informed unity . . . is intelligibly structured towards the ends of the whole person . . . by the natural law, when the human being is in good functioning order', so 'that the person is enabled and empowered'. In so proposing 'the reality of a determinate human nature', he endorses the arguments of Edith Stein and Karol Wojtyla, John Paul II, as well as those of Aquinas, and can therefore be understood as arguing from within a veritable tradition of Thomistic Aristotelianism (1994b: 186–7).

For a human being to flourish, MacIntyre now specifies, is for her to become an *independent* practical reasoner (1999b; cf. 1988a: 138). In this, he follows Aristotle in identifying human flourishing with a uniquely human characteristic. Other species can reason about their practice, but what language uniquely gives us is a capacity to engage in higher level critical reflection upon our and others' practice and, therefore, to judge and to act independently. Such independence has nothing to do with Humean internalism, as MacIntyre remains Wittgensteinian about the publicness of language and about what he once called 'the connectedness of the inner life and the outer'. Nor, therefore, does 'independence' imply any Aristotelian self-sufficiency to the *theoretical* reasoner, as thinking is a social activity and as forms of enquiry and theorizing are social practices. He agrees, again, with Kant 'that thinking for oneself always does require thinking in cooperation with others' (2006d: 176).

MacIntyre argues against Aristotle (and in this differs from Aquinas; cf. Aquinas 1993: 236–51 [735–91]) regarding the ethical implications of our natural capacity for independent practical reasoning in at least one important respect. He had claimed in *After Virtue* that Nietzsche takes 'the name and notion of "the great-souled man" from the *Ethics*' (1985a: 117; cf. Kaufman 1974: 382–4; Magnus 1980), and noted that Aristotle considered the magnanimity characteristic of this noble man to be a central virtue (1985a: 182; see above, p. 27). Now such a *megalopsychos*, who is ashamed to acknowledge the help of others, he condemns as of 'bad character'. Such a man represents 'an illusion of self-sufficiency . . . that is all too characteristic of the rich and powerful in many times and places, an illusion that plays its part in excluding them from certain types of communal relationship' that are constitutive of the human good. (1999b: 127) This illusion, shared with Aristotle by Nietzsche, is such because the individual really owes their independence to others. One such debt is that their wealth is produced by others, but MacIntyre's point goes deeper than this. What he now emphasizes is that we are mutually *dependent* animals.

Human beings need the virtues, he argues, because of the kind of biological being we are. To become a freely willing reasoner, we require the generous help of others. We are not born as such reasoners, and nor is it in our own power to become such. We are vulnerable creatures, dependent on unconditional care from others for our coming into being and for long thereafter. Nor is this all. We require care and teaching from others if ever we are to become independent of those others and capable ourselves of independent reasoning and acting, and the kind of care we receive cannot but profoundly affect the kind of person we become. To become excellent human beings we depend greatly upon the virtue of others and upon those networks of giving and receiving within which we grow and upon which we are likely to depend again in illness or old age. If we fail to acknowledge our past (or present) dependence and our always present vulnerability, we are prone to fail as practical reasoners. This is why it is mistaken to regard us as distinct and apart from our social relationships and why we need each other to have the virtues, excluding magnanimity but including what MacIntyre calls 'just generosity'; 'just' because it is something upon which we have all depended, naturally, and which we should therefore extend to others. This is the kind of unconditional generosity that is commonly practised by parents – and, MacIntyre happily acknowledges, most often by mothers – towards their children, and sometimes by adults towards their parents, but it is a virtue that may be exercised much more widely and should be institutionalized politically (1999b: 81–123, 155–62).

MacIntyre chides himself for having previously disregarded the facts of dependence, but this is unfair. True, at the time of *After Virtue* – even though he acknowledged 'just and generous criticism' (1985a: x), as well as moral philosophers' neglect of the 'residual category' of ' "caring" ' (1982b: 294) – he was far from appreciating that which he appreciates in *Dependent Rational Animals*, but, as with so much else in his revision of Aristotelianism, we can refer back to when he was an active Marxist. Then, too, he combined his argument for free self-activity with recognition that 'the individual who recognizes his dependence on others has taken a path which can lead to an authentic independence of mind' (1960c: 24).

The argument of *Dependent Rational Animals* may be regarded as radically Aristotelian in the way that it links virtues to animality via the teleological concept of flourishing. To this, a post-Heideggerian neo-Aristotelian might object that, although its combination of theoretical with practical philosophies is true to the tradition of Thomistic Aristotelianism, it is not true to their separation by Aristotle himself. It might also be objected that the naturalistic way in which MacIntyre effects this combination offends against the way in which Aristotle argues for the superiority of the specifically human life of theoretical contemplation. Aristotle argues that the human good resides in the activity of contemplation precisely because this is the most uniquely human activity, distinguishing us from all other animals, whereas MacIntyre argues from the facts of other animals' practices and of our physical vulnerability to the naturalness of human virtue.

To ethics from nature?

It is commonly observed that 'the Aristotle of tradition was committed to a historically invariant account of proper human functioning' (O'Neill 1996: 14), and Bernard Williams has imputed to the Aristotle of history a naturalistic foundationalism (Williams 1985). Martha Nussbaum has combined such an 'Aristotelian' and universalist conception of human 'functioning' with a moderate moral particularism (Nussbaum 1986; 1995; and 2001: 290–306). MacIntyre's stress on the importance of recognizing our animality and, consequently, our potentialities, vulnerabilities, essential functions and universal human needs, such as our need for external goods, matches themes basic to Nussbaum, including themes in which she acknowledges that Stoicism cannot substitute for Aristotle (e.g. Nussbaum 2001: xxii–xxiv) and in which she, too, identifies with 'the Aristotelian/ Marxian idea of truly human functioning' (Nussbaum 1998: 283). She has now retreated from this Aristotelian/Marxian idea to what she presents as a more liberal and permissive 'capabilities approach', and criticizes MacIntyre for not having done likewise. To prioritize capabilities over 'truly human functioning' is, of course, to abandon the Aristotelian prioritization of actuality to potentiality.

MacIntyre's philosophical ambition remains the Aristotelian/Marxian one of an 'ethics and politics [that] are explanatory as well as prescriptive', and in which 'the soundness of prescriptive claims depends in key part on the success of . . . explanatory claims'. His 'Aristotelian ethics is naturalistic' in the sense that 'its conception of human goods and human flourishing finds application within an explanatory scheme of cause and effect'. 'This causality is to be understood in terms of Aristotle's fourfold classification of causes', so that final and formal causality may be understood in distinction from the nomological heuristic of scientific enquiry into material and efficient causality. His naturalism is not of the kind imputed to Aristotle by Williams, and he intends his Aristotelian 'ethics and politics' to be 'vulnerable to refutation by empirical findings of the psychological and social sciences, and, where they are relevant, of biological science' (2005: 204–5).

MacIntyre argues that different cultures' norms are subject to identical natural constraints so that, for example, 'within many languages-in-use color vocabularies have developed in remarkably uniform and systematic patterns, patterns which reflect the social use of discriminations made possible by the physics and neurophysiology of color vision' (2006n: 47). The practice of painting is therefore constrained by the nature of our perceptual capacities, as well as by the nature of objects perceived (cf. Charles 2000: 130–5, 370; 2003: 105ff.). It is also constrained by the natural capacities of the materials used, as is the similarly productive practice of Aristotle's master builder (cf. Charles 2003: 112–14, 118–120). MacIntyre therefore argues that 'criteria for the identity of practices are in important respects transcultural' (2006n: 47). Nonetheless, standards of 'aesthetic evaluation' as well as of 'artistic practice' are advanced 'from *within* the practice of painting' (ibid.: 47–8; cf. Charles 2003: 120–3). These are goods internal and particular to the practice. It is not at all the case that these goods are simply given by and deducible from our nature, but culturally and historically specific understandings of goods are nonetheless constrained by a universal human nature. Reality limits incommensurability, and MacIntyre's ethics is now informed by a robust philosophical realism.

To practice from theory?

Even if Gadamer's use of a Heideggerian Aristotle suggested to MacIntyre the possibility of detaching Aristotle's practical philosophy from the universalism of his theoretical philosophy, MacIntyre has nonetheless never interpreted Aristotle's own practical philosophy as predicated upon any radical division from his theoretical philosophy. 'What ethics is about', on Aristotle's account, according to MacIntyre, is 'the education of the passions into conformity with pursuit of what theoretical reasoning identifies as the *telos* and practical reasoning as the right action to do in each particular time and place' (1985a: 162). In this way, the particular is informed by the universal, action by truth.

It is not only post-Heideggerian commentators upon Aristotle who object to MacIntyre's interpretation. *Whose Justice?* has been accused by

Sarah Broadie of advancing a 'Grand End theory' of the human good (Broadie 1991), supported by a 'Grand End interpretation' of Aristotle's account of practical wisdom (Broadie 1998). On Broadie's account of this Grand End view, the function of action is reduced to the production of a human *telos* specified by theory. As MacIntyre notes (2006a: 22–6), her critique of such a theory and interpretation is supported by John McDowell. Indeed, McDowell goes further. He criticizes not only the comprehensive grandness of such an end or technical ' "blueprint" ' but also the deductive and deliberative end-means reasoning that it involves, and which Broadie retains in her more pluralistic account of ends (McDowell 1996b; cf. Whiting 2002). As noted in chapter 1, McDowell, like our German practical philosophers, would (now, even more clearly than earlier; cf. McDowell 1998c: 66) have us draw the sharpest of distinctions between practical and productive reasoning. In productive reasoning 'deliberation is such as to be *effective*' in achieving 'the proposed end', so that we can 'exploit the idea of effectiveness to explain excellence' (McDowell 1996b: 20–1), whereas excellence in practical reasoning has nothing to do with effecting any end. Therefore, in maintaining the importance of 'deductive arguments employed in deliberation' about means to the end that is the human good, MacIntyre's 'Aristotle [is] seriously at odds with McDowell's Aristotle' (1997: 242).

Does, then, MacIntyre now understand the human *telos* as a 'state of affairs' to be effected? Certainly he denies that a human *telos* can be just anything and affirms that constraints upon practical rationality can be specified by theory and by science; ' "Ensure that children . . . receive adequate iodine" is now . . . a moral imperative' (1998f: 865). However, in responding to Broadie's charge he says that theory's job is only the 'justification' of practice and that theory's retrospective 'deduction can never take the place of the exercise of *phronesis*' (2006a: 37). What theory can posit is:

> an outline sketch of what it would be for any rational animal to achieve its specific good, constructing by dialectical argument an account of what *eudaimonia* cannot consist in, that is, in such lives as the life of money-making, the life of sensual pleasure, or the life for which political honor is a sufficient end, and what it must be, a life of activities that give expression to the several moral and intellectual virtues, a life of friendships and of engagement in political activity, a life that moves towards a perfected understanding of that life and of its place in the universe. What such philosophical enquiry also constructs is a specification of the forms of deductive argument by which we would, if everything relevant to our judgments, passions and actions were made explicit, move from premises

concerning the nature of the good life for rational animals and the function of the virtues in achieving the ends of such a life through intermediate steps concerning what particular virtues require in particular types
of circumstance to ultimate conclusions about what it is good and best
for me to do in these circumstances here and now. (Ibid.: 35–6)

Reasoning about our lives as human beings and about the place in our
lives of various practices is primarily dialectical, and such reasoning is best
conducted with others from whose experience, ideas and judgement we can
learn in forming our own. Anyone engages in moral enquiry who articulates 'the rational grounds for her or his rank ordering of goods in this way
rather than that'. Such a 'rational moral agent' becomes 'a moral and political philosopher' insofar as they find they need to 'justify some conception
of the human good' in order to justify their action, and such a conception
serves 'as the terminus for the rational justification of practical judgment
and action' (ibid.: 35–7). That there is such a final end is the first, theoretical
principle of Aristotelian practical reasoning. MacIntyre does not shy from
specifying further principles. 'Goods have to be rank ordered in at least three
ways', he says. One of these ways has already been adequately discussed:
that of the ordering of external to internal goods, of activities that are only
good instrumentally to activities that are good in themselves. Secondly,
there is more conditional judgement about what 'it is here and now open to
me to achieve. That will depend in key part on my particular talents, opportunities, and responsibilities.' Thirdly, there is judgement about the different
activities in which one and the same individual should engage at different
stages in their lives (2003: 34). The latter two forms of argument might be
thought to provide reasons why the human *telos* should not be conceived as
a single 'state of affairs', as individuals occupy different places within networks of giving and receiving both from one another and at different ages.
But MacIntyre has moved on from 1977's denunciation of any but a
metaphorical *telos*, and even from *After Virtue*'s 'provisional conclusion' that
the good life is one spent in pursuit of some ever elusive, grail-like conception of the human good. Now he criticizes Lacan for 'the fantasy of an
impossible quest for finality of achievement, in which it is of crucial importance that the attainment of any final end should be rendered impossible'
(2004d: 33). It would be wrong for any philosopher to claim the last word
about the human good, but it does not follow that there is no truth about
the human good to be discovered or that we cannot judge our progress
towards its specification. Crucially, such progress is something in which all
can participate who engage in moral enquiry about their own lives, and such
specification is not something which can be a compartmentalized preserve

of professional philosophers. Against the intellectualist conceit that the good life is the life devoted to philosophy for its own sake, MacIntyre objects that 'Aristotle's conception of the activity of *theória* as that which completes and perfects a human life is open to radical criticism' (2004d: 33–4). Truth is 'constitutive of the human good' but it may be attained through both 'practical and theoretical enquiry', so that 'all human beings "are in some sense philosophers"' (2006m: 215, 212–13, quoting *Fides et Ratio*).

Second nature

MacIntyre's Aristotelian attempt to combine the philosophy of mind and action with ethics and a type of naturalism may be compared with that of McDowell (who was, like MacIntyre, brought up in something of a cultural 'boundary situation' and then trained in classics), just as his interpretation of Aristotle can be compared with 'McDowell's Aristotle'. But McDowell shares more with Gadamer, philosophically and interpretively. Like Gadamer, he urges us to read Aristotle through a Hegelianized Kant. His 'invocation of tradition' in his major work, *Mind and World*, 'was inspired by Gadamer' (McDowell 2002b: 173) and this invocation was, indeed, of something unitary, pre-philosophical and cultural. More importantly, he resembles Gadamer in the way in which he uses Aristotle's account of *phronesis* as a base from which to strike deep into the territory of theoretical philosophy. Although he makes far less of Kant's third *Critique* than does Gadamer, McDowell (translator of the *Theaetetus*) makes much of the same Platonic analogy between *phronesis* and *aisthesis*. Our capacity to perceive and apprehend moral reasons is, he tells us, analogous to our capacity to perceive objects. This is not only because they are both human powers, but also because, just as physical objects have an independent reality that we can spontaneously perceive, so too do moral norms have an independent, cultural existence that is apparent to the trained and habituated eye of the properly enculturated mind.

For McDowell, as for Gadamer, practical wisdom subsumes what is valuable in theoretical wisdom. ' "Practical wisdom" is the right sort of thing to serve as a model for the understanding, the faculty that enables us to recognize and create the kind of intelligibility that is a matter of placement in the space of reasons' (McDowell 1996c: 79). This space is not bounded by the categorial limits ordained by Kant's first *Critique*, and nor is the spontaneous power of apperception that we exercise within this open space. What the space *is* shaped by is the tradition that we share with its other inhabitants.

Central to McDowell's presentation of this argument in *Mind and World* is the concept of 'second nature'. Our habituation into a culturally normative space of reasons endows us with a second nature, similar to our actualization of the perceptual and other powers belonging to our first nature. 'Practical wisdom is second nature to its possessors' (ibid.: 84). Once we have acquired practical wisdom, we exercise it as naturally and spontaneously as we do our inborn power of visual perception.

The concept of second nature, if not the term, McDowell attributes to Aristotle (ibid.: 78, 91; 1998d: 184; cf. Vasiliou 1996), although both term and concept are prominent in Hegel, who calls 'the system of right . . . the world of spirit produced from within itself as a second nature' (Hegel 1991: 35 [§4]; see also Ferrarin 2001: 262–83. Riedel argues that Hegel took the concept from Hobbes's contrast with our original or first 'state of nature', although Hegel should indeed have been familiar with it from Aristotle's *hexis*, both directly and through the mediation of Cicero's terminology, of Augustine, and of medieval ideas of *habitus*.) When McDowell agrees with Pippin that Hegel, like Kant, tends to leave nature behind, the nature to which he refers is only first nature and not the second nature implicated in Aristotle's practical philosophy. When read in the light of his earlier interpretive work on Aristotle's account of practical reasoning, McDowell's insistence that Aristotle is the source of his concept of second nature might suggest that an implicit but distinctly Aristotelian metaphysical biology must be central to his own thought. Accordingly, the relation of second nature to first nature is that of actuality to potentiality, and our intellectual maturation and entry into 'the space of reasons' is, as McDowell repeatedly puts it, a process of 'actualization'. Besides the actualization of our physical powers, we actualize 'powers of second nature' (McDowell 1996c: 88). In drawing an analogy between those perceptual capacities that we share with some other animals and that apperceptual capacity of 'insight' which he proposes is uniquely human, McDowell is not obviously inconsistent with Aristotle. Nor is he inconsistent in what he says of the relation of such capacities to action. 'Intentional bodily actions are actualizations of our active nature in which conceptual capacities are inextricably implicated' (ibid.: 90). Rather as he sees Hegel naturalizing Kant, still more he sees Aristotle naturalizing Plato, and therefore his Aristotelianism can be equally understood as a 'naturalized platonism'.

McDowell wishes to reconceptualize a robust philosophical realism (cf. Charles 1995). He hopes to reconcile 'is' and 'ought', world and mind. He hopes to do so neither epistemologically nor within any architectonic theory but therapeutically and with 'a postlapsarian or knowing counterpart of Aristotle's innocence' (McDowell 1996c: 109). What we know, which Aristotle did not, is what we have learnt through modern, nomological science. For Kant, we are therefore presented with an antinomy of nature and reason but, following the philosophically quietist approach of Wittgenstein – another naturalized platonist (ibid.: 95) – McDowell thinks that even if Kant's antinomy cannot be solved it can be conceptually 'dissolved' or 'exorcized'. We can then knowingly return to something like our prior conception of our embodied selves (ibid.: 101–4) as peculiarly rational animals, living within a normative world. The antinomy is, after all, a creation of modern philosophy, in defiance of 'common sense'. A rehabilitated Aristotelianism can embrace our 'normative' and 'logical' sense of the reality of our second nature without renouncing 'the logical space of nature' (ibid.: xiv–xv) revealed to us by science.

'What makes a virtue a virtue – a capacity to get things right in one's conduct – cannot be the fact that it is second nature to its possessors' (McDowell 2000: 108) because one can be habituated also into vices. Ethical 'habits of thought and action' result from what McDowell – in acknowledgement of his debt to post-Kantian German thought – calls *Bildung* (McDowell 1996c: 84). He identifies this with 'our upbringing' (ibid.: 87), apparently intending by this *our* upbringing; not the upbringing of just anyone into any kind of reasoning, but the education of his already ethical audience into a space of ethically right reasons. Aristotle, he often proposes, addressed the *Ethics* to those who already had the right kind of upbringing and therefore did not need to be persuaded to be virtuous but wanted a better understanding of what their virtue is. Aristotle's adult audience had already been instructed in 'the that' of morality, and his own task was the altogether more advanced and theoretical one of teaching 'the because'. In explaining what virtue is himself, McDowell employs the concept of *Bildung*; the formation of the right kind of character, involving the right kind of thought and the right kind of action. 'We can easily correct' any 'tendency to smugness' (ibid.: 81), he assures us.

As with 'second nature', McDowell presents *Bildung* as a non-Aristotelian term signifying an Aristotelian idea (which is consistent with the Graecophilia that originally informed *Bildung*'s institutionalized promotion in Germany). Indeed, what he signifies by the term shares more with Aristotle, and with Ackrill, than with Schiller, Hegel or Marx. Ackrill proposes that one can 'inculcate good principles by . . . saying in the right tone of voice "it would be brave (kind, honourable, . . .) to do this, that, and the other"' (Ackrill 1973: 30). Such a didactic style of education may indeed work with a child. It is the form of education apparently envisaged by

Hugh of St Victor, and by those Renaissance Aristotelians admonished by MacIntyre for supposing that moral virtue can be taught in the same way as theoretical knowledge. Although Aristotle was in the Socratic tradition, his conception of ethical *paideia* seems to have been, as McDowell suggests, that of a process of instructing the young.

McDowell and MacIntyre, Gadamer or Marx?

The task that McDowell has set himself is not a normative one concerning 'the that' of morality, and nor is it a theoretical one concerning 'the because'. He simply ignores Aristotle's political argument for a hierarchy of 'for the sake of' relations and, also, Aristotle's intellectualist argument that this hierarchical order is for the final sake of the life of *theoria*. The only human excellence with which McDowell's Aristotle is concerned is moral virtue. The intellectual virtue of *phronesis* is concerned with apprehension of a 'because' that is neither theoretical nor political. Nor is practical wisdom deliberative or productive. It is unconcerned with means and ends. Rather, it resembles perception in the immediacy of its apprehension of pre-existing moral reasons for action. The action of the *phronimos* is therefore good in itself in the thoroughly Aristotelian sense of being complete, final and atemporal. There is therefore no warrant for *theoria*'s superiority to *praxis*. On the contrary, theory is concerned only with the perfection of other beings; action is concerned with the perfection of one's own being in the world.

To act within the space of moral reasons is to have an excellent character. It is *not* for the individual to follow some universalizable law, as McDowell argues by reference to Wittgenstein's critique of rule-following (McDowell 1998c and 1998e; see O'Neill 1996: 79–87 for a Kantian riposte). Nonetheless, he matches Kant's moral rigorism with an Aristotelian 'rigorism' that sacrifices faring well to doing well (Wiggins 1995: 226–9). As we noted in chapter 1 (see also e.g. McDowell 1998b: 16; 1998d: 169), he has revived the idea of the 'noble' individual as the highest criterion and judge of what it is to do and live well. To 'do well' is simply to do what is 'noble [*kalon*]'. Those for whom nobility is a fixed attribute are those whose characters 'silence' any reason to act in other than a virtuous way. One is habituated into virtue and then acts as and when virtue requires (McDowell 1998f: 90ff; 1998b: 17–18; 1998c), and what virtue requires is given by conventional reason. For McDowell, as for Gadamer, what is most important ethically is 'the self-projection of human Dasein' 'towards the *kalon*' (Gadamer 1999: 148, Greek transliterated; cf. Gadamer 1989: 477ff.).

The concept of 'nobility', like that of 'aristocracy', reinforces the identification of ethical excellence with social elitism. The one term is Latin, the other Greek. Both convey an idea that is veritably Aristotelian, and in using the one McDowell is indeed faithful to Aristotle's practical philosophy. The question is whether this faith is justifiable.

MacIntyre takes issue with *Mind and World* for consigning human babies and non-human animals to the realm of an unreasoning first nature (1999b: 60; see also Charles 1995: 148–51), which McDowell argues in following that account of 'language as experience of the world' by which Gadamer attempts 'to learn from Hegel' how to return to 'the basis of logos philosophy' in 'the old co-ordination between man and world' (Gadamer 1989: 438–56, 460, 459). McDowell regards babies as 'mere animals' because of their lack of participation in the linguistic practices of the space of reasons. He often refers to adults as if fully and finally formed characters. It is as if babies, as human beings, are *nothing* but potentiality, whilst adults lack *any* potentiality. The process of *Bildung*, of individuals' educative formation into moral agents, appears to be coextensive with children's education into adulthood. Therefore, nobility is not a goal for adults. Rather, it is an attribute that is fixed in some by their upbringing and denied to others.

McDowell considers it 'essential' to our 'conceptual capacities' and faculty of spontaneity . . . that they can be exercised in an activity of thinking responsibly undertaken by a subject who is in control of the course of the activity' (McDowell 1998g: 367). Animals and babies lack our self-consciousness of subjectivity within an objective world. They live not in an 'objective world' but in an 'environment' which continually confronts them with 'problems and opportunities' which they cannot conceive as such but to which they have continuously to respond. Their lives are 'determined' by their 'enslavement to immediate biological imperatives' and they 'need to produce behaviour', not action. (McDowell 1996c: 114–17, cf. 182). This distinction between 'world' and 'environment' McDowell takes from Gadamer, who in turn takes it from Heidegger. Nonetheless, McDowell refers to Marx in illustrating its social implications. Marx's *Economic and Philosophical Manuscripts* of 1844 (cf. MacIntyre above, p. 107, and Nussbaum 1988a: 183f.; 1990: 226f., 214f.) describe productive activity as 'the part of human life that should be most expressive of humanity' but which, 'in wage slavery', 'is reduced to the condition of merely animal life, the meeting of merely biological needs'. This he assimilates to Gadamer: 'in Marx as in Gadamer, the point is . . . that a properly human life is . . . distinctively free'. He then implicitly echoes Kant, Schiller and Gadamer, whilst explicitly following Marx, in saying that what makes 'art' a human 'experience of the world' is 'its freedom from the need to be useful' (McDowell 1996c: 117–19).

We have called Gadamer an apolitical Aristotelian, but Gadamer has ventured further than McDowell into social theory. Gadamer recognizes that Hegel differs from Aristotle regarding productive activity and the 'self-consciousness of "vocation"'. If we agree with Hegel that 'all handwork is a matter of the spirit', but also with Marx that 'industrial society do[es] not permit the worker to find a significance for himself in his work, which alone would make self-consciousness possible', what then follows? Not, for Gadamer, the revolutionary conclusion drawn by Marx, but rather the conclusion drawn by Weber: 'if there is to be freedom, then first of all the chain attaching us to things must be broken. The path of mankind to universal prosperity . . . could be a path to the unfreedom of all' (Gadamer 1976: 71, 73–4). For Weber, who already considered the Protestant work ethic to have expired in Europe, and for Gadamer, contemporary capitalism expresses the enslavement of our reason by our passion to consume. MacIntyre agrees that capitalism's structure corresponds to such a 'Humean' practical rationality (1998h). What he disagrees with is their understanding of capitalism as a system encompassing all practices and unchallenged by any. 'It seems inevitable: economics is our fate', says Gadamer, departing from Weber in claiming that 'every function is subordinated to a system' in which 'nobody has power and everybody is in service' (Gadamer 1998c: 95–6). That nobody has power because we live in a providential system of functionally interdependent parts operating in accordance with some impersonal rationale is a claim that a Marxist would regard as paradigmatically ideological.

Interpretive tales

McDowell's account of a singular ethical second nature into which children are more or less well habituated resembles the account of ethical tutoring propounded by MacIntyre before he elaborated his account of Humean practical reasoning as constitutive of a rival tradition. For McDowell, virtue is the condition of our having overcome the natural causation of our actions by our passions and desires. MacIntyre would object only that virtue, even if it needs to enslave the passions, needs not to silence but to educate desire. True moral knowledge may not derive from universal laws but it does derive from education into ideas of the human good, and of that good as constituted by virtues. Conversely, moral non-cognitivism denies both universal laws and universal goods, even when it identifies natural or artificial virtues or a need for education into virtues and rules. Whilst MacIntyre agrees with McDowell about the non-instrumentality of virtue, he also acknowledges that what they both deny is affirmed by a rival tradition that is both philosophical and institutionalized. Therefore, despite their shared concern with habituation into virtue, where McDowell speaks of a single space of reasons and of second nature, MacIntyre allows of rivalry between conceptual schemes.

When McDowell speaks of 'the philosophical tradition', it is usually clear that he is referring to the modern, epistemological tradition, the foundationalist concerns of which he wishes to quieten and dissolve. Like Gadamer and Heidegger, he argues that theory provides no basis for practice. Their agreement might be thought to go deeper than this. Even if McDowell does not explicitly go all the way down through Wittgenstein's linguistic bedrock to Heidegger's sense of being in the world, he, like Heidegger (Heidegger 2002), conceives of truth, including moral truth, as a perceiving of particulars.

Foundationalism is, McDowell notes, an attempted solution to modern philosophy's peculiar and misconceived epistemological anxieties. As he considers Aristotle innocent of such concerns, he declares the naturalistic foundationalism of Williams's Aristotle to be an 'historical monstrosity' (McDowell 1998d: 195). Significantly, he detects 'something similar' in the anti-Nietzscheanism of *After Virtue*'s Aristotle (McDowell 1996c: 79). For his part, MacIntyre has said of McDowell's early work on Aristotle's ethics that it was erroneous in the same way as was 'my own misguided attempt in *After Virtue* to excise all references to Aristotle's "metaphysical biology" from his ethics', because Aristotle's 'account of the moral life is at one and the same time action-guiding and explanatory' in combining 'conceptions of . . . natural and human causality' (1991: 191; cf. Gill 1990). Only by being explanatory as well as action-guiding is Aristotelianism able to answer sociological and other arguments advanced from within rival traditions, as MacIntyre attempts to do.

MacIntyre would include McDowell alongside Williams amongst those philosophers who 'share a disregard for the place in morality of . . . what I have called practices' (1983b: 119–20). McDowell himself accuses others of disregarding 'an individual's allegiance to a practice', as when he accuses 'Brandom's Hegel' of disregarding this as an alternative to an individual being held to some commitment by having '"norms *administered* by someone else"' (McDowell 1999: 192, quoting Brandom 2002a; McDowell's emphasis). Robert Brandom takes his own concept of a normatively authoritative practice primarily and explicitly from a Heidegger whom he understands as in the tradition of Hegel (Brandom 2002b: 76–83), and his Hegel insists that the best example of a norm being authoritatively administered by someone else is of a law being administered by a judge in the tradition of the common law (Brandom 2002a: 230–3; 2005: 432). Having norms administered by someone else contravenes the independence of McDowell's noble man, who should be in 'control of the course of [his] activity'. Nonetheless, what McDowell calls a practice is something very different from what MacIntyre calls a practice, and McDowell's conception admits of no opposition of practices to institutions. McDowell's 'practices' include 'languages, traditions' (McDowell 1999: 192), and his traditions are things that express but do not aim at actualizing truths. As with Brandom's particularized but nonetheless Hegelian conception of normative traditions, they are 'lived forward but understood backward' (Brandom 2002b: 45). McDowell's normative practices also lack ends, and to this extent lack what MacIntyre calls internal goods. For McDowell and his Hegel, as well as Brandom's, the only end is that of the individual herself. All she has to actualize is her self. There is no idea of any ethically educative function in pursuing the actualization of goods initially external to the individual but which the individual may then internalize. There are no goods greater than individuals, in cooperative pursuit of which individuals might collectively act. For Brandom, and for Brandom's Hegel, the social project is one of mutual recognition, including the recognition of others' official authority. Ethical education would appear to reduce to the inculcation of norms by some institutionalized authority – for McDowell, a parent; for Brandom, also a paternal state. Brandom is concerned with individuals' accountability to others for their commitments, and with individuals' mutual '*normative* independence and dependence' (Brandom 2002b: 54), whereas McDowell resists this idea in the cause of individual self-mastery. MacIntyre certainly shares something here with Brandom. He, like Brandom, is concerned with '*instituting* . . . norms' (Brandom 2002a: 228). The political question is *how* norms are to be instituted.

From ethics to politics

MacIntyre's conception of ethical formation is not, like McDowell's, of a process that finishes along with our upbringing by our parents and our entry into a space of adult reason. 'To be a rational individual is to participate in' some systematic and ongoing form 'of activity within which goods are unambiguously ordered and within which individuals occupy and move between well-defined roles [so] that the standards of rational action directed towards the good and the best can be embodied' (1988a: 141). Within such forms of activity individuals are held accountable to such standards by each other *and* by administrative institutions, insofar as those institutions subserve the good of the practice. Within such practices individuals are also encouraged to hold themselves accountable to those standards, but MacIntyre does not presume that individuals' virtue is ever so complete that it cannot benefit from others' scrutiny and criticism. As he said when a Leninist, 'the knowledge which liberates' is 'a continually growing consciousness'.

Although MacIntyre agrees with Hegel that *Bildung*, or ethical tutoring, is a matter for adults as well as for children, he agrees with McDowell in resisting the thought that normative excellence is best ensured by institutionalized administration. To Aristotle's case for the educative function of laws and of the noble craft of legislation, Hegel added a case for the more particularistic function of corporate institutions in educating their adult members and mediating between them and the modern, bureaucratic state. Where MacIntyre differs from Brandom's Hegel, and from Ritter's Hegel, and from Hegel's Hegel, is in differentiating goods internal to practices from norms formalized by such institutions.

Although McDowell agrees with MacIntyre in resisting the Hegelian celebration of institutionalized administration, he poses no political alternative. It falls to MacIntyre alone to theorize how norms can be instituted and excellence politicized in a way that is not bureaucratically hierarchical and paternalist. As against this, McDowell explicitly refuses MacIntyre's critique of managerial 'manipulation' (McDowell 1998h: 155–6, 164). We have already noted MacIntyre's reference to Kant in advancing this critique, and we may add that MacIntyre is not so comprehensively antipathetic to Kant's account of practical rationality as is sometimes alleged (e.g. Nussbaum 1999: 169ff.). He regards the emancipatory projects of both Kant and Marx to have been defeated by institutionalized power of a kind that they mistakenly regarded as a means to their ethical ends (2006d, 1998a). He proposes his account of social practices as the kind of theory of self-activity and self-changing that he argues is necessary to recommence what Marx, impatient to leave behind interpretation and engage in revolution, left behind as 'unfinished philosophical business' (1998a: 232).

MacIntyre's, like Marx's, is an 'ontology of individuals-in-relation' (ibid.: 225). This he contrasts to a 'materialist' ontology of the kind that informs an empiricist epistemology, capable of perceiving only what Hobbes called 'bodies in motion' and of understanding causation in terms only of the motive effects of such bodies upon one another in pursuing their individual desires. An ontology of individuals-in-relation is an ontology that acknowledges the primary being of individuals of specific kinds, but which perceives also the prior reality of those relations into which human beings are born and socialized and which may help or hinder individuals to actualize their natural potentials. Having said that practices 'are constitutive means to the end of our flourishing', MacIntyre adds that they also generally 'give expression to established hierarchies of power and of the uses of power, hierarchies and uses that, as instruments of domination and deprivation, often frustrate us in our movement towards our goods'. A social theory capable of informing genuinely liberatory activity must be one that distinguishes between 'two kinds of rules': those that we have identified with practices, and those that we have identified with institutions. A moral theory capable of justifying such activity must be one that says why power should 'serve the ends to which the rules of giving and receiving are directed' (1999b: 102–3). But such a theory cannot be one that prescribes rules or ends to actors. Any universalizing theoretical distinction between institutions and practices must afford to practices and practitioners the setting and revising of their aims and standards.

This, MacIntyre proposes, is the standpoint of what Marx called 'human society, or social humanity' (Marx 1976: 5). This standpoint is opposed to that of those would-be revolutionaries who deny that revolution should be a process of self-changing and who take it upon themselves to achieve socialism through institutional manipulation, dividing society between those whose actions are to be causally explained in social scientific or psychological terms and those who can freely employ such knowledge to manage the former. 'They understand others in terms of a determinist theory. They understand themselves in terms of a rational voluntarism' (1998a: 230). The standpoint of social humanity is also opposed to that of 'civil society', according to which actors are understood as acquisitive consumers. In opposition to this (and in engagement with other analytic moral philosophers; 2003: 1–26), MacIntyre advances a critique of rational choice theorists' attempts to apply the assumptions and methods of microeconomic calculation to broader practical and political reasoning (1998k: 239–43; 2003: 69–75).

Concerned only with the self-activity of some, Aristotle celebrated their management of others. Concerned with the potential self-activity of all, MacIntyre condemns everything that prevents their free cooperation. He takes from theism his prioritization of moral over intellectual virtue and his admission of productive work to the ambit of personal excellence. Productive and other social practices he conceives as the ever-present actualization of human goods. Whereas Marx saw future freedom latent only in actual technology and proletarian alienation, and even though he agrees with Marx in denying that human potential can be fulfilled within capitalist social relations, MacIntyre agrees with Hegel to the extent of seeing ethical life lived here and now. As Gadamer observes, Hegel understood that 'for self-consciousness the actual purpose of work is fulfilled in the non-alienated work world'; that is, in 'material work' but not in the work of 'capitalism's wage slave' (Gadamer 1976: 73). MacIntyre remains close to Marx regarding the irreconcilability of present conflict, and regarding the need to overcome the social division of mental from manual labour, but he is closer to Hegel in denying that self-actualization involves individuals' practical transcendence of their own social particularity and their elevation into some realm of universality beyond material need and beyond any social division of labour. MacIntyre's conception of human completion is not that of the Renaissance man revived by many 'left Kantians' and Left Hegelians; that of a person who can freely turn their hand to any art. This he regards as an impossible ideal for the kind of mutually dependent beings that we are, naturally. Rather than any abolition of the division of skill and function between particular practices, his hope is that of liberating workers' own practical rationality and institutionalizing their cooperative self-management at the level of political community.

Aristotle, as Broadie says, attempts no general answer to the question of what should be done at 'the ground level of quotidian practicality' and advocates 'architectonic thinking', an 'architectonic goal' and 'architectonic practice' only as the preserve of politicians and not of ordinary practical reasoners (Broadie 2006: 351–2). MacIntyre agrees on the desirability of a veritably political rationality ordered to our common good, whilst objecting that this architectonic rationality should be based in, rather than simply directive of, more quotidian practices and their rationalities. Politics, for MacIntyre, is a practice that should necessarily encompass and involve other practices and practitioners.

In response to Broadie's 'Grand End' critique, MacIntyre has appealed to Richard Kraut (2006a: 26; Kraut 1993). Nonetheless, their positions differ. As noted in chapter 1, Kraut has argued that we should 'reject [Aristotle's] conception of the for-the-sake-of relation' because of its elitism in subordinating craft reason to political reason and political reason to philosophy (Kraut 1989: 357). MacIntyre rejects any such rejection, even whilst agreeing with Kraut's anti-elitism. I have argued that where he disagrees with Aristotle is, first, in refusing any social division of managed from managers and, secondly, in overriding Aristotle's conceptual distinction between actions and productions and condemnation of the latter to an unethical servility. He remains Aristotelian in holding that practical reasoning should indeed comprise a chain of ' "for the sake of" relationships' (1988a: 131) and terminate in some conception of a common good. Where he again differs from Aristotle is in holding that this common good should be socially inclusive.

MacIntyre shares with Hegel the hope for a political order in which ordinary actors will understand their work as functional to an inclusive common good. As with the identification of such a good by Aquinas and by those medievals whom Nederman calls communal functionalists, this hope may be understood as inspired by a theistic universalism. Where MacIntyre differs from both Hegel and communal functionalists, as well as from more recent communitarians and sociological functionalists, is in imputing such an order to contemporary reality and explaining it in terms of some socially or historically necessary logic. Unlike Hegel and his contemporary followers, MacIntyre denies that modern societies, administered by bureaucratic states, are really ordered to what an Aristotelian should regard as the common good. To understand such societies as so ordered is to make a theoretical mistake and, for MacIntyre, to act on such a theoretical understanding is to make a practical error. In contrast, to understand ourselves as alienated from society's dominant institutions is to understand our real situation under capitalism. If MacIntyre has himself inherited a degree of philosophical quietism from Wittgenstein in what he says of practices (e.g. 1998g), this is negated in his juxtaposition of practices to institutions. He remains 'anti-Wittgensteinian' in denying that there can be any 'philosophical cure' (1998a: 229) to social and ethical conflict.

History, politics and philosophy

We may suppose that MacIntyre still agrees with Hegel that 'history, informed by philosophical understanding, provides a more ultimate kind of knowledge of human beings than inquiries whose theoretical structure is modeled on that of the natural sciences' (2006f: 85), and this notwithstanding his acknowledgment of the crucial fact of our animality. Where he differs most fundamentally from Hegel is in his philosophical understanding of history. The philosophies of both MacIntyre and Hegel may be regarded as Aristotelian in the sense that they include a teleological understanding of beings of a kind that is denied by the various followers of Hobbes, Hume, Nietzsche, Dewey or Heidegger. Moreover, the Aristotelian philosophy of MacIntyre resembles that of Hegel more closely than that of Aristotle or Aquinas in understanding itself historically. That said, MacIntyre indeed sides with Aristotle and Aquinas and against Hegel in denying that history is a whole with a *telos*. Humanity is a universal kind, and therefore individuals universally have a common *telos*, but there is no human universal existing apart from individual human beings in relation to which individuals can be no more than particular constituents. In posing such a universal, Hegel is indeed an absolute idealist rather than an Aristotelian.

In denying Hegel's universal, MacIntyre is not denying reality to any human progress. However, real progress is only the progress of particular enquiries and practices, and such progress lacks any kind of logical necessity. He looks to history in rejecting the Enlightenment's search for apodictic foundations for knowledge. The lessons of history are the lessons of tradition; of traditions of practical rationality, of their institutional embodiments, and of their articulation at the level of philosophical enquiry into human being, the human good, and the best practical and institutional means to further that good. For MacIntyre, this is quite enough. He has said that the most certain knowledge we can attain is no more than that of the best theory so far, and the history of ideas is the testing ground of rival traditions and their rival theories. The 'best test' of the truth of any theory 'is that it is able to withstand the strongest objections available from every known rival point of view' (2006m: 212). He would therefore still say that Hegel was 'mistaken in supposing that anyone can ever have the last word' (1990a: 261). However, he can no longer justify being 'irremediably anti-Hegelian' in the way that he did, because he now accepts that 'the notion of an absolute standpoint' is entailed by his idea of truth as the *telos* of enquiry. 'The mind cannot dispense with a conception of an absolute standpoint, a divine standpoint, that from which things would be viewed as they truly are' (2006m: 211), and MacIntyre intends by this more than a merely regulative ideal.

Hegel is post-Kantian in accepting that ethics is not premised in any atemporally universal human nature. Our ethical life is determined not by first nature but by history. We legislate for ourselves, but the ways in which we do so are necessarily constrained by our society and its history. Hegel therefore leaves nature behind in elaborating a theoretical history of the progress of ethical life towards the rational and institutional reconciliation of individuals' free wills with communal constraints. This history might be regarded as teleological in the sense that the end it actualizes is one that exists as a potential in humanity's original condition. But although Hegel's 'actualization' is no Hobbesian event, nor does it have the atemporal quality attributed by Aristotle to *praxis* (let alone *theoria*). Actualization is a process. This transgression of Aristotle's conceptual divide poses a problem for those post-Heideggerians who would assimilate Hegel to their Aristotelian tradition, but it might be thought to pose no such problem for MacIntyre. He, after all, follows Hegel in repeating theism's dissolution of the distinction between action and production, activity and process. The Aristotelianism of *After Virtue* is not, therefore, obviously anti-Hegelian. Even though history is no kind of Aristotelian being, nor is a social practice.

To this we may add the young MacIntyre's point that the understanding of history that Marx took from Hegel is less philosophical and teleological in inspiration than theistic and eschatological. Rather as with Hugh of St Victor's postulation of a historical 'improvement of human action' and 'restoration of our nature', so too Hegel and Marx argue that the historical development of human activity is leading to the restoration of an original (whether Hellenic or primitive communist) communal harmony, but now in combination with individual freedom and rational self-consciousness. The atemporal providentialism propounded by Leibniz and Wolff is replaced by a providentialism of history. What both the young and the old MacIntyre resist in any such eschatology is the danger of dogmatic closure. MacIntyre refuses to bring faith down to history in any way that presents past and present activity as a temporal means to some future end, as pronounced by some unfalsifiable theory. Such historicism may pretend to answer, but instead only begs, the Enlightenment's epistemological questions.

Certainty of faith should no more pretend to historical than to biological certainty, and faith in the beneficence of an existing social order (whether as historically evolved or party-imposed) should never substitute for actors' own reasoning about the ends and means of their own activity. What theistic faith can do – and did do for Leibniz, for Newton, for Hegel, and for many others – is provoke, inspire and guide philosophical enquiry. The way in which it guided Aquinas's philosophical enquiries, and therefore directed that tradition of Thomistic Aristotelianism within which MacIntyre now locates his own philosophizing, inclines him to extend the scope of teleology beyond that of Aristotle (see above, p. 6) to the universe as a providentially ordered whole and to explain things by reference to their 'function . . . within the overall order' (2006m: 206). Nonetheless, as yet, at least, this metaphysical commitment has not altered his account of ethics, politics or practices.

Even though MacIntyre attributes no *telos* to history, his philosophical understanding of history shares something with Western and, more precisely, Lukácsian Marxism. He understands history in terms of self-activity, or *praxis*, or self-making, and attempts to identify activity that is 'entitled to be called "revolutionary" ' (1998a: 231). Teleology enters when our everyday reasoning is informed by reasoning about the human good. MacIntyre's appeal to teleology is, therefore, no simple appeal to the authority of Aristotelian tradition. It is an appeal that tradition inform practice and that our understanding of practice reform tradition. Most of all, it is an appeal that Aristotelian tradition and ordinary practice inform our active reformation of the social conditions of our own consciousness.

MacIntyre's hope for a veritably political order in which ordinary actors will understand their work as functional to an inclusive common good differs from Hegel's in being little more than a hope. It is not elevated to a historical necessity, nor even a programmatic goal. MacIntyre attributes no such order to our contemporary social structure and denies that it could be generated by the state. In this he differs from the Hegelian tradition which, in Britain, informed the politics of Green and his liberal and social democratic followers. For them, the modern state had institutionalized Aristotle's idea of justice within a more inclusive political community than that possible in his own time, whilst liberty was reconceptualized in teleological (or 'positive') terms. The ambition of social democrats was to extend political and ethical principles into social and economic relations through the use of state power and the construction of corporatist institutions, whereas, for those liberals who were inspired as much by Kant and Mill as by Hegel, the coercive and bureaucratic machinery of the state was to be extended only as an educative example to be voluntarily but progressively followed by individuals and civil associations. Now, following their political defeat, the original hopes of social democrats have been abandoned, whilst liberals once again celebrate capitalism as the arena of a 'negative' liberty of unconstrained choice. That this has happened is no surprise to those, such as MacIntyre, who have followed Marx in regarding the state as an instrument of capitalist order rather than of ethical principle or political community.

What distinguishes MacIntyre's politics from that of most other followers of Marx (even if not of those council communists who helped inspire Lenin's *State and Revolution*) is his denial that the modern state can ever be an instrument of revolution against capitalism. Those who followed Lenin failed to produce any more than a state capitalism that combined the evils of exploitation and alienation with those of blatantly coercive repression. MacIntyre's hope is for another kind of political and economic order, based in practices and practical reasoning. Such order requires organization and institutions, and power and money, but cannot be simply produced by using the unreformable institutions of the state and corporate capital. Its institutions must be those of ordinary actors pursuing and producing quotidian goods. Such an order can, he claims, be found in some localities and some institutions. The hope for Aristotelians must be that it can be built up into a more extensive and inclusive social structure, and this can only be done by practitioners themselves. However, denying that theory can be liberatory in isolation from the everyday practice and rationality of ordinary actors, and having had his hopes dashed before, MacIntyre proposes no party programme.

Such a philosophy may appear apolitical to Marxists, and to Aristotelians. Aristotle, after all, refused Plato's communist utopianism and related his politics to a comparative study of existing *poleis*. I have argued that MacIntyre's revision of Aristotle's political ethics is informed by that revision of Aristotelianism previously effected by its combination with theism. MacIntyre emphasizes how, in the work of Aquinas, that combination challenged existing regimes, whilst Nederman argues that it inspired more widely held and inclusivist ideals of communal functionalism and Christian republicanism. Many of Christianity's founders had posed the Church as a separate order from that of temporal *imperium*, even whilst asserting the need to coexist with that other order in a condition of dual authority. Dominican Aristotelianism provided that position with philosophical support, reinforcing (irrespective of Aquinas's own intentions) ecclesiastical conservatism in a way that provoked oppositional attempts at institutional reformation. However, it was only through the development of 'left Kantianism' and Left Hegelianism, culminating in the work of the early Marx, that a philosophical understanding of historical difference and change – in social structures, in theoretical ideas and practical rationalities, and in their mutual influence – was to inform an opposition to the dominant institutions of modernity. It is, then, to Marx that MacIntyre owes his thoroughgoing critique of the institutions of state and capital, but to a Marx informed by philosophical understanding and not to that Marx who rejected philosophy 'at a stage at which his own philosophical enquiries were still incomplete'. A Marx informed by philosophical understanding would be, claims MacIntyre, a Marx who distinguishes communal practices from capitalist institutions. MacIntyre therefore understands his own work as continuing that of Marx, as well as of Aristotle and Aquinas. This is a task that is unlikely ever to be complete, and MacIntyre's most frequent refrain is that there is further work to be done.

MacIntyre's explicit disagreement with Marx (or, at least, with Marx as understood by Marxism's traditional orthodoxy) now shares something with what I have proposed is his implicit but continuing disagreement with aspects of Aristotle's metaphysics. Marx, like Hegel, is wrong to impute a *telos* to history, just as Aristotle is wrong to impute a *telos* to products. We can reason teleologically about natural kinds, including human beings, but the social, intellectual and material products of human agency should always be understood in terms of the reasoning of such actors and not of any innate goal of their own. Actors' reasoning is of two kinds: that which understands such goods of effectiveness as money and power to be good only for the sake of goods of practical and personal excellence, and that which denies any such distinction. The distinction between these two kinds of reasoning MacIntyre understands to be drawn by Aristotle and, since Aristotle, to be still best drawn in Aristotelian terms. Goods of excellence are those that comprise the human *telos*, the good for human beings as such, including goods internal to the activities of humans as naturally social and political beings. Sociologically, this may be understood as a distinction between the kind of reasoning internal to practices and that which is characteristic of institutions. The distinction is denied by those traditions that deny the validity of teleological claims, in a rivalry that MacIntyre traces back to the Greek origins of philosophy.

To express in this way the distinction between goods of excellence and goods of effectiveness, or between practices and institutions, is to demonstrate the extent to which MacIntyre has moved beyond Wittgenstein. Practices no more comprise a natural kind than does history, and when MacIntyre first spoke about social practices rather than about the *energeiai* of individuals he followed Wittgenstein more than Aristotle. When he described practices as having a teleological structure, because ordered to 'internal goods', this teleology inhered not in practices as beings but in the intentionality of individuals as participants in language games. By the time of *After Virtue*, however, he already differed from the standard Wittgensteinian account in two important respects: first, in posing practices' rules as secondary to their goals; secondly, in juxtaposing practices to institutions. In since elaborating these thoughts, MacIntyre has combined Wittgenstein's insights with those of Aristotle, and of Marx, and of Aquinas.

This philosophical synthesis has enabled MacIntyre to move far beyond Gadamer and Heidegger. In tracing philosophical tradition back to Greece, alone, MacIntyre follows the later Heidegger. In at first attempting to reconstruct an Aristotelian practical philosophy apart from the history of metaphysics, he followed Gadamer. In then attempting to save Aristotelian tradition as a whole from those who would deconstruct it, he turned to Aquinas. In this, he reversed the path taken by the young Heidegger. In posing a primordial rivalry between traditions, rather than speaking of 'the tradition', he differs from Thomists and Heideggerians alike. His Aristotelianism is, now, the ontological philosophy that Aristotelianism was understood to be, 'at the most fundamental level' (1990b: 166), by both Aquinas and Heidegger. But his Aristotelianism is also more than this. Whereas traditional Aristotelian doctrine identifies a being's good, its *telos*, only with the actualization of its innate potential, MacIntyre locates human goods also within shared practices. It is in acting for the sake of such common goods, he argues, that humans achieve real excellence. His central ethical argument is that if one fails to pursue common goods, then one cannot actualize one's own good, and this is an argument the origins of which are not Greek. Nonetheless, it is still to Aristotelianism that he attributes the task of articulating the self-understanding of those engaged in cooperative and progressive social practices and of contesting the claims of those who would deny the good of such activity. In fulfilling this task, he hopes, Aristotelianism will be freed from its academic compartmentalization and become the philosophy of an ethical and political *praxis* that is transformative of selves and societies.

Conclusion

This book is victim to the author's overnumerous intentions. My first intention has been to present an interpretive narrative of the formation of MacIntyre's philosophy. The conceptual subtleties and political implications of this philosophy have often been misconstrued, and my hope is that some of these will be better understood through such a mode of presentation. MacIntyre began his project of combining social science with moral theory as a Marxist, and this source informed his subsequent account of a tradition of philosophical reflection upon practical rationality that he calls Aristotelian. My case is not that there was once 'another MacIntyre' (Blackledge 2005: 696) but that there has always been one and the same MacIntyre, and that his thought has progressed in ways that are important to contemporary Aristotelianism, to contemporary moral and political theory, and to our understanding of our own social and ethical practice.

My second intention has been to chart the main course through the history of ideas taken by MacIntyre's Aristotelian tradition, from Aristotle to himself. It has *not* been my intention to trace either the philosophical rationale of his metatheory of traditions or the development of his Thomism, as these have already been mapped in a way that construes correctly what he says of tradition as an exercise in philosophical partisanship rather than epistemological theory (Lutz 2004). Freed from these tasks, I have explored more widely what he identifies as the confluence of Aristotelianism with a previously rival and theistic tradition of Augustinianism. His conviction that it was revitalized by this combination distinguishes his Aristotelianism from that of many contemporaries. Apart from his account of Aquinas' successful synthesis of the two traditions, the main episode MacIntyre has recounted is that of the unsuccessful attempt at synthesis by Scottish Calvinists (MacIntyre 1988a: 219–332). His appreciation of the Scottish Enlightenment and its Humean aftermath has been important for his own intellectual formation (as I hope to elaborate elsewhere), but still more important has been that 'Prussian tradition in which public law and Lutheran theology were blended' (ibid.: 11) and which, he suggests, culminated in Hegel's similarly abortive attempt at a universalizing synthesis. Rather as the Scottish failure was marked by the success of Hume, so the German failure was marked by the success of Nietzsche and Heidegger. Nonetheless, I suggest that the significance for Aristotelianism of this German history is not so clear-cut. Hegel was to influence Marx in one way and Gadamer in another, whilst Heidegger's reinterpretation of Aristotle has proven massively influential, and MacIntyre has felt the influence of them all.

My third and unifying intention has been to argue that Aristotelianism has now been revitalized once again, by MacIntyre. This argument is based in an interpretation of both Aristotle and later tradition that is more critical than MacIntyre's own. Traditionally, Aristotelianism's promotion of ethical excellence has legitimated elitism and oppression. In this, post-Heideggerian Aristotelianism is at one with the tradition. My argument is that MacIntyre's account of social practices provides a socially inclusive understanding of ethical excellence that fills a gap between Aristotelianism's universalist theoretical philosophy and its particularistic practical philosophy. On this account, practices are the social means by which individuals may actualize their natural potential. They are such because they are the sources of normative standards for individuals to emulate. This thought owes much to modern philosophy, and especially to what Wittgenstein said about following the rules of mathematics, of grammar, and of chess. On this view, the basic subjects of philosophy are not Aristotle's beings or kinds but language games, conceptual schemes, traditions. Numerous analytic philosophers, including McDowell, have made an ethics out of this view by explaining how the following of customary rules is internalized by individuals, as virtue. Where MacIntyre goes beyond these other philosophers is in elaborating what, in *After Virtue*, he calls a 'teleological' account of practices. On this teleological account, the precepts that are internal to practices and reproduced in the thought and action of practitioners are secondary to shared aims internal to the practices, which give 'point and purpose' to those rules (cf. Wittgenstein 1958: 150 [§564]). Following Aristotle, MacIntyre calls these aims 'goods'. On his account, what defines a practice is not the intentionality of shared rule-following but the intentionality – and, indeed, the social reality – of what he calls a shared 'telos'. Whereas he had once, when conceiving morality as a matter of convention and usage, said that moral precepts could not be justified in non-moral terms, in *After Virtue* he argued that his sociological account of practices formed the first stage of a 'core concept of virtue' that permitted a successful justification of morality, substituting for Aristotle's metaphysical conception of a human *telos*.

The similarly teleological terms of this justification he identified with an Aristotelian tradition. In thinking through his theoretical commitment to this broader conceptual scheme, he advanced from Wittgensteinian conventionalism to Aristotelian metaphysics. His sociological account of practices no longer substitutes for but complements Aristotle's metaphysical account of the human *telos*. In this way, MacIntyre has demonstrated how an Aristotelian practical philosophy of human excellence can be saved and rehabilitated; not by discarding the entirety of Aristotle's theoretical philosophy, as done by post-Heideggerians, but by reconceiving Aristotelianism as a conceptual scheme and by quietly adding to that scheme insights from modern linguistic and social philosophy.

MacIntyre's ethic is also theistic. As with Hegel's earlier dissolution of Aristotelianism's traditional distinction between action and production, MacIntyre's revision of Aristotle's conceptual scheme is informed by theism's replacement of an elitist ethic of self-sufficiency with an inclusive ethic of mutual service. Much of what Aristotle says of justice, of courage, of friendship, of liberality and of magnanimity recommends action that may benefit others, but he nonetheless contrasts what is noble to what is servilely done for the sake of something or someone else. MacIntyre translates this contrast into one between goods of excellence and goods of effectiveness, whereby the latter should be used for the sake of the former. He then opposes Aristotelianism, which maintains this claim that power and money are only instrumentally good, to a tradition that rejects the idea of a human *telos* and therefore any separation of instrumental from internal goods.

Marxism MacIntyre understands to have originated as a secularized form of a religious ethic, and from an immanent but abortive critique of a German philosophical tradition that owed much to Aristotle. Whereas Aristotelians have wished to conserve political and economic order, Marxists have worked for its overthrow. Whilst MacIntyre warns of the corruptiveness of power and against the idea of revolution as an eschatological event, his juxtaposition of practices to institutions provides an ethical and political argument for resistance to manipulation. Therefore, MacIntyre's is more than a merely rehabilitated Aristotelianism. In relation to the tradition, it is a reformed Aristotelianism. In relation to capitalism and to the liberal, national and bureaucratic state, it is what I have called a revolutionary Aristotelianism. MacIntyre has revised and revitalized Aristotelianism's conceptual scheme by, most especially, reintroducing to it ideas that have progressed via the detour of Marxism.

But this book must not be allowed to replace old misconstruals of MacIntyre's philosophy with a new one. MacIntyre's regard for practice is greater than his regard for theory, and he is more concerned to raise questions than to provide answers. In cursorily contrasting some of the propositions that he has advanced with the standpoints of other philosophers, and in problematizing Aristotelianism's concepts of action, production and teleology, this book, too, may have raised more questions than it has answered. It is, in any case, intended as part of a tradition of enquiry.

References

Ackrill, J. L. 1973. 'Introduction', in Ackrill, ed., *Aristotle's Ethics*, Faber and Faber.

—— 1997a. 'Aristotle on Action', in Ackrill, *Essays on Plato and Aristotle*, Oxford University Press.

—— 1997b. 'Aristotle's Distinction between *Energeia* and *Kinesis*', in ibid.

—— 1997c. 'Aristotle on *Eudaimonia*', in ibid.

Adkins, Arthur W. H. 1960. *Merit and Responsibility: A Study in Greek Values*, Oxford University Press.

Albert the Great. 2001. 'Questions on Book X of the Ethics', trans. Arthur Stephen McGrade, in McGrade et al. eds., *The Cambridge Translations of Medieval Philosophical Texts*, vol. 2: *Ethics and Political Philosophy*, Cambridge University Press.

Anscombe, G. E. M. 1958 'Modern Moral Philosophy', *Philosophy* 33(124): 1–19.

—— 1963. *Intention*, Basil Blackwell (2nd edn.).

—— 1965. 'Thought and Action in Aristotle: What is "Practical Truth"?', in Renford Bambrough, ed., *New Essays on Plato and Aristotle*, Routledge and Kegan Paul.

—— 1971. *An Introduction to Wittgenstein's* Tractatus, Hutchinson (4th edn.).

—— 1981. 'Mr Truman's Degree', in Anscombe, *The Collected Philosophical Papers of G. E. M. Anscombe*, vol. 3: *Ethics, Religion and Politics*, Basil Blackwell.

—— 1991. 'Wittgenstein: Whose Philosopher?', in A. Phillips Griffiths, ed., *Wittgenstein Centenary Essays* (Royal Institute of Philosophy supplement 28), Cambridge University Press.

Aquinas, St Thomas. 1963. *Commentary on the Politics*, trans. Ernest L. Fortin and Peter D. O'Neill, in Ralph Lerner and Muhsin Mahdi, eds., *Medieval Political Philosophy: A Sourcebook*, Free Press.

—— 1993. *Commentary on Aristotle's Nicomachean Ethics*, trans. C. I. Litzinger O.P., Dumb Ox Books.

—— 1999. *A Commentary on Aristotle's De anima*, trans. Robert Pasnau, Yale University Press.

Arendt, Hannah. 1958. *The Human Condition*, University of Chicago Press.

—— 1965. *On Revolution*, Viking Press.

Arendt, Hannah. 1982. *Lectures on Kant's Political Philosophy*, ed. Ronald Beiner, University of Chicago Press.

Aristotle. 1925. 'Ethica Nicomachea', trans. W. D. Ross, in Ross, ed., *The Works of Aristotle Translated into English*, vol. 7, Oxford University Press.

—— 1948. *The Politics of Aristotle*, trans. Ernest Barker, Oxford University Press (2nd edn.).

—— 1998. *Politics*, trans. C. D. C. Reeve, Hackett.

Augustine, St. 1953. 'To Simplician – on Various Questions. Book 1', in John H. S. Burleigh, trans., Augustine, *Earlier Writings*, Westminster Press.

—— 1997. *The Confessions*, trans. Maria Boulding O.S.B., Hodder and Stoughton.

—— 1998. *The City of God against the Pagans*, trans. R. W. Dyson, Cambridge University Press.

Austin, J. L. 1961. 'The Meaning of a Word', in J. O. Urmson and G. J. Warnock, eds., *Austin, Philosophical Papers*, Oxford University Press.

Baum, Manfred. 2004. 'Common Welfare and Universal Will in Hegel's *Philosophy of Right*', trans. Nicholas Walker, in Robert B. Pippin and Otfried Höffe, eds., *Hegel on Ethics and Politics*, Cambridge University Press.

Barker, Ernest. 1906. *The Political Thought of Plato and Aristotle*, Oxford University Press.

Beadle, Ron, and Geoff Moore. 2006. 'MacIntyre on Virtue and Organisation', *Organization Studies* 27(6).

Beiner, Ronald. 2002. 'Community Versus Citizenship: MacIntyre's Revolt Against the Modern State', *Critical Review* 14(4): 459–79.

Beiser, Frederick. 2005a. *Schiller as Philosopher: A Re-Examination*, Oxford University Press.

—— 2005b. *Hegel*, Routledge.

Bielskis, Andrius. 2005. *Towards a Post-Modern Understanding of the Political: From Genealogy to Hermeneutics*, Palgrave Macmillan.

Blackledge, Paul. 2005. 'Freedom, Desire and Revolution: Alasdair MacIntyre's Early Marxist Ethics', *History of Political Thought* 26(4): 696–720.

Blackledge, Paul, and Neil Davidson. 2007. 'Introduction: The Unknown Alasdair MacIntyre', in Blackledge and Davidson, eds., *Alasdair MacIntyre's Marxist Writings*, Brill.

Blickle, Peter. 1981. *The Revolution of 1525: The German Peasants' War from a New Perspective*, trans. Thomas A. Brady, Jr. and H. C. Erik Midelfort, Johns Hopkins University Press.

Blythe, James M. 1997. 'Introduction', in Ptolemy of Lucca, *On the Government of Rulers: De Regimine Principium*, trans. Blythe, University of Pennsylvania Press.

—— 2000. ' "Civic Humanism" and Medieval Political Thought', in James Hankins, ed., *Renaissance Civic Humanism: Reappraisals and Reflections*, Cambridge University Press.

Blythe, James M. 2002. 'Aristotle's *Politics* and Ptolemy of Lucca', *Vivarium* 40(1): 103–36.

Booth, William James. 1993. *Households: On the Moral Architecture of the Economy*, Cornell University Press.

Brandom, Robert B. 2002a. 'Some Pragmatist Themes in Hegel's Idealism', in Brandom, *Tales of the Mighty Dead: Historical Essays in the Metaphysics of Intentionality*, Harvard University Press.

—— 2002b. 'Talking with a Tradition', in ibid.

—— 2005. 'Responses to Pippin, Macbeth and Haugeland', *European Journal of Philosophy* 13(3): 429–41.

Breen, Keith. 2002. 'Alasdair MacIntyre and the Hope for a Politics of Virtuous Acknowledged Dependence', *Contemporary Political Theory* 1(2): 181–201.

—— 2005. 'Compartmentalization and the Turn to Local Community: A Critique of the Political Thought of Alasdair MacIntyre', *The European Legacy* 10(5): 485–501.

Brentano, Franz. 1975. *On the Several Senses of Being in Aristotle*, trans. Rolf George, University of California Press.

Broadie, Sarah. 1988. 'The Problem of Practical Intellect in Aristotle's *Ethics*', *Proceedings of the Boston Area Colloquium in Ancient Philosophy* 3: 229–52.

—— 1990. 'Nature and Craft in Aristotelian Teleology', in Daniel T. Devereux and Pierre Pellegrin, eds., *Biologie, logique et métaphysique chez Aristote*, Éditions du CNRS.

—— 1991. *Ethics with Aristotle*, Oxford University Press.

—— 1998. 'Interpreting Aristotle's Directions', in Jyl Gentzler, ed., *Method in Ancient Philosophy*, Oxford University Press.

—— 2006. 'Aristotle and Contemporary Ethics', in Richard Kraut, ed., *The Blackwell Guide to Aristotle's* Nicomachean Ethics, Blackwell.

Brudney, Daniel. 1998. *Marx's Attempt to Leave Philosophy*, Harvard University Press.

Charles, David. 1984. *Aristotle's Philosophy of Action*, Duckworth.

—— 1986. 'Aristotle: Ontology and Moral Reasoning', in Michael Woods, ed., *Oxford Studies in Ancient Philosophy* 4: 119–44.

—— 1988. 'Perfectionism in Aristotle's Political Theory: Reply to Martha Nussbaum', in Julia Annas and Robert Grimm, eds., *Oxford Studies in Ancient Philosophy*, supp. vol.: 185–206.

—— 1991. 'Teleological Causation in the *Physics*', in Lindsay Judson, ed., *Aristotle's* Physics: *A Collection of Essays*, Oxford University Press.

—— 1995. 'Aristotle and Modern Realism', in Robert Heinaman, ed., *Aristotle and Moral Realism*, Westview Press.

—— 2000. *Aristotle on Meaning and Essence*, Oxford University Press.

—— 2003. 'Wittgenstein's Builders and Aristotle's Craftsmen', in R. W. Sharples, ed., *Perspectives on Greek Philosophy: S. V. Keeling Memorial Lectures in Ancient Philosophy 1992–2002*, Ashgate.

Cole, Eve Browning. 1994. 'Women, Slaves, and "Love of Toil" in Aristotle's Moral Philosophy', in Bat-Ami Bar On, ed., *Engendering Origins: Critical Feminist Readings in Plato and Aristotle*, State University of New York Press.

Collingwood, R. G.1939. *An Autobiography*, Oxford University Press.

Cooper, John. 1975. *Reason and Human Good in Aristotle*, Harvard University Press.

Davidson, David. 2005. 'Aristotle's Action', in Davidson, *Truth, Language, and History: Philosophical Essays Volume 5*, Oxford University Press.

Dewey, John. 1979. 'The Logic of Judgments of Practice', in Jo Ann Boydston, ed., Dewey, *The Middle Works, 1899–1924*, vol. 8, Southern Illinois University Press.

—— 1988a. 'Means and Ends: Their Interdependence, and Leon Trotsky's Essay on "Their Morals and Ours"', in Jo Ann Boydston, ed., Dewey, *The Later Works, 1925–1953*, vol. 13, Southern Illinois University Press.

—— 1988b. 'Theory of Valuation', in Jo Ann Boydston, ed., Dewey, *The Later Works, 1925–1953*, vol. 13, Southern Illinois University Press.

Dover, K. J. 1974. *Greek Popular Morality in the Time of Plato and Aristotle*, Basil Blackwell.

Engels, Frederick. 1987. 'Anti-Dühring: Herr Eugen Dühring's Revolution in Science', trans. Emile Burns, in Eric Hobsbawm et al., eds., Karl Marx and Engels, *Collected Works*, vol. 25, Lawrence and Wishart.

Ferrarin, Alfredo. 2001. *Hegel and Aristotle*, Cambridge University Press.

Fink, Hans, and Alasdair MacIntyre. 1997. 'Introduction', in Knud Ejler Løgstrup, *The Ethical Demand*, University of Notre Dame Press.

Gadamer, Hans-Georg. 1976. 'Hegel's Dialectic of Self-consciousness', trans. P. Christopher Smith, in Gadamer, *Hegel's Dialectic: Five Hermeneutical Studies*, Yale University Press.

—— 1981a. 'Hermeneutics as Practical Philosophy', trans. Frederick G. Lawrence, in Gadamer, *Reason in the Age of Science*, MIT Press.

—— 1981b. 'Hermeneutics as a Theoretical and Practical Task', trans. Frederick G. Lawrence, in ibid.

—— 1986a. *The Idea of the Good in Platonic-Aristotelian Philosophy*, trans. P. Christopher Smith, Yale University Press.

—— 1986b. 'Natural Science and Hermeneutics: The Concept of Nature in Ancient Philosophy', trans. Kathleen Wright, *Proceedings of the Boston Area Colloquium in Ancient Philosophy* 5: 39–52.

—— 1989. *Truth and Method*, trans. W. Glen-Doepel et al., Sheed and Ward (2nd edn.).

—— 1997a. 'Reflections on My Philosophical Journey', trans. Richard E. Palmer, in Lewis Edwin Hahn, ed., *The Philosophy of Hans-Georg Gadamer*, Open Court.

—— 1997b. 'Reply to P. Christopher Smith', trans. Matthias Lütkehermölle and Dennis J. Schmidt, in ibid.

Gadamer, Hans-Georg. 1998a. 'Einführung', 'Zusammenfassung' and 'Nachwort: Die Begründung der praktischen Philosophie', in Aristotle, *Nikomachische Ethik VI*, trans. Gadamer, Klostermann.

—— 1998b. 'On the Political Incompetence of Philosophy', trans. John Fletcher, *Diogenes* 46(2): 3–11.

—— 1998c. 'The Idea of Tolerance 1782–1982', trans. Chris Dawson, in Gadamer, *Praise of Theory: Speeches and Essays*, Yale University Press.

—— 1999. 'Aristotle and Imperative Ethics', trans. Joel Weinsheimer, in Gadamer, *Hermeneutics, Religion, and Ethics*, Yale University Press.

Gerson, Lloyd P. 2005. *Aristotle and Other Platonists*, Cornell University Press.

Gewirth, Alan. 1951. *The Defender of Peace: Marsilius of Padua and Medieval Political Philosophy*, Columbia University Press.

—— 1956. 'Appendix II: Natural Desire, the Unity of the Intellect, and Political Averroism', in Marsilius of Padua, *Defensor Pacis*, trans. Alan Gewirth, Columbia University Press.

Gill, Christopher. 1990. 'The Human Being as an Ethical Norm', in Gill, ed., *The Person and the Human Mind: Issues in Ancient and Modern Philosophy*, Oxford University Press.

Gilson, Etienne. 1936. *The Spirit of Mediaeval Philosophy*, trans. A. H. C. Downes, Sheed and Ward.

Gorovitz, Samuel, and Alasdair MacIntyre. 1976. 'Toward a Theory of Medical Fallibility', *The Journal of Medicine and Philosophy* 1(1): 51–71.

Gottschalk, Hans B. 1990. 'The Earliest Aristotelian Commentators', in Richard Sorabji, ed., *Aristotle Transformed: The Ancient Commentators and their Influence*, Duckworth.

Greenwood, L. H. G. 1909. 'Introduction', in Aristotle, *Nicomachean Ethics Book Six: With Essays, Notes, and Translation*, trans. Greenwood, Cambridge University Press.

Habermas, Jürgen. 1974. 'The Classical Doctrine of Politics in Relation to Social Philosophy', trans. John Viertel, in Habermas, *Theory and Practice*, Heinemann.

—— 1979. 'Legitimation Problems in the Modern State', trans. Thomas McCarthy, in Habermas, *Communication and the Evolution of Society*, Heinemann.

Hardie, W. F. R. 1965. 'The Final Good in Aristotle's Ethics', *Philosophy* 40(154): 277–95.

—— 1968. *Aristotle's Ethical Theory*, Oxford University Press.

Hayek, F. A. 1973. *Law, Legislation and Liberty*, vol. 1: *Rules and Order*, Routledge and Kegan Paul.

—— 1988. *The Fatal Conceit: The Errors of Socialism*, ed. W. W. Bartley III, Routledge.

Hegel, G. W. F. 1892. *Hegel's Lectures on the History of Philosophy*, vol. 1, trans E. S. Haldane, Routledge and Kegan Paul.

Hegel, G. W. F. 1894. *Hegel's Lectures on the History of Philosophy* vol. 2, trans. E. S. Haldane and Frances H. Simson, Routledge and Kegan Paul.

—— 1977. *Phenomenology of Spirit*, trans. A. V. Miller, Oxford University Press.

—— 1979. *System of Ethical Life* and *First Philosophy of Spirit*, trans. H. S. Harris and T. M. Knox, State University of New York Press.

—— 1991. *Elements of the Philosophy of Right*, trans. H. B. Nisbet, ed. Allen W. Wood, Cambridge University Press.

Heidegger, Martin. 1962. *Being and Time*, trans. John Macquarrie and Edward Robinson, Basil Blackwell.

—— 1984. *The Metaphysical Foundations of Logic*, trans. Michael Heim, Indiana University Press.

—— 1988. *The Basic Problems of Phenomenology*, trans. Albert Hofstadter, Indiana University Press (2nd edn.).

—— 1995. *Aristotle's Metaphysics Θ 1–3: On the Essence and Actuality of Force*, trans. Walter Brogan and Peter Warnek, Indiana University Press.

—— 1996. 'On the Essence and Concept of Φύσις in Aristotle's *Physics* B, Γ', trans. Thomas Sheehan, in William McNeill, ed., Heidegger, *Pathmarks*.

—— 1997. *Plato's Sophist*, trans. Richard Rojcewicz and André Schuwer, Indiana University Press.

—— 2001. *Phenomenological Interpretations of Aristotle: Initiation into Phenomenological Research*, trans. Richard Rojcewicz, Indiana University Press.

—— 2002. *The Essence of Truth: On Plato's Cave Allegory and* Theaetetus, trans. Ted Sadler, Continuum.

Hennis, Wilhelm. 1959. 'Zum Problem der deutschen Staatsanschauung', *Vierteljahreshefte für Zeitgeschichte* 7: 1–23.

—— 1963. *Politik und praktische Philosophie: Eine Studie zur Rekonstruktion der politischen Wissenschaft*, Luchterhand.

—— 2000. 'Political Science as a Vocation: A Personal Account', trans. Keith Tribe, in Hennis, *Max Weber's Central Question*, Threshold Press.

—— 2003. 'Die "Hellenische Geisteskultur" und die Ursprünge von Webers politischer Denkart', in Hennis, *Max Weber und Thukydides: Nachträge zur Biographie des Werkes*, Mohr Siebeck.

Hobbes, Thomas. 1994. *Leviathan: With Selected Variants from the Latin Edition of 1688*, ed. Edwin Curley, Hackett.

Hoven, Birgit van den. 1996. *Work in Ancient and Medieval Thought: Ancient Philosophers, Medieval Monks and Theologians and their Concept of Work, Occupations and Technology*, J. C. Gieben.

Hugh of St Victor. 1961. *The Didascalion of Hugh of St Victor: A Medieval Guide to the Arts*, trans. Jerome Taylor, Columbia University Press.

Hume, David. 2000. *A Treatise of Human Nature*, ed. David Fate Norton and Mary J. Norton, Oxford University Press.

Ilting, K.-H. 1971. 'The Structure of Hegel's *Philosophy of Right*', in Z. A.

Pelczynski, ed., *Hegel's Political Philosophy: Problems and Perspectives*, Cambridge University Press.

—— 1984. 'Hegel's Concept of the State and Marx's Early Critique', trans. H. Tudor and J. M. Tudor, in Z. A. Pelczynski, ed., *The State and Civil Society: Studies in Hegel's Political Philosophy: Problems and Perspectives*, Cambridge University Press.

Inwood, Michael. 1992. *A Hegel Dictionary*, Blackwell.

Joachim, Harold H. 1926. 'Introduction', in Aristotle, *On Coming-To-Be and Passing-Away*, ed. Joachim, Oxford University Press.

—— 1951. *Aristotle* The Nicomachean Ethics: *A Commentary by the Late H. H. Joachim*, ed. D. A. Rees, Oxford University Press.

John of Salisbury. 1990. *Policraticus: Of the Frivolities of Courtiers and the Footprints of Philosophers*, trans. Cary Nederman, Cambridge University Press.

Johnson, Monte Ransome. 2005. *Aristotle on Teleology*, Oxford University Press.

Jordan, Mark D. 1986. *Ordering Wisdom: The Hierarchy of Philosophical Discourses in Aquinas*, University of Notre Dame Press.

Kant, Immanuel. 1987. *Critique of Judgment*, trans. Werner S. Pluhar, Hackett.

—— 1996. *Critique of Pure Reason*, trans. Werner S. Pluhar, Hackett.

—— 2002. *Groundwork for the Metaphysics of Morals*, trans. Arnulf Zweig, ed. Thomas E. Hill, Jr. and Zweig, Oxford University Press.

Kaufman, Walter. 1974. *Nietzsche: Philosopher, Psychologist, Antichrist*, Princeton University Press (4th edn.).

Kempshall, M. S. 1999. *The Common Good in Late Medieval Political Thought*, Oxford University Press.

Kenny, Anthony. 1979. *Aristotle's Theory of the Will*, Oxford University Press.

Keyt, David. 1991. 'Three Basic Theorems in Aristotle's *Politics*', in David Keyt and Fred D. Miller, Jr., eds., *A Companion to Aristotle's Politics*, Blackwell.

Kraut, Richard. 1989. *Aristotle on the Human Good*, Princeton University Press.

—— 1993. 'In Defense of the Grand End', *Ethics* 103(2): 361–74.

Kullmann, Wolfgang. 1998. *Aristoteles und die moderne Wissenschaft*, Franz Steiner.

La Salle, John, and James M. Blythe. 2005. 'Was Ptolemy of Lucca a Civic Humanist?: Reflections on a Newly-Discovered Manuscript of Hans Baron', *History of Political Thought* 26(2): 236–65.

Langholm, Odd. 1979. *Price and Value in the Aristotelian Tradition: A Study in Scholastic Economic Sources*, Universitetsforlaget.

—— 1998. *The Legacy of Scholasticism in Economic Thought: Antecedents of Choice and Power*, Cambridge University Press.

Lear, Gabriel Richardson. 2004. *Happy Lives and the Highest Good: An Essay on Aristotle's* Nicomachean Ethics, Princeton University Press.

Lobkowicz, Nicholas. 1967. *Theory and Practice: History of a Concept from Aristotle to Marx*, University of Notre Dame Press.

Lobkowicz, Nicholas. 1977. 'On the History of Theory and Praxis', trans. Jere Paul Surber, in Terence Ball, ed., *Political Theory and Praxis: New Perspectives*, University of Minnesota Press.

Löwy, Michael. 2003. *The Theory of Revolution in the Young Marx*, Brill.

Luther, Martin. 1961a. 'The Pagan Servitude of the Church', trans. Bertram Lee Woolf, in John Dillenberger, ed., *Martin Luther: Selections From His Writings*, Doubleday.

—— 1961b. 'An Appeal to the Ruling Class of German Nationality as to the Amelioration of the State of Christendom', trans. Bertram Lee Woolf, in ibid.

Lutz, Christopher Stephen. 2004. *Tradition in the Ethics of Alasdair MacIntyre: Relativism, Thomism, and Philosophy*, Rowman and Littlefield.

McCarthy, George E. 1990. *Marx and the Ancients: Classical Ethics, Social Justice, and Nineteenth-Century Political Economy*, Rowman and Littlefield.

—— 1992, ed. *Marx and Aristotle: Nineteenth-Century German Social Theory and Classical Antiquity*, Rowman and Littlefield.

MacDonald, Scott. 1991. 'Ultimate Ends in Practical Reasoning: Aquinas's Aristotelian Moral Psychology and Anscombe's Fallacy', *The Philosophical Review* 100(1): 31–66.

McDowell, John. 1995. 'Eudaimonism and Realism in Aristotle's Ethics', in Robert Heinaman, ed., *Aristotle and Moral Realism*, Westview Press.

—— 1996a. 'Incontinence and Practical Wisdom in Aristotle', in Sabina Lovibond and S. G. Williams, eds., *Essays for David Wiggins: Identity, Truth and Value*, Blackwell.

—— 1996b. 'Deliberation and Moral Development in Aristotle's Ethics', in Stephen Engstrom and Jennifer Whiting, eds., *Aristotle, Kant, and the Stoics: Rethinking Happiness and Duty*, Cambridge University Press, 1996.

—— 1996c. *Mind and World*, Harvard University Press (2nd edn.).

—— 1998a. 'Some Issues in Aristotle's Moral Psychology', in McDowell, *Mind, Value, and Reality*, Harvard University Press.

—— 1998b. 'The Role of *Eudaimonia* in Aristotle's Ethics', in ibid.

—— 1998c. 'Virtue and Reason', in ibid.

—— 1998d. 'Two Sorts of Naturalism', in ibid.

—— 1998e. 'Non-Cognitivism and Rule-Following', in ibid.

—— 1998f. 'Are Moral Requirements Hypothetical Imperatives?', in ibid.

—— 1998g. 'Précis of *Mind and World*', *Philosophy and Phenomenological Research*, 58(2): 365–8.

—— 1998h. 'Projection and Truth in Ethics', in McDowell, *Mind, Value, and Reality*, Harvard University Press.

—— 1999. 'Comment on Robert Brandom's "Some Pragmatist Themes in Hegel's Idealism"', *European Journal of Philosophy* 7(2): 190–3.

—— 2000. 'Responses', in Marcus Willaschek, ed., *John McDowell: Reason and Nature*, Lit Verlag.

McDowell, John. 2002a. 'Responses', in Nicholas H. Smith, ed., *Reading McDowell: On Mind and World*, Routledge.

—— 2002b. 'Gadamer and Davidson on Understanding and Relativism', in Jeff Malpas et al., eds., *Gadamer's Century: Essays in Honor of Hans-Georg Gadamer*, MIT Press

—— 2003. 'The Apperceptive I and the Empirical Self: Towards a Heterodox Reading of "Lordship and Bondage" in Hegel's *Phenomenology*', *Bulletin of the Hegel Society of Great Britain* 47/48: 1–16.

McEvoy, James. 2000. *Robert Grosseteste*, Oxford University Press.

McGrade, Arthur Stephen. 1974. *The Political Thought of William of Ockham: Personal and Institutional Principles*, Cambridge University Press.

McGrath, Alister E. 1998. *Iustitia Dei: A History of the Christian Doctrine of Justification*, Cambridge University Press (2nd edn.).

MacIntyre, Alasdair. 1953. *Marxism: An Interpretation*, SCM Press.

—— 1956. 'Marxist Tracts', *The Philosophical Quarterly* 6(25): 366–70.

—— 1957a. 'Determinism', *Mind* 66(261): 28–41.

—— 1957b. 'The Logical Status of Religious Belief', in MacIntyre, ed., *Metaphysical Beliefs: Three Essays*, SCM Press.

—— 1958a. *The Unconscious: A Conceptual Analysis*, Routledge and Kegan Paul.

—— 1958b. 'On Not Misrepresenting Philosophy', *Universities and Left Review* 5: 72–3.

—— 1958c. 'The Algebra of Revolution', *Universities and Left Review* 5: 79–80.

—— 1959. 'The "New Left"', *Labour Review* 4(4): 98–100.

—— 1960a. *What is Marxist Theory For?*, Socialist Labour League.

—— 1960b. 'Breaking the Chains of Reason', in E. P. Thompson, ed., *Out of Apathy*, Stevens and Sons.

—— 1960c. 'Freedom and Revolution', *Labour Review* 5(1): 19–24.

—— 1960d. *From MacDonald to Gaitskell*, Socialist Labour League.

—— 1961a. 'Rejoinder to Left Reformism', *International Socialism* 6: 20–3.

—— 1961b. 'Marxists and Christians', *The Twentieth Century* 170(1011): 28–37.

—— 1963a. 'Prediction and Politics', *International Socialism* 13: 15–19.

—— 1963b. 'Labour Policy and Capitalist Planning', *International Socialism* 15: 5–9.

—— 1964a. 'A Mistake About Causality in Social Science', in Peter Laslett and W. G. Runciman, eds., *Philosophy, Politics and Society: Second Series*, Basil Blackwell.

—— 1964b. 'Existentialism', in D. J. O'Connor, ed., *A Critical History of Western Philosophy*, Free Press.

—— 1964c. 'Against Utilitarianism', in T. H. B. Hollins, ed., *Aims in Education: The Philosophic Approach*, Manchester University Press.

—— 1964d. 'Marx', in Maurice Cranston, ed., *Western Political Philosophers*, Bodley Head.

MacIntyre, Alasdair. 1966. 'Recent Political Thought', in David Thomson, ed., *Political Ideas*, Penguin.

—— 1967a. *A Short History of Ethics: A History of Moral Philosophy from the Homeric Age to the Twentieth Century*, Routledge and Kegan Paul.

—— 1967b. *Secularization and Moral Change*, Oxford University Press.

—— 1968a. *Marxism and Christianity*, Duckworth.

—— 1968b. 'Son of Ideology', *New York Review of Books* 10(9): 26–8.

—— 1969. 'Nietzsche's Titanism', *Encounter* 32(4): 79–82.

—— 1970a. *Marcuse*, Fontana.

—— 1970b. Review of Immanuel Wallerstein, *University in Turmoil*, inter alia, *American Journal of Sociology* 75(4): 562–4.

—— 1971a. 'The Antecedents of Action', in MacIntyre, *Against the Self-Images of the Age: Essays on Ideology and Philosophy*, Duckworth.

—— 1971b. 'How Not to Write About Stalin', in ibid.

—— 1971c. 'Rationality and the Explanation of Action', in ibid.

—— 1971d. 'The Idea of a Social Science', in ibid.

—— 1971e. 'Marxism of the Will', in ibid.

—— 1971f. 'Tell Me Where You Stand On Kronstadt', *New York Review of Books* 17(2): 24–5.

—— 1971g. ' "Ought" ', in MacIntyre, *Against the Self-Images of the Age: Essays on Ideology and Philosophy*, Duckworth.

—— 1971h. 'The End of Ideology and the End of the End of Ideology', in ibid.

—— 1971i. 'Marxist Mask and Romantic Face: Lukács on Thomas Mann', in ibid.

—— 1973. 'Ideology, Social Science, and Revolution', *Comparative Politics* 5(3): 321–42.

—— 1976a. 'Causality and History', in Juha Manninen and Raimo Tuomela, eds., *Essays on Explanation and Understanding: Studies in the Foundations of Humanities and Social Sciences*, D. Reidel.

—— 1976b. Review of C.B. Macpherson, *On Democratic Theory: Essays in Retrieval*, *Canadian Journal of Philosophy* 6(2): 177–81.

—— 1977. 'Can Medicine Dispense with a Theological Perspective on Human Nature?', in H. Tristram Engelhardt, Jr. and Daniel Callahan, eds., *Knowledge, Value and Belief*, Hastings Center.

—— 1980. 'Contexts of Interpretation: Reflections on Hans-Georg Gadamer's Truth and Method', *Boston University Journal* 26: 173–8.

—— 1981. *After Virtue: A Study in Moral Theory*, Duckworth.

—— 1982a. 'How Moral Agents Became Ghosts Or Why the History of Ethics Diverged from that of the Philosophy of Mind', *Synthese* 53(2): 295–312.

—— 1982b. 'Comments on Frankfurt', *Synthese* 53(2): 291–5.

—— 1983a. 'Moral Rationality, Tradition, and Aristotle: A Reply to Onora O'Neill, Raymond Gaita, and Stephen R. L. Clark', *Inquiry* 26(4): 447–66.

—— 1983b. 'The Magic in the Pronoun "My" ', *Ethics* 94(1): 113–25.

MacIntyre, Alasdair. 1984a. 'After Virtue and Marxism: A Response to Wartofsky', *Inquiry* 27(2–3): 251–4.

—— 1984b. 'Bernstein's Distorting Mirrors: A Rejoinder', *Soundings* 67(1): 30–41.

—— 1985a. *After Virtue: A Study in Moral Theory*, Duckworth (2nd edn.).

—— 1985b. 'Rights, Practices and Marxism: Reply to Six Critics', *Analyse und Kritik* 7(2): 234–48.

—— 1986a. 'Positivism, Sociology, and Practical Reasoning: Notes on Durkheim's Suicide', in Alan Donagan et al., eds., *Human Nature and Natural Knowledge: Essays Presented to Marjorie Grene*, D. Reidel.

—— 1986b. 'Which God Ought We to Obey and Why?', *Faith and Philosophy* 3(4): 359–71.

—— 1988a. *Whose Justice? Which Rationality?*, Duckworth.

—— 1988b. 'Sōphrosunē: How a Virtue Can Become Socially Disruptive', *Midwest Studies in Philosophy* 13: 1–11.

—— 1990a. 'The Form of the Good, Tradition and Enquiry', in Raimond Gaita, ed., *Value and Understanding: Essays for Peter Winch*, Routledge.

—— 1990b. *Three Rival Versions of Moral Enquiry: Encyclopaedia, Genealogy, and Tradition*, Duckworth.

—— 1990c. 'The Privatization of Good: An Inaugural Lecture', *The Review of Politics* 52(2): 344–61.

—— 1991. 'Persons and Human Beings', *Arion (third series)* 1(3): 188–94.

—— 1994a. 'A Partial Response to my Critics', in John Horton and Susan Mendus, eds., *After MacIntyre: Critical Perspectives on the Work of Alasdair MacIntyre*, Polity.

—— 1994b. 'How Can We Learn What Veritatis Splendor Has to Teach?', *The Thomist* 58(2): 171–95.

—— 1995. 'Is Patriotism a Virtue?', in Ronald Beiner, ed., *Theorizing Citizenship*, State University of New York Press.

—— 1997. Review of Engstrom and Whiting, eds., *Aristotle, Kant, and the Stoics*, *Philosophical Books* 38(4): 239–42.

—— 1998a. 'The Theses on Feuerbach: A Road Not Taken', in Kelvin Knight, ed., *The MacIntyre Reader*, Polity.

—— 1998b. 'Notes from the Moral Wilderness', in ibid.

—— 1998c. 'An Interview with Giovanna Borradori', in ibid.

—— 1998d. 'Preface', in *A Short History of Ethics: A History of Moral Philosophy from the Homeric Age to the Twentieth Century*, Routledge (2nd edn.).

—— 1998e. 'Social Science Methodology as the Ideology of Bureaucratic Authority', in Knight, ed., *The MacIntyre Reader*, Polity.

—— 1998f. 'What Can Moral Philosophers Learn from the Study of the Brain?', *Philosophy and Phenomenological Research*, 58(4): 865–9.

—— 1998g. 'Plain Persons and Moral Philosophy: Rules, Virtues and Goods', in Knight, ed., *The MacIntyre Reader*, Polity.

MacIntyre, Alasdair. 1998h. 'Practical Rationalities as Forms of Social Structure', in ibid.

—— 1998i. 'An Interview for Cogito', in ibid.

—— 1998j. 'First Principles, Final Ends and Contemporary Philosophical Issues', in ibid.

—— 1998k. 'Politics, Philosophy and the Common Good', in ibid.

—— 1998l. 'Aquinas's Critique of Education: Against His Own Age, Against Ours', in Amélie Oksenberg Rorty, ed., *Philosophers on Education: New Historical Perspectives*, Routledge, 1998.

—— 1998m. 'Moral Relativism, Truth and Justification', in Knight, ed., *The MacIntyre Reader*, Polity.

—— 1999a. 'John Case: An Example of Aristotelianism's Self-Subversion?', in John P. O'Callaghan and Thomas S. Hibbs, eds., *Recovering Nature: Essays in Natural Philosophy, Ethics, and Metaphysics in Honor of Ralph McInerny*, University of Notre Dame Press.

—— 1999b. *Dependent Rational Animals: Why Human Beings Need the Virtues*, Open Court.

—— 2002a. 'On Not Having the Last Word: Thoughts on Our Debts to Gadamer', in Jeff Malpas et al., eds., *Gadamer's Century: Essays in Honor of Hans-Georg Gadamer*, MIT Press

—— 2002b. 'Alasdair MacIntyre on Education: In Dialogue with Joseph Dunne', *Journal of Philosophy of Education* 36(1): 1–19.

—— 2003. 'Impoverished Moral Discourse, Insoluble Philosophical Problems: Three Lectures Delivered at the University of Essex in May 2003', unpublished manuscript.

—— 2004a. 'Dialogue with Alasdair MacIntyre' (London School of Economics, 26 May).

—— 2004b. 'Questions for Confucians: Reflections on the Essays in Comparative Study of Self, Autonomy, and Community', in Kwong-loi Shun and David B. Wong, eds., *Confucian Ethics: A Comparative Study of Self, Autonomy, and Community*, Cambridge University Press.

—— 2004c. 'The Only Vote Worth Casting in November', <http://ethicscenter.nd.edu/macintyrevote.shtml>.

—— 2004d. 'Preface to the Revised Edition', in MacIntyre, *The Unconscious: A Conceptual Analysis*, Routledge (2nd edn.).

—— 2005. 'Artifice, Desire, and Their Relationship: Hume against Aristotle', in Joyce Jenkins et al., eds., *Persons and Passions: Essays in Honor of Annette Baier*, University of Notre Dame Press.

—— 2006a. 'Rival Aristotles: 1. Aristotle Against Some Renaissance Aristotelians. 2. Aristotle Against Some Modern Aristotelians', in MacIntyre, *Ethics and Politics: Selected Essays Volume 2*, Cambridge University Press.

—— 2006b. 'The Ends of Life, the Ends of Philosophical Writing', in MacIntyre, *The Tasks of Philosophy: Selected Essays Volume 1*, Cambridge University Press.

MacIntyre, Alasdair. 2006c. 'Truthfulness and Lies: 1. What is the Problem and What Can We Learn from Mill? 2. What Can We Learn from Kant?', in MacIntyre, *Ethics and Politics: Selected Essays Volume 2*, Cambridge University Press.

—— 2006d. 'Some Enlightenment Projects Reconsidered', in ibid.

—— 2006e. 'Epistemological Crises, Dramatic Narrative and the Philosophy of Science', in MacIntyre, *The Tasks of Philosophy: Selected Essays Volume 1*, Cambridge University Press.

—— 2006f. 'Hegel on Faces and Skulls', in ibid..

—— 2006g. 'Three Perspectives on Marxism: 1953, 1968, 1995', in MacIntyre, *Ethics and Politics: Selected Essays Volume 2*, Cambridge University Press.

—— 2006h. 'Moral Philosophy and Contemporary Social Practice: What Holds Them Apart?', in MacIntyre, *The Tasks of Philosophy: Selected Essays Volume 1*, Cambridge University Press.

—— 2006i. 'Toleration and the Goods of Conflict', in MacIntyre, *Ethics and Politics: Selected Essays Volume 2*, Cambridge University Press.

—— 2006j. 'Natural Law as Subversive: The Case of Aquinas', in ibid.

—— 2006k. 'Poetry as Political Philosophy: Notes on Burke and Yeats', in ibid.

—— 2006l. Review of Raymond Geuss, *Outside Ethics*, <http://ndpr.nd.edu/review.cfm?id=5922>.

—— 2006m. 'Truth as a Good: A Reflection on Fides et Ratio', in MacIntyre, *The Tasks of Philosophy: Selected Essays Volume 1*, Cambridge University Press.

—— 2006n. 'Colors, Culture, and Practices', in ibid.

MacIntyre, Alasdair, et al.1959. 'Discussion', *The Newsletter* 3(127): 330–4.

Magnus, Bernd. 1980. 'Aristotle and Nietzsche: "Megalopsychia" and "Uebermensch"', in David J. Depew, ed., *The Greeks and the Good Life*, California State University, Fullerton.

Markovic, Mihailo, and Gajo Petrovic. 1979, eds. *Praxis: Yugoslav Essays in the Philosophy and Methodology of the Social Sciences*, D. Reidel.

Marshall, Gordon. 1982. *In Search of the Spirit of Capitalism: An Essay on Max Weber's Protestant Ethic Thesis*, Hutchinson.

Marsilius of Padua. 1956. *Defensor pacis*, trans. Alan Gewirth, Columbia University Press.

Marx, Karl. 1975a. 'Economic and Philosophic Manuscripts of 1844', trans. Martin Milligan and Dirk J. Struik, in Jack Cohen et al., eds., Marx and Frederick Engels, *Collected Works*, vol. 3, Progress Publishers.

—— 1975b. 'Critical Marginal Notes on the Article "The King of Prussia and Social Reform. By a Prussian"', trans. Clemens Dutt, in ibid.

—— 1976. 'Theses on Feuerbach', trans. anon., in Jack Cohen et al., eds., Marx and Frederick Engels, *Collected Works*, vol. 5, Progress Publishers.

—— 1981. *Capital: A Critique of Political Economy*, vol. 3, trans. David Fernbach, Penguin.

Marx, Karl, and Frederick Engels. 1976. 'The German Ideology' (part 1), trans. W. Lough, in Jack Cohen et al., eds.,Marx and Engels, *Collected Works*, vol. 5, Progress Publishers.

Meikle, Scott. 1985. *Essentialism in the Thought of Karl Marx*, Open Court.

—— 1995. *Aristotle's Economic Thought*, Cambridge University Press.

—— 2002, ed. *Marx*, Ashgate.

Melanchthon, Philip. 1999a. 'On the Rôle of the Schools', trans. Christine F. Salazar, in Sachiko Kusukawa, ed., Melanchthon, *Orations of Philosophy and Education*, Cambridge Univerity Press.

—— 1999b. 'On Aristotle', trans. Christine F. Salazar, in ibid.

Michels, Robert. 1962. *Political Parties: A Sociological Study of the Oligarchical Tendencies of Modern Democracy*, trans. Eden Paul and Cedar Paul, Free Press.

Miles, Steven H. 2004. *The Hippocratic Oath and the Ethics of Medicine*, Oxford University Press.

Mill, J. S. 1987. *The Logic of the Moral Sciences*, Duckworth.

Morsel, Joseph. 2001. 'Inventing a Social Category: The Sociogenesis of the Nobility at the End of the Middle Ages', trans. Pamela Selwyn, in Bernhard Jussen, ed., *Ordering Medieval Society: Perspectives on Intellectual and Practical Modes of Shaping Social Relations*, University of Pennsylvania Press.

Mure, G. R. G 1932. *Aristotle*, Oxford University Press.

—— 1940. *An Introduction to Hegel*, Oxford University Press.

Murphy, James Bernard. 1993. *The Moral Economy of Labor: Aristotelian Themes in Economic Theory*, Yale University Press.

—— 1994. 'The Kinds of Order in Society', in Philip Mirowski, ed., *Natural Images in Economic Thought: 'Markets Read in Tooth and Claw'*, Cambridge University Press.

Najemy, John M. 1982. *Corporatism and Consensus in Florentine Electorial Politics, 1280–1400*, University of North Carolina Press.

—— 2000. 'Civic Humanism and Florentine Politics', in James Hankins, ed., *Renaissance Civic Humanism: Reappraisals and Reflections*, Cambridge University Press.

Nederman, Cary J. 1986. 'Royal Taxation and the English Church: The Origins of William of Ockham's *An princeps*', *Journal of Ecclesiastical History* 37(3): 377–88.

—— 1987a. 'The Physiological Significance of the Organic Metaphor in John of Salisbury's *Policraticus*', *History of Political Thought* 8(2): 211–23.

—— 1987b. 'Sovereignty, War and the Corporation: Hegel on the Medieval Foundations of the Modern State', *Journal of Politics* 49(2): 500–20.

—— 1989. 'Nature, Ethics, and the Doctrine of "Habitus": Aristotelian Moral Psychology in the Twelfth Century', *Traditio*, 45: 87–110.

—— 1991. 'Aristotelianism and the Origins of "Political Science" in the Twelfth Century', *Journal of the History of Ideas* 52(2): 179–94.

—— 1992. 'Freedom, Community and Function: Communitarian Lessons of Medieval Political Theory', *American Political Science Review* 86(4): 977–86.

Nederman, Cary J. 1995. *Community and Consent: The Secular Political Theory of Marsiglio of Padua's* Defensor Pacis, Rowman and Littlefield.

—— 1996. 'The Meaning of "Aristotelianism" in Medieval Moral and Political Thought', *Journal of the History of Ideas* 57(4): 563–85.

—— 1998. 'The Puzzling Case of Christianity and Republicanism: A Comment on Black', *American Political Science Review* 92(4): 913–18.

—— 2000. *Worlds of Difference: European Discourses of Toleration, c.1100—c.1550*, Pennsylvania State University Press.

—— 2002a. 'Mechanics and Citizens: The Reception of the Aristotelian Idea of Citizenship in Late Medieval Europe', *Vivarium* 40(1): 75–102.

—— 2002b. *Political Thought in Early Fourteenth-Century England: Treatises by Walter of Milemete, William of Pagula, and William of Ockham*, Arizona Center for Medieval and Renaissance Studies.

—— 2005. 'Beyond Stoicism and Aristotelianism: John of Salisbury's Skepticism and Moral Reasoning in the Twelfth Century', in Istvan Bejczy and Richard Newhauser, eds., *Virtue and Ethics in the Twelfth Century*, Brill.

Newman, W. L. 1887. *The Politics of Aristotle: With an Introduction, Two Prefatory Essays and Notes Critical and Explanatory*, vol. 1, Oxford University Press.

Nightingale, Andrea Wilson. 2004. *Spectacles of Truth in Classical Greek Philosophy: Theoria in its Cultural Context*, Cambridge University Press.

Nussbaum, Martha C. 1978. *Aristotle's* De Motu Animalium, Princeton University Press.

—— 1986. 'The Discernment of Perception: An Aristotelian Conception of Private and Public Rationality', *Proceedings of the Boston Area Colloquium in Ancient Philosophy* 1: 151–207.

—— 1988a. 'Nature, Function, and Capability: Aristotle on Political Distribution', in Julia Annas and Robert Grimm, eds., *Oxford Studies in Ancient Philosophy* supp. vol.: 145–84.

—— 1988b. 'Reply to David Charles', in ibid.: 207–14.

—— 1989. 'Recoiling from Reason', *New York Review of Books* 36(19): 36–41.

—— 1990. 'Aristotelian Social Democracy', in R. Bruce Douglass et al., eds., *Liberalism and the Good*, Routledge.

—— 1992. 'Human Functioning and Social Justice: In Defense of Aristotelian Essentialism', *Political Theory* 20(2): 202–46.

—— 1995. 'Aristotle on Human Nature and the Foundations of Ethics', in J. E. J. Altham and Ross Harrison, eds., *World, Mind, and Ethics: Essays on the Ethical Philosophy of Bernard Williams*, Cambridge University Press.

—— 1998. 'Political Animals: Luck, Love, and Dignity', *Metaphilosophy* 29(4): 273–87.

Nussbaum, Martha C. 1999. 'Virtue Ethics: A Misleading Category?', *The Journal of Ethics* 3(3): 163–201.

―――― 2000. 'Aristotle, Politics, and Human Capabilities: A Response to Antony, Arneson, Charlesworth, and Mulgan', *Ethics* 111(1): 102–40.

―――― 2001. *The Fragility of Goodness: Luck and Ethics in Greek Tragedy and Philosophy*, Cambridge University Press (2nd edn.).

O'Neill, Onora. 1996. *Towards Justice and Virtue: A Constructive Account of Practical Reasoning*, Cambridge University Press.

Otter, Sandra M. Den. 1996. *British Idealism and Social Explanation: A Study in Late Victorian Thought*, Cambridge University Press.

Pike, Jonathan E. 1999. *From Aristotle to Marx: Aristotelianism in Marxist Social Ontology*, Ashgate.

Pinkard, Terry. 2003. 'MacIntyre's Critique of Modernity', in Mark C. Murphy, ed., *Alasdair MacIntyre*, Cambridge University Press.

Pippin, Robert B. 1989. *Hegel's Idealism: The Satisfactions of Self-Consciousness*, Cambridge University Press.

―――― 1997. 'Introduction: Hegelianism?', in Pippin, *Idealism as Modernism: Hegelian Variations*, Cambridge University Press.

Ptolemy of Lucca. 1997. *On the Government of Rulers: De Regimine Principium*, trans. James M. Blythe, University of Pennsylvania Press.

Pocock, J. G. A. 1975. *The Machiavellian Moment: Florentine Political Thought and the Atlantic Republican Tradition*, Princeton University Press.

Reeve, C. D. C 1992. *Practices of Reason: Aristotle's* Nicomachean Ethics, Oxford. University Press.

―――― 1998. 'Introduction', in Aristotle, *Politics*, trans. Reeve, Hackett.

―――― 2000. *Substantive Knowledge: Aristotle's* Metaphysics, Hackett.

Richardson, Henry S. 1994. *Practical Reasoning about Final Ends*, Cambridge University Press.

Riedel, Manfred. 1972a, ed. *Rehabilitierung der praktischen Philosophie*, vol. 1: *Geschichte, Probleme, Aufgaben*, Rombach.

―――― 1972b. 'Vorwort', in ibid.

―――― 1972c. 'Über einige Aporien in der praktischen Philosophie des Aristoteles', in ibid.

―――― 1974, ed. *Rehabilitierung der praktischen Philosophie*, vol. 2: *Rezeption, Argumentation, Diskussion*, Rombach.

―――― 1984. *Between Tradition and Revolution: The Hegelian Transformation of Political Philosophy*, trans. Walter Wright, Cambridge University Press.

―――― 1996. 'In Search of a Civic Union: The Political Theme of European Democracy and Its Primordial Foundation in Greek Philosophy', in Reginald Lilly, ed., *The Ancients and the Moderns*, Indiana University Press.

Ritter, Joachim. 1982. 'Morality and Ethical Life: Hegel's Controversy With Kantian Ethics', trans. Richard Dien Winfield, in Ritter, *Hegel and the French Revolution: Essays on the Philosophy of Right*, MIT Press.

Ritter, Joachim. 1983. 'On the Foundations of Practical Philosophy in Aristotle', trans. Alfonso Gomez-Lobo, in Darrel E. Christensen et al., eds., *Contemporary German Philosophy*, vol. 2, Pennsylvania State University Press.

Rockmore, Tom. 1980. *Fichte, Marx, and the German Philosophical Tradition*, Southern Illinois University Press.

Rosler, Andrés. 2005. *Political Authority and Obligation in Aristotle*, Oxford University Press.

Ross, W. D. 1936. 'Commentary', in Aristotle, *Physics*, ed. Ross, Oxford University Press.

Salzman, Michele Renee. 2002. *The Making of a Christian Aristocracy: Social and Religious Change in the Western Roman Empire*, Harvard University Press.

Shields, Christopher. 1999. *Order in Multiplicity: Homonymy in the Philosophy of Aristotle*, Oxford University Press.

Southern, R. W. 1986. *Robert Grosseteste: The Growth of an English Mind in Medieval Europe*, Oxford University Press.

Steiner, Franz. 1956. *Taboo*, Cohen and West.

Stocks, John Leofric. 1925. *Aristotelianism*, Harrap.

Strauss, Leo. 1953. *Natural Right and History*, University of Chicago Press.

—— 1964. *The City and Man*, University of Chicago Press.

Taylor, Charles. 1964. *The Explanation of Behaviour*, Routledge and Kegan Paul.

Taylor, Jerome. 1961. 'Introduction', in Hugh of St Victor, *The Didascalion of Hugh of St Victor: A Medieval Guide to the Arts*, trans. Taylor, Columbia University Press.

Thompson, E. P. 1978a. 'An Open Letter to Leszek Kolakowski', in Thompson, *The Poverty of Theory and Other Essays*, Merlin Press.

—— 1978b. 'The Poverty of Theory or An Orrery of Errors', in ibid.

Thomson, George. 1973. *Aeschylus and Athens: A Study in the Social Origins of Drama*, Lawrence and Wishart (4th edn.).

Troeltsch, Ernst. 1931. *The Social Teaching of the Christian Churches*, trans. Olive Wyon, Allen and Unwin (2 vols.).

Trotsky, Leon. 1973. 'Their Morals and Ours', in Trotsky et al., *Their Morals and Ours: Marxist vs. Liberal Views on Morality*, Pathfinder Press.

Turner, Stephen. 1994. *The Social Theory of Practices: Tradition, Tacit Knowledge and Presuppositions*, Polity.

Vasiliou, Iakovos. 1996. 'The Role of Good Upbringing in Aristotle's Ethics', *Philosophy and Phenomenological Research* 66(4): 771–97.

Viroli, Maurizio. 1992. *From Politics to Reason of State: The Acquisition and Transformation of the Language of Politics 1250–1600*, Cambridge University Press.

Waszek, Norbert. 1988. *The Scottish Enlightenment and Hegel's Account of 'Civil Society'*, Kluwer Academic Publishers.

Weber, Max. 2002. *The Protestant Ethic and the Spirit of Capitalism*, trans. Stephen Kalberg, Blackwell.

Weber, Max. 2004. *The Vocation Lectures*, trans. Rodney Livingstone, ed. David Owen and Tracy B. Strong, Hackett.

Whiting, Jennifer E. 2002. 'Stong Dialectic, Neurathian Reflection, and the Ascent of Desire: Irwin and McDowell on Aristotle's Methods of Ethics', *Proceedings of the Boston Area Colloquium in Ancient Philosophy* 17: 61–116.

Wiggins, David. 1995. 'Eudaimonism and Realism in Aristotle's Ethics: A Reply to John McDowell', in Robert Heinaman, ed., *Aristotle and Moral Realism*, Westview Press.

—— 1996. 'Replies', in Sabina Lovibond and S. G. Williams, eds., *Essays for David Wiggins: Identity, Truth and Value*, Blackwell.

—— 2002. 'Deliberation and Practical Reason', in Wiggins, *Needs, Values, Truth: Essays in the Philosophy of Value*, Oxford University Press (3rd edn.).

Wildberg, Christian. 2004. '*On Generation and Corruption* I. 7: Aristotle on *poiein* and *paschein*',in Frans de Haas and Jaap Mansfeld, eds., *Aristotle's* On Generation and Corruption *Book 1*, Oxford University Press.

Williams, Bernard. 1985. *Ethics and the Limits of Philosophy*, Fontana.

Wittgenstein, Ludwig. 1958. *Philosophical Investigations*, trans. G. E. M. Anscombe, Basil Blackwell.

Wood, Allen W. 1981. *Karl Marx*, Routledge and Kegan Paul.

Woods, Michael. 1992. 'Commentary', in Aristotle, *Eudemian Ethics: Books I, II, and VIII*, trans. Woods, Oxford University Press (2nd edn.).

Wright, Georg Henrik von. 1963. *The Varieties of Goodness*, Routledge and Kegan Paul.

—— 1971. *Explanation and Understanding*, Routledge and Kegan Paul.

—— 1989. 'A Reply to My Critics', in Paul Arthur Schilpp and Lewis Edwin Hahn, eds., *The Philosophy of Georg Henrik von Wright*, Open Court.

Yack, Bernard. 1986. *The Longing for Total Revolution: Philosophic Sources of Social Discontent from Rousseau to Marx and Nietzsche*, Princeton University Press.

Index